Freelancing Expertise

A Volume in the Series

COLLECTION ON TECHNOLOGY AND WORK

edited by Stephen R. Barley

Between Craft and Science: Technical Work in the United States
edited by Stephen R. Barley and Julian E. Orr

Talking about Machines: An Ethnography of a Modern Job
by Julian E. Orr

Finding Time: How Corporations, Individuals, and Families Can Benefit from New Work Practices
by Leslie Perlow

Putting Work in Its Place: A Quiet Revolution
by Peter Meiksins and Peter Whalley

Surgeons and the Scope
by James R. Zetka Jr.

Selling Technology: The Changing Shape of Sales in an Information Economy
by Asaf Darr

FREELANCING EXPERTISE

Contract Professionals in the New Economy

DEBRA OSNOWITZ

ILR PRESS

AN IMPRINT OF

CORNELL UNIVERSITY PRESS

ITHACA AND LONDON

First published 2010 by Cornell University Press
First printing, Cornell Paperbacks, 2010

Printed in the United States of America

Library of Congress Cataloging-in-Publication Data

Osnowitz, Debra.
   Freelancing expertise : contract professionals in the new economy / Debra Osnowitz.
      p. cm. — (Collection on technology and work)
   Includes bibliographical references.
   ISBN 978-0-8014-4936-9 (cloth : alk. paper) —
   ISBN 978-0-8014-7656-3 (pbk. : alk. paper)
   1. Self-employed—United States.   2. Independent contractors—United States.   3. Consultants—United States.
   4. Professional employees—United States.
   5. Temporary employment—United States.   I. Title.
   II. Series: Collection on technology and work.

   HD8037.U5O75 2010
   658'.041—dc22   2010015246

Cornell University Press strives to use environmentally responsible suppliers and materials to the fullest extent possible in the publishing of its books. Such materials include vegetable-based, low-VOC inks and acid-free papers that are recycled, totally chlorine-free, or partly composed of nonwood fibers. For further information, visit our website at www.cornellpress.cornell.edu.

Cloth printing   10 9 8 7 6 5 4 3 2 1
Paperback printing   10 9 8 7 6 5 4 3 2 1

to the memory of my father

CONTENTS

Acknowledgments

Writing a book is both a solitary task and a group effort. In developing this book I have incurred many debts of gratitude. I first thank my informants, who gave me their time and attention when they had much else to do, and I thank those who allowed me to observe their daily practices and routines as my research proceeded. Several informants also offered ongoing updates as my work progressed. This project has benefited from their generosity.

This book came about through my graduate work in the Department of Sociology at Brandeis University, where my advisors—Carmen Sirianni, George Ross, and Karen Hansen—offered critical feedback and support. I am forever grateful for the education they made possible. Vicki Smith provided insightful comments as I completed a first draft. I have since been especially fortunate to have a team of reviewers in Mignon Duffy, Kathleen (Kay) Jenkins, and Karen Hansen. Separately and together, they have provided analytical insights and thoughtful comments that have prodded my thinking and enhanced the result. Their efforts underscore the value of reciprocity in practice.

Later drafts have benefited from Steve Barley's careful review and support for this project and from Fran Benson's commitment to seeing it through. George Gonos, Kevin Henson, and Rachel Rockenmacher also read work in progress and helped me hone the analysis. Encouragement came as well from the Sloan Foundation Early Career Scholars Program, especially Steve Sweet, who offered advice and support. To my students at the University of Massachusetts, both Boston and Lowell, I am grateful for many questions that clarified my thinking. I thank Judy Hanley and Elaine Brooks for much assistance and the Department of Sociology at Clark University for providing a supportive environment in which to complete the project.

Many more people assisted along the way. Hope Steele was a constant source of clarity and strategic thinking. Linda Dunn showed me that I could return to school, despite the odds. To John Croll I owe the very substance of this project, born years ago in our late-night conversations, and much thanks for jump-starting my fieldwork. Karen McAninch and Steve Markovitz offered ongoing perspective as the project unfolded. Claire Cummings and Larry Elle offered neighborly assistance, as did Ferdinand Steer when I needed technical help. Sylvia Stocker and Steve Wellcome helped me find a number of informants. As I presented pieces of this project at conferences, I enjoyed the hospitality of Steven Osnowitz, Kay Jenkins and Mark Lerman, Lynn Lerman, Ray Knapp and Ahuva Brauerman, and David Teutsch and Betsy Platkin Teutsch.

Books take a long time to research and write. As I worked on this one, Emily and Amanda Markovitz grew into fine young women. As I finish it, Sophie Croll and Anna Steele are on the verge of the same transition, and Kathryn and Jackie Lerman will soon be as well. For them, I hope to have contributed to rethinking policy and practice in ways that provide greater opportunity and equality.

FREELANCING EXPERTISE

Introduction

The afternoon I spent with Ben discussing his work, career, and family life, was, in his words, "a chance to think about the big picture. With so much to manage and never enough time," he explained, "that little screen gets all my attention." Gesturing to several computer terminals crowded on to a corner table, Ben compared his work as a contract software engineer to "the people who made the Industrial Revolution. They changed they way people lived, where they lived, where they worked. A lot of it was for the good. But if you read history, you find out there were a lot of problems along the way." Reflecting on his experience as an independent contractor, Ben believed he was witnessing a shift analogous to industrialization, a challenge to long-established patterns of paid employment. "There's a fundamental change going through the workplace," he elaborated. "I think the freelance consultant is probably one of the best things that's happening over the next several years, but it will take a while for society to catch up with us."

A white man in his early forties, college educated and middle class, Ben saw himself on the cutting edge of a trend. For six years he had been working as a "freelance consultant," or contractor, from the suburban home he shared with his wife and two daughters. There he had the office equipment needed for a small business and had invested further in the technological "gear" that software development required. From his home office, Ben could communicate both with companies large and small and with colleagues who shared his passion for developing technology. At work but without a regular office routine, he could also attend to family needs without jeopardizing his job. "The Industrial Revolution put people in factories and destroyed a lot of cottage industries," he mused, "but we're bringing them back." For Ben, contracting from home offered the autonomy to direct his own small-scale operation.

Emily was also a contractor, although she rarely worked at home and had few of the trappings of a home office. Instead, she moved from one work site to the next. At the time of our interview, she was dividing her time between a small publishing company and a much larger law firm, where she worked as an editor and proofreader. At each site, she occupied a small space, which she sometimes shared. "I hear it's the wave of the future, this kind of moving around and working short term," she explained, "and it's fine as long as they give me work, and I like that I'm learning new things everywhere I go." A single white woman in her late forties, Emily had been a contractor for little more than a year, and as our conversation continued, she weighed the pros and cons of long-term contract employment. "Knowing how to do this is probably a good thing," she reflected, "but I still don't feel like I understand it. I don't know if it's dependable.... I wonder about doing it in twenty years."

Emily, too, sensed a shift in the world of work, away from the long-term steady job with a well-marked career path. By her own account, she was doing well, with an income at least equivalent to what she had earned as a "regular, permanent employee." When her former employer relocated, she had discovered a ready market for her services. "I know how to do what I do," she assured me. Even so, Emily seemed somewhat less sanguine than Ben about her long-term prospects in the workforce. She was confident in her abilities but uncertain about her future. "I guess I could use an advice manual," she mused. "Maybe I should be planning for something." Emily's unease stemmed less from day-to-day experience than from the recognition that she was assuming ever-more responsibility for charting her own course. Any direction she took incurred risks. Should she, like Ben, invest in a home office? Learn new skills? Seek new markets for her services? "They say it's a new economy," she reflected. "I guess I'm trying to figure out what that means."

Emily and Ben share a set of questions and observations about work and careers with social scientists, policymakers, and workers alike. Across the economic spectrum, employment has become less secure and careers less predictable. New work practices—with such terms as reengineering, lean production, or just-in-time staffing—have generated a new sense of precariousness.[1] Jobs calling on a specific body of knowledge or set of skills may be eliminated, outsourced, or replaced with new requirements. Technological change may demand adaptation as new technologies threaten long-standing practices. Likening these developments to the Industrial Revolution, Ben underscored the dislocation that segments of the workforce now experience, even as many workers embrace change. Echoing Ben, Emily also gave voice to a pervasive sense of insecurity in the wake of organizational downsizing and internal restructuring through which employing organizations have shed jobs and realigned expectations. As contractors no longer working for a single employer, Ben and Emily represent one facet of a shift in employment relations that have become increasingly tenuous.

Had she investigated popular sources of advice, Emily would probably have found a growing literature offering guidance for self-identified freelancers, consultants, or contractors.[2] Some of these sources date back decades, indicating that contract employment is far from new. But a recent stream of books, magazines, and websites now celebrates the potential for liberation from work in a bureaucratic hierarchy. Some advocates of change invoke a new entrepreneurial culture and encourage all workers to seize opportunities and pursue their dreams. Others take a more cautionary tone and equate individual success with such personal traits as independence and self-motivation, or they admonish would-be entrepreneurs to remain conscientious in plying their trade, managing their resources, and maintaining good business relations. Encouraged simultaneously to embrace risk and guard against danger, Emily might well have found advice about the new economy contradictory.

In the first few years of the twenty-first century, two headlines highlighted these contradictions. "The Liberated, Exploited, Pampered, Frazzled,

Uneasy New American Worker," read the cover of the *New York Times Magazine* on March 5, 2000. Inside, articles celebrated the free agent, who moves easily from project to project, unbound by formal employment or even, in some cases, by a physical address. Free agents avoid stagnation and worry little about job security, rights, or benefits. Riding the wave of new technology, they can reap the rewards of innovation. By April 23, 2003, however, a front-page story in the *Wall Street Journal* chronicled the crash that followed the heady days of an expanding economic bubble; the headline read, "Once Stars of the New Economy, Free-Lance Workers Take the Brunt of Its Downfall." By then, the free agent had become one casualty of a downturn. No longer commanding high fees, freelancers were the first to scramble for work when companies began to cut costs. Few journalistic accounts reported estimates of the size or scope of this unanchored workforce. Instead, most stories illustrated either free-ranging possibility or ongoing unemployment.

Such signals can be hard to decipher. Evidence of changing patterns of employment may appear in the press, in advice literature, and in talks among friends and acquaintances whose working lives are taking new directions. Increasing numbers of people appear to change jobs with increasing frequency. Staffing agencies offer to link individuals with specific skill sets to employers who seek their services. Career counseling offers advice for those "outplaced" and unemployed. New forms of employment represent options and alternatives, sometimes approximating the notion of free agency, occasionally defined as self-employment,[3] and variously termed temp work, freelancing, consulting, or contracting. As Ben and Emily observed, such developments are notable less for a unified pattern than for a multiplicity of trends that appear uneven and often paradoxical.

This book is about contract professionals, people such as Ben and Emily who sell their expertise in a market for their services. Contract professionals are mobile workers hired temporarily to apply specific knowledge and skills. Rather than salaries, they receive hourly wages or, less often, project fees. Rather than having employers, contractors have clients, with whom they forge short-term agreements, sometimes through staffing agencies acting as third-party intermediaries in the labor market. Their clients are businesses, large and small; nonprofit institutions; and occasionally individuals seeking specific services. Like Ben, some of the contract professionals whose stories appear on these pages work at a distance from their clients, usually from offices in their homes, where e-mail, fax, and phone can connect them around the globe. Others work mainly at clients' sites of business and, like Emily, may be so integrated into organizational life that they seem indistinguishable from the employees around them. A sub-group of contractors is geographically mobile, relocating periodically as they move from one client site to the next.

The contractors who are the subject of this book work in one of two occupational groups: (1) writers and editors or (2) programmers and engineers. In these two occupations, contract employment is well institutionalized, and both contractors and their clients are familiar with its practices. For them, contracting is a relational system that operates in tandem with standard organization-based employment. The system provides staffing options for employers seeking flexibility in the size and composition of a workforce, but it also requires ongoing negotiation with contractors to define the scope and content of each new assignment. For contractors, therefore, informally defined work relations supplant formal affiliation and structural authority in an office hierarchy. Contract professionals must, therefore, depend on their own expertise to enact competence and instill confidence in their abilities.

I set out to investigate the strategies and structures of contracting at the turn of the twenty-first century, at the height of a booming economy and plentiful employment. I interviewed contractors and, at a series of work sites, observed them at work with colleagues and clients. My investigation lasted well into an economic recession, when the boom-gone-bust was front-page news. By then, however, I had heard one contractor after another dismiss both the high-flying rhetoric of free agency and the dismal predictions of downward mobility. Instead, I heard a more nuanced account of plans, choices, and constraints, all of which spanned economic cycles, then as now.[4] Many of the people I met were exuberant about the challenge and variety that contract employment provided. Others were less sanguine about their prospects or less satisfied with their work. Yet all saw themselves as skilled professionals making their way in a time of change. Neither workforce mavericks nor labor market victims, they were navigating a system of employment with its own norms, processes, and mechanisms of control.

The accounts of the contractors I interviewed revealed much about the workings of this system. My informants related strategies for finding contract assignments, developing work-based relationships, and remaining employable over time. Their stories illustrated a complex calculus by which they weighed their risks and sought opportunities. Keenly aware that their contractual status set them apart from normative notions of holding a job, many offered their own interpretations of changing employment relations and raised questions that I shared as I began this investigation. In a time of accelerated social and economic change, what constitutes a good job? A satisfying career? What does contract employment portend for work and careers in a new economy?

I had other questions as well. I knew that contracting is one of a number of work arrangements associated with increasing workforce flexibility, and I wondered how contracting in these two occupational groups compared with other forms of short-term employment. I wondered, too, how the processes and practices associated with contracting might differ between or within these two groups. How, for example, might demographic differences—especially gender, race, and age—affect contractors' options? What organizational practices and employment policies are significant? How do these skilled professionals manage the risks of a volatile economy and understand their contractual status? What, then, might their experiences reveal about changing employment relations and new patterns for work and careers?

Changing Employment and the Standard Job

Contracting is one of a range of alternative forms of paid work that contrasts with standard jobs, the institutionalized system of social relations that defines regular employment. Lodged in an organization, a standard job represents a position, fixed vertically and horizontally. With it comes a set of formal responsibilities, often classified in a status hierarchy and elaborated in a job description, along with informal expectations governing workplace interaction. Although informal processes may influence hiring, firing, and mobility within a firm, the standard job is a formal arrangement. A job connotes stability, an individual's ongoing relationship with a single employer, a steady paycheck, and established patterns of authority and accountability. Measured against this standard, most alternative forms of employment—contracting included—provide less stability or at least less regularity. They may be part-time, intermittent, casually arranged, temporary, or seasonal. Individual workers may experience high mobility, periods of unemployment, and multiple employers and work sites.

The standard job has a relatively short history. It was forged in the early twentieth century and institutionalized in U.S. policy during the New Deal and the decades that followed. Its dominance corresponds with the industrial era, a period of national corporations and vertically integrated firms. A standard job in such settings came to imply steady work, even lifetime tenure, and the prospect of a career with one employer. Social insurance— the benefits tied to standard employment in the United States—protected employees from the risks of illness and disability and often protected their families as well. Having a job meant going out to work. It separated paid employment from household labor. Having a good job, especially for full-time male employees, meant earning a family wage high enough to support a middle-class household. In the mid-twentieth century, therefore, the standard job complemented the normative nuclear family, with its single primary wage earner. Social policies protected employees with standard jobs by extending legal rights, covering occasional periods of unemployment, and elaborating standards for regulated work-site practices.[5]

Even at its mid-century high-water mark, however, the standard job was never universal. Rather, its formal practices applied most broadly to employment in large organizations with internal personnel systems. There, corporate policies or collective bargaining agreements prevailed, and job classifications defined relative status. For a great many professional and managerial employees, employers further promised lifelong careers in return for commitment and competent performance. In the mid-century corporation, therefore, layoffs for those in white-collar jobs were exceedingly rare.[6] Layoffs did periodically affect workers in mass production, but under union contracts, they too could depend on established procedures, usually based on seniority, for determining who would be dismissed and called back. Although the mechanisms might differ, therefore, both white-collar and blue-collar workers were secure, subject to standard practices and regulations.

The standard job, in turn, became the basic unit in what came to be known as an internal labor market, a system of hiring and promotion bounded within an organization. Where internal labor markets regulated employment, employees were typically hired at the bottom rungs of a hierarchy and then retained and promoted from within its ranks.[7] Analysts have offered different explanations for the expansion of internal labor markets, but all stress the order and regularity they imposed.[8] Within an employing organization, an internal labor market structured mobility. It also provided a rationale for employers to invest in a workforce and for employees to commit their efforts to organizational goals.

Changes in this rational, ordered process, the destabilizing of standard employment, are one key to understanding the contradictions that contract professionals face in the new economy. Rather than well-marked paths and clear criteria for success, segments of the workforce have encountered new calls for entrepreneurialism, initiative, and adaptability. Employers offer fewer promises and demand less adherence to formal rules. Individuals exercise greater latitude and decision making. The standard job has thus shed some of the rigidity that characterized employing organizations in the mid-twentieth century. Yet, despite the loosening of its strictures, the standard job, the fixed position in an employing organization, continues to provide both a system of regulation and a cultural ideal, a set of norms associated with "permanent," full-time work. Other forms of employment, contracting among them, are thus alternatives to this standard.

Signs of strain in this system had appeared by the last decades of the twentieth century. Long-term employment had become less dependable and promotion through internal labor markets less assured. Researchers seeking explanations for this new instability have pointed to the parallel processes of downsizing and restructuring, which in the 1980s began to sweep through entire industries, dislodging systems and displacing employees.[9] Downsizing directly threatens job security, even for those who survive layoffs. Restructuring, in turn, flattens hierarchies and shrinks the ranks of managers and supervisors. In the aftermath of restructuring, organizations tend to depend less on formal rules and procedures and, instead, stress communication and collaboration. Under these conditions, problem solving devolves downward, to lower levels of the hierarchy;[10] control becomes less centralized; and workers exercise greater discretion. The scope of jobs may also expand. Rather than narrow classifications and predetermined duties, for example, job descriptions may identify knowledge and skills to be applied to broad functional areas.[11]

The reconfiguring of organizations and internal labor markets has, in turn, altered career trajectories. Whereas employees' advancement once depended on loyalty to a single employer and progression along a career path, employees now more readily move across organizational boundaries, from one employer to another.[12] In the wake of downsizing, of course, changing jobs may well be a forced choice and not necessarily a means for career advancement.[13] Nevertheless, in some occupations mobility between employers has become a well-established strategy for gaining varied experience.[14] Considering this evidence of greater mobility, some analysts have proposed employability, rather than job security, as the basis for longevity in the workforce.[15] Even employees who remain with a single employer, they suggest, must be prepared to move from project to project, as work teams convene and dissolve. Mobility, they argue, can provide opportunities and expand choices, especially for knowledge workers with essential expertise.

More varied patterns of mobility indicate more variation across opportunity structures. Whereas holding a specific job once defined an individual's future prospects and marked individual progress, opportunities for advancement now more often take a career in unanticipated directions. In its extreme form, employment in this fluid, dynamic universe becomes less a sequence of positions than a series of opportunities, each building on the next, a trajectory that unfolds through individual initiative as employees develop both their own expertise and the knowledge that allows their employers to succeed. The optimism reflected in these images coincides with the rhetoric of free agency that pervades much of the popular advice now offered to workers in the new economy. Although the possibilities for endless opportunity appearing in some advice literature are surely overstated, such analyses do suggest a stark departure from earlier models of career success through loyalty to a company and adherence to its protocols.

The new economy, therefore, represents a broad cultural shift through which employees no longer exchange loyalty for security and no longer expect their careers to follow a scripted progression of stages. Work relations have generally become more fluid and open to frequent change. Still, despite challenges to its uniformity and stability, the standard job remains associated with a relatively stable organizational position, however tenuously held. For most of the workforce, too, the standard job remains the dominant model for defining relations of employment. Against its promise of regularity, most alternative forms of work necessitate greater self-reliance and mobility. Analysts of alternative work arrangements distinguish a number of these forms with the term *contingent work*.

Nonstandard, Contingent Work

Contingency connotes instability, and the term *contingent work* has been applied to a constellation of work arrangements, each differing in one or more ways from the standard, "permanent," full-time job.[16] As a concept, contingent work lacks a clear definition. Nonetheless, the notion of contingent employment has generated much debate about the causes and consequences of the short-term and alternative work arrangements that have proliferated in the new economy. Although these alternatives depend on the standard job as a basis for comparison, many such forms have long existed in tandem with standard employment, and some predate the standard job. Among these segments of the workforce are on-call workers, day laborers, seasonal employees, and migrant workers, all of whom experience sporadic or intermittent episodes of paid work.[17] In many ways, these long-standing arrangements exemplify the instability associated with contingency. The notion of contingent work, however, is broader and more inclusive.

Common definitions of contingent work also encompass temporary arrangements, including short-term assignments mediated by staffing agencies or contracting companies.[18] These relatively recent forms of employment are similar in that they are both triangular—that is, an intermediary in the labor market and its client firm divide responsibility for hiring employees and overseeing their work. Broader definitions of *contingent work* add part-time work to the mix, especially when a worker would prefer or is seeking a full-time job.[19] Still broader definitions include all part-time workers as well as those who work independently on contract and consider themselves self-employed. Defined this broadly, *contingent work* is synonymous with an array of nonstandard work arrangements.

These differing definitions underlie a debate over the number of contingent workers in the United States. Addressing the perception of a developing problem, the U.S. Census Bureau, in 1995, began collecting data to document the size and scope of the contingent workforce and then conducted several more counts in alternating years.[20] Questions added to the Current Population Survey (CPS) ask workers about their formal work arrangement; the expected duration of their current jobs; and various related aspects of employment, including earnings, benefits, and union membership.[21] Analyses of these successive surveys, using different definitions of contingency, have yielded widely divergent estimates, with different implications for employment policy and practice.

Applying a series of narrow definitions, analysts with the U.S. Bureau of Labor Statistics (BLS) initially estimated the size of the contingent workforce at 2.2–4.9 percent of the total working population, a low range that captures only those respondents who expected their current employment to end within a year. In contrast, a separate team of researchers analyzed the same data but applied a much broader definition that generated a much larger figure: 29.4 percent of the workforce.[22] Over time, the two perspectives represented by these estimates have converged principally on one point: the size of the contingent workforce, however defined, has shown little change from the mid-1990s into the twenty-first century.[23] Indeed, later waves of data collection, spanning an economic cycle, verified that contingent work encompasses a stable segment of overall employment.

The debate over numbers and definitions also represents different views about the causes and consequences of contingent work. Analysts who apply a narrow definition suggest that these arrangements are evidence of expanded opportunities for certain segments of the workforce. Correlating contingent status with workers' social characteristics, they identify a disproportionate number of women, younger workers, and older workers near retirement. In these groups, they suggest, individuals might well be choosing arrangements that allow them to reduce their hours or to enter or exit the workforce with relative ease.[24] Other analysts, however, see in the same correlations evidence of limited opportunity, especially for populations that are already disadvantaged.[25] They identify patterns of lower compensation, fewer employment benefits, and very low levels of union membership, and they see in the disproportionate numbers of women and racial minorities a pretext for ongoing economic inequality and social marginality. Most nonstandard work arrangements, they suggest, reinforce barriers to upward mobility and so constrain opportunity over time.

Unfortunately, the debate over numbers can obscure larger questions about the changing structures of employment and new sources of opportunity and constraint. The emergence of nonstandard work arrangements across industries, occupations, and sectors of the economy, taken together, represents a structural shift that has, in turn, shifted risk from institutions to individuals and from employers to workers. In contrast to the relative security and regularity that much standard employment still provides, contingent status increases risk in multiple ways: greater uncertainty, fewer formal rights and legal protection, and greater individual responsibility for finding sources of work and remaining employable.[26] The erosion of internal labor markets and the formal regulation of the standard job occur along many dimensions.

The larger debate over contingent work, therefore, is about risk and opportunity. Questions of risk underlie the challenge to standard employment that contingency represents. The standard job and its legacy provide shelter from labor market risk by protecting workers from at least some of the uncertainty inherent in economic exchange. Social insurance and the system of rights associated with standard employment further provide protection from chance events that affect an individual's employability and labor market prospects. The standard employment relationship thus manages and distributes risk. Employers that provide standard jobs, even with the limited commitments that characterize work in the new economy, assume the risks of keeping a business sound and a workforce employed. By externalizing a segment of the workforce and limiting the terms of their commitment still further, employers shed elements of risk, which individual workers must then assume.

Researchers concerned with the consequences of increased risk for a segment of the workforce often characterize nonstandard work as "substandard" and equate contingent status with the proliferation of "bad" jobs.[27] For contract professionals, such reasoning suggests, contingent work represents a problem. Lack of commitment to long-term employment makes relations with clients uncertain. Selling their services in a sometimes volatile market becomes a constant imperative. The insecurity inherent in this unregulated system is evident in Emily's unease about her new employment status. Wondering whether contracting can be "dependable" over time, she too raises questions about the risks and consequences of contingency. At the same time, however, both Emily and Ben describe contracting as an opportunity made possible, as Ben explains, by "a fundamental change" in work relations that can also offer steady employment and professional challenge. How can we reconcile these two facets of experience?

Vicki Smith, a sociologist, offers a perspective that moves past the dichotomy between "good" and "bad" jobs and looks instead at the interplay between risk and opportunity.[28] As employment relations have become unstable and careers unpredictable, she asserts, variation across settings and circumstances structures risk and opportunity differently. In the new economy, most workers face some degree of uncertainty and may take risks and assume responsibilities that were both inconceivable and unavailable several decades ago. Rather than a clear distinction between "good" jobs and unstable work arrangements, workers encounter a range of institutional contexts.

Variation across the Contingent Workforce

The shifting dimensions of risk and opportunity point to variation across occupations, industries, and labor markets that employ contingent workers. Institutionalized differently, specific nonstandard arrangements present different labor market structures, industry practices, and occupational norms. Variation extends, as well, to the terms of the standard job. Although standard employment once provided clear—although by no means equal—opportunity structures for those situated within internal labor markets, it too has absorbed some of the risks of the new economy. Variation and volatility, experienced across the workforce, thus confront individuals with a new calculus for making choices.

Much of the analysis of nonstandard, contingent work has focused on lower-wage occupations and has identified conditions that offer multiple means of subordinating contingent workers. Clerical and industrial temps, for example, earn lower wages than their counterparts in standard jobs; forgo most benefits of standard employment; and contend with isolation, disrespect, and frequent readjustment to the changing demands of supervisors, coworkers, and staffing agency recruiters, who demand deference and control labor market access.[29] When a divided workforce encompasses a marginal segment of workers, these studies suggest, contingent status is a mechanism of subordination that augments individual risk and limits access to better opportunities.

Nonstandard work arrangements may also exacerbate race and gender inequalities. For example, case studies of clerical temps document discriminatory practices that might well be deemed illegal for workers who hold standard jobs.[30] Studies of part-time workers reveal a common assumption that part-time hours benefit women but justify lower wages.[31] Studies of home-based contingent workers reveal similar assumptions that paid work performed at home is appropriate for women, whose low wages are secondary to family concerns.[32] Contingent status, together with accommodation of work and family, may thus provide a pretext for inequality, as family needs delimit a worker's options and drive individual choices.[33]

Across professional occupations, however, different opportunity structures offer a varying mix of risk and choice. For example, attorneys working through staffing agencies on temporary assignments report marginality in their profession as a whole but greater control over their time and choice of assignments than jobs in law firms typically allow.[34] Traveling nurses, who move from one locale to the next, similarly avoid the heavy workloads and mandatory overtime so often demanded of their counterparts on hospital staffs.[35] Unlike attorneys, however, traveling nurses also report ready access to standard jobs without loss of professional standing. In contrast, adjunct faculty members, working outside the tenured core of the internal labor market of academia, find their experience as teachers and researchers devalued and their options foreclosed.[36] Here contingent status marginalizes one segment of an occupation.

Despite evident variation, professional occupations tend to offer those with nonstandard work arrangements a greater measure of autonomy than other contingent workers exercise. Professional work is traditionally associated with a status that confers prestige.[37] Professionals possess expert knowledge, usually gained through formal education, an investment in human capital expected to pay off in relatively high incomes and positions of authority. Indeed, professionals employed in standard jobs lodged in internal labor markets do, in general, exercise more authority over their work than lower-level workers are allowed. Professionals are trusted workers.[38] They adhere to occupational standards that help to maintain their status. Professionalism thus includes adherence to principles of practice. It provides both a mechanism of control and a source of identity for professional practitioners.

Studies of Contract Professionals

What, then, do we know about contract professionals? Which occupations constitute the workforce segment of these contingent workers? What norms and practices prevail on each side of the divide between standard and nonstandard employment? Contract employment, by definition, is governed by short-term agreements, which typically last for a defined period of time or for the term of a project. Contracting usually means much mobility and frequent negotiation as individuals move from one project to the next. Professionals involved in artistic production—among them screenwriters, film editors, and sound and light technicians—have long worked through contract arrangements, in fluid skill-based labor markets, with teams that are assembled for the duration of a project and dissolved when the effort ends.[39] On contract, these workers apply their well-defined expertise and then move on, finding new projects through networks of colleagues, clients, and brokers of talent. Labor markets for artistic production thus resemble the structure of craft work before the industrial-era factory with its narrow jobs and institutionalized assembly line.[40]

Contract professionals in print media evidence some of the same patterns. For example, two groups of researchers analyzing self-employed freelancers in Britain, one focusing on translators and the other on copy editors and proofreaders, found emerging occupational groups of contractors working on a project-by-project basis. Most of these workers expressed overall satisfaction with their work arrangement, despite having been "pushed" into freelancing when their former employers downsized.[41] Both studies identified a preponderance of women among these contract workers, and both found many who considered their work arrangement a strategy for accommodating paid work with family responsibilities. Echoing debates about the contingent workforce in the United States, these studies document conditions in which social characteristics rationalize the contingent status of one segment of a labor market.

Contractors also encompass a segment of the technical professionals—engineers, computer experts, and technical writers—who, as Peter Meiksins and Peter Whalley (2002, 11) explain, "customize" their working time.[42] These researchers focus on experienced professionals, both women and men, who opted to limit their hours at work, either through contracting or through organization-based jobs defined as part-time. For these workers, standard employment had come to demand more of life than they were willing to give, and contingent status became a strategy for achieving more autonomy to control their daily schedules. Contractors in this study exercised enough leverage to select assignments that allowed them to limit their working time. Avoiding staffing agencies for finding work, they relied instead on informal networks of colleagues and clients, together with professional associations that helped them establish connections. Despite their limited hours, these contract professionals navigated effectively within a system of employment that depends on informal social relations.

To date, Stephen R. Barley and Gideon Kunda have provided the most comprehensive analysis of contract work.[43] These researchers, too, studied technical professionals, identifying a broad swath of workers, from "gurus," who develop and implement cutting-edge computer systems, to technical administrators, who maintain work stations and in-house networks. Their analysis thus offers a bird's-eye view of an employment sector that is more a set of occupations requiring technical expertise than a single, unified body of knowledge and skills. Most of the technical professionals in this study contracted with staffing agencies, which not only identified sources of work but also brokered "deals" between contractors and clients (96). Here, too, contractors moved within a system of employment relations, but one in which a triangular arrangement, with a staffing agency as intermediary, had become the norm. Like the technical professionals studied by Meiksins and Whalley, these contractors exercised more negotiating leverage than most lower-wage contingent workers are able to exert. Market conditions, human capital, and experience in the market all mitigated some of the uncertainty and powerlessness found among clerical and industrial temps.

Barley and Kunda equate contracting with an "itinerant professionalism" (285), through which contractors apply their expertise for a series of clients and maintain up-to-date skills, usually understood as knowledge of the latest technical tools. Itinerant professionalism conceptualizes contract employment as a shift from organization to occupation. Whereas employees with standard jobs look first to their employing organizations as sources of social identity and connection, contractors look to their occupations. Whereas organizations depend on administrative measures—incentives, sanctions, rewards—to exert control over employees, contractors turn to the market, where reputations affect their long-term employability.

Barley and Kunda depict contractors as strategic actors seeking to negotiate the best deals while simultaneously managing a set of contradictions that pervade the experience of contracting: respect versus resentment, technical challenge versus routine work, high pay versus high exposure to the vagaries of market forces. These contradictions surface in contractors' dealings with agency recruiters, hiring managers, and employees in standard jobs—that is, with all actors involved in this three-way institutional arrangement. Presumably, then, the experience of contract work is distinct from comparable standard employment. Some of the differences, however, invite closer examination. What is it, for example, that causes so many of these professionals to continue to contract despite at least occasional offers of regular jobs? How do organizational practices and patterns of interaction reflect the differences between contracting and standard employment? How do labor markets for contractors differ across occupations?

Taken together, the studies by Meiksins and Whalley and by Barley and Kunda present another contradiction. Just how flexible is contract work? Although Meiksins and Whalley find contractors taking advantage of temporal flexibility to limit their working time, Barley and Kunda find just the opposite effect: the contractors in their study seemed to work constantly. Far from limiting their work hours, they became absorbed in efforts to stay abreast of technical change. How do we reconcile these two, apparently contradictory findings? Is one group of contractors merely more cognizant of the risks of technical obsolescence? Are Barley and Kunda's informants merely more driven by the pace of change in Silicon Valley, a region well known for high-tech innovation? Do they face special constraints on their autonomy? For example, does the intercession of a staffing agency somehow affect the expectations and options associated with contracting?

A comparison with standard employment might be instructive here. Indeed, the tension between autonomy and constraint is far from unique to contracting; rather, it pervades much professional work. The administrative demands of organizational employment are one source of constraint; clients, or customers, are another. Practitioners in the classic professions—medicine, law, and the clergy—have long had to package their services for a market of consumers, even though they claim expertise based on formal credentials and exercise authority over the services they provide.[44] In the new economy, as standard jobs expand and the shelter of standard employment becomes less secure, organization-based professionals are also subject to the demands of customers, whose requirements may dictate product specifications and determine staffing needs. How, then, does contracting affect a professional's exposure and accountability to these external forces? With all workers more directly exposed to the risk of the labor market, do contractors merely accumulate additional risk? Or does extra-organizational employment so restructure risk and opportunity that contractors experience their options and work relations differently?

A Distinct Occupational Focus

I focus in this book on two groups of contract professionals representing two distinct occupations that span a number of industries. My informants are writers and editors, who work in print and web communications, and programmers and engineers, who work in software development and its applications. This study, therefore, surveys some of the same landscape identified in recent studies of technical contracting. Like other researchers, I began my study having seen much evidence that technical work, sometimes facilitated by technology itself, had come to incorporate a segment of workers in nonstandard arrangements. I knew, too, that the computer industry, with its reputation for geeks and nonconformity, had long supported work cultures and practices that had (at least) stretched the limits of the standard job. And I had witnessed the emergence of new occupational categories, such as technical writing and information technology (IT) administration, which support the use of information technology.

I also knew something about contracting. For many years, I had worked as an editorial freelancer, selling my services to a clientele that produced documents and publications, and before that I had worked as a hiring manager, engaging contractors to perform much the same work. I knew the labor processes associated with the development and production of print materials. I also knew that contractors in this occupation may work not only as editors and writers but also as proofreaders, indexers, translators, and project managers, all sets of skills that need not correspond to the titles attached to standard jobs in any particular organization or industry. Contract professionals, I had learned, often establish a breadth of expertise, a menu of services that might provide options and, presumably, leverage in the labor market.

For the purposes of this study, therefore, my definition of *occupation* is wider than the dimensions of most standard jobs in the same line of work. Standard jobs and the fixed positions they represent rarely provide the range of skills and experience that contract employment allows. Rather, the relative stability of most positions limits their scope, so that practitioners seeking broader experience must usually change jobs. At the same time, however, my definition is narrower than those in recent studies of technical contracting. Rather than equating occupation with technical facility, I separate technology from expertise and define an *occupation* as a central set of skills and related tasks, activities, and knowledge. For the writers and editors in this study, the central skills were the ability to write and revise copy.[45] My informants, therefore, all contributed to something in print: a book, article, report, website, or other document. Unlike freelance journalists, who also write, their work was crafted to meet clients' specifications, and so they marketed their services rather than products of their own design. Beyond their common skills, they might work in any number of substantive areas, including many technical fields. As in other studies, therefore, some of my informants worked as technical writers and editors.

The programmers and engineers I interviewed also shared a central set of skills: the ability to write and revise code. Like writers and editors, many of these practitioners applied their expertise to a number of related functions. Some of these informants, for example, worked as test engineers, reviewing portions of code for bugs; others designed system architecture that linked any number of related computer programs. These tasks also required a facility with programming,[46] whereas IT administration, in contrast, does not. Unlike recent analyses of technical contractors, therefore, this study excludes those who work principally as technicians.[47] A few of my informants had worked in this capacity at a different stage of their careers. At the time of our interview, however, they were either developing new technologies or maintaining the functionality of technical products.

All my informants had made contracting their principal source of employment. Although some had other sources of income or sometimes worked only intermittently, none was a moonlighter supplementing a standard, organization-based job. Many asked me to emphasize that contracting is a legitimate, above-board arrangement, neither an informal, under-the-table exchange nor a euphemism applied to unemployment. Although many were familiar with the term *contingent work,* only one embraced this as a self-defining category. To be a contingent worker, apparently, implied qualifying as a full-fledged professional only some of the time. Most of the contractors I interviewed similarly rejected the designation *temp,* although they universally characterized their agreements with clients as temporary and were under no illusions about the tenuous nature of their working relationships.

The term *contractor,* for most of my informants, connoted greater equality in their relations with clients, but the language they used also reflected a lack of uniform terminology to describe their employment status. Some spoke of their jobs, but the word meant a specific project or assignment with a specific client, not a position in an employing organization. A few preferred to call themselves consultants, and some made fine distinctions between terms. Consultants, they asserted, exercised greater latitude and authority, whereas contractors took direction and more closely resembled employees with standard jobs. As I found throughout my fieldwork, however, the nomenclature distinguishing a contractor from a consultant is far from universal. For example, in one setting I observed that contractors functioned much like employees but were called consultants by the client that employed them. As I came to understand, contract professionals are acutely aware of fine gradations of difference in their work relations, but the terms that describe them remain fluid and, across contexts, fail to capture the differences that practitioners experience.

A few of the contractors I met also vehemently objected to the word *freelancer.* The term, they pointed out, contains the word *free,* suggesting that a freelancer's services should be donated or at least carried little value. The etymology of the word, in fact, dates from the social relations of medieval Europe, where a free lance was a knight unsworn to an overlord and so free to sell his services. The hiring of editorial freelancers—or, in the United Kingdom, freelances—is both established practice and common parlance in the publishing industry, and among my informants, therefore, writers and editors more often used the term. In parts of Europe today, they might instead call themselves portfolio workers, indicating the portability of their expertise.[48] Although a few of my informants self-identified as portfolio workers, none reported hearing the term applied in the United States.

Contractors' concerns over the terminology that marks them reflected both pride in their work and the liminal status they occupy. Although many of the contractors I interviewed had spent long careers working without formal employment and organizational affiliation, they had experienced questions frequently enough, usually from those outside their occupations, to have learned to characterize contracting carefully. It was employment, they made clear, but they were not employees. Employees worked on staff, in jobs fixed in an organizational hierarchy. They had employers, not clients. Most employees worked full-time, so contractors sometimes distinguished themselves by saying that these colleagues held full-time jobs. The distinction, however, meant not that contactors worked part-time, according to some measure, but that their time was ultimately divided among clients. Even when they worked full-time for a single client, they would eventually move on to another. Contractors, they emphasized, are mobile professionals, marketing their expertise in an occupational labor market.

Overview of This Book

In this book, I analyze the experience of contracting from the perspectives of those who do it. I seek to explain the rationales, processes, and conditions that shape their experiences. By addressing two distinct occupations—and thus two different groups of workers—I widen the angle of vision beyond a single industry or occupational case study and so identify common elements that define this alternative system of employment. Attention to two occupations in which contract work is well institutionalized allows me to examine the strategies by which these two groups of contractors make their way in the labor market, to analyze occupational norms and patterns. In the chapters that follow, therefore, I consider the social organization of contract employment and ask what this system can reveal, not only about contracting but also about the institutionalized standard job. With close attention to one form of nonstandard, contingent work, therefore, I consider the implications of a structural and cultural shift that affects organizations, occupations, and individuals in the new economy.

Chapter 1, "Two Occupations with Divided Labor Markets," considers flexibility. Here I explore different arrangements that promote or limit flexible work relations for workers and employers in the new economy. I explain the legal distinctions that differentiate forms of contracting and, in some cases, obscure their similarities. I chronicle the development of contract employment in two key industries—book publishing and computer software—in which many of my informants acquired their expertise, and I consider demographic similarities and differences in these two occupations. I conclude with an explanation of the research design.

Chapter 2, "Assessing Options, Making Choices," is about opportunity and choice. Contractors consider their arrangement a positive choice, but their reasoning depends largely on available options in the same occupation. Here I chronicle the transitions that most have made to contract work. I relate my informants' accounts of workforce restructuring and the experiences in standard jobs that inform their decisions. I consider, too, the implications of working time in distinguishing contract from standard employment and in creating different logics, risks, and opportunities for different groups of practitioners in these two occupations.

Chapter 3, "Performing Expertise," reveals patterns of negotiation between contractors and clients. Lacking the structural authority of an organizational position, contractors negotiate working relationships as they develop a clientele. Rather than relying on formal credentials, they depend on social interaction. To promote their abilities and exercise authority over their work, they display competence and strive for an effective performance that will establish occupational equality with clients and counterparts on staff. Analyzing expertise as a form of impression management, I reveal the backstage processes that support these efforts.

In chapter 4, "Managing Marginality," I consider the contractor's structural position outside the organization and the shelter of the internal labor market. Here I elaborate the processes through which contractors seek to maintain client relations, and I consider the components of expert performance that sustain a contractor over time. Contractors, I argue, must simultaneously assert expertise and remain disengaged from organizational conflict. Identifying patterns of interaction that support contract employment, I elaborate the contradictions between exclusion and participation that characterize client relations.

In chapter 5, "Collegial Networking, Occupational Control," I shift attention from contractors' marginality in client organizations to their inclusion in occupational communities. Here I analyze the processes through which contractors establish and maintain connections with colleagues, and I explain the significance of occupational networks that support a social identity and an occupational culture. Collegial interaction, I argue, contributes to patterns of workforce mobility based on reciprocity, referral, and informal exchange. Networks of colleagues that enforce occupational norms thus provide mechanisms of occupational control.

Chapter 6, "Extra-Organizational Careers," focuses on contractors' careers outside the organization and the career paths associated with standard employment. Here I analyze the multiple trajectories that constitute contractors' careers, the many mixes of skills they offer their clients, and the effort required for them to remain employable in an occupational labor market. I consider the trade-offs that contractors make as they forgo standard jobs but seek occupational advancement without formal organizational positions. For many contractors, I explain, career choices constitute strategies for accommodating paid work with family obligations.

Chapter 7, "Work Relations Reconsidered," documents the downside of an unregulated system of work relations. Here I identify difficulties that may affect contractors only occasionally but nonetheless demonstrate the limits of informality as the basis for managing conflict and resolving disputes. I note the influence of the staffing industry, which appears to be increasing. I consider, too, the prospects for collective advocacy among contractors, in light of impediments posed by existing labor and employment law. I conclude with an overview of public policies and organizational practices that would benefit contract professionals.

In the conclusion to this book, I turn again to the broader context of the new economy with its structures and cultures of flexibility. Here I address the intersection of risk and opportunity that characterizes contracting in the two occupations. I consider the implications of a mobile workforce and dispersed occupational communities. I argue, too, for an expanded system of employment relations that would protect the interests of all workers without sacrificing choice or demanding uniformity. Such a system, I suggest, should accommodate a range of contractual differences and promote equality in the workforce as a whole.

1

Two Occupations with Divided Labor Markets

Why do firms hire contractors? Short-term need and flexibility are the key reasons. Because employers no longer retain enough staff for periods of peak demand, contractors can temporarily augment the workforce of a firm. Contractors also enhance managerial options. Hired for a defined period or the duration of a project, they can be chosen for expertise that employers need only occasionally. Rather than employers, however, contractors speak of clients, usually firms that engage their services for short-term work. For their clients, contractors collectively constitute an external labor market that facilities flexibility in two ways: numerical flexibility allows an organization to adjust the size of its workforce; functional flexibility can reconfigure an organizational mix of specific skills and experience to meet changing needs.[1]

Flexibility, then, is the essence of contract employment. But flexibility is a slippery, sometimes contradictory concept. In the last decades of the twentieth century, calls for flexibility were heard both from employers seeking to reshape the workforce and from employees seeking greater control over the spatial and temporal expectations of their jobs. In response, some employers have instituted flexible work arrangements—such measures as teleworking, job sharing, and flextime—which alter the dimensions of the standard job without fundamentally changing its terms. When offered as options, flexible arrangements can be appealing. When, instead, flexibility demands that workers accede to altered schedules and changing expectations, flexible practices can limit options and impose instability on individuals' lives.

This dichotomy of flexibility reflects a broad cultural shift in which unpredictability has become a norm and adaptability a virtue.[2] Flexible practices promote versatility and accommodation to change, and flexibility can thus be an attribute of both employing organizations and the individuals who work for them. Contractors practice flexibility as they span the boundaries of multiple client firms. Organizations, in turn, demonstrate flexibility by responding to the environments in which they operate. Yet organizational responsiveness can also impose flexibility on workers, who may or may not welcome its demands. Flexible staffing may offer variety, but short-term, tenuous arrangements also limit commitments to a segment of workers who can be quickly hired and dismissed. What, then, facilitates flexible staffing practices? What formal and legal distinctions mark the different segments of the occupations in this study? What are their similarities and differences?

Flexible Staffing and Employing Organizations

Contract employment—like other forms of nonstandard, contingent work—supports a change in organizational structure, an erosion of internal labor markets and the development of a peripheral segment of workers who can serve as a buffer for a more protected core of employees. On the margins of the organization, therefore, contractors may well be the first dismissed during periods of retrenchment. Like most nonstandard work arrangements, contracting circumvents collective bargaining agreements or internal organizational policies. Whereas temporary employment serves principally to cut costs, the presence of a peripheral labor market segment may also exert downward pressure on wages and employment standards.[3]

For some firms, however, cost cutting may be secondary to "head count," a vernacular expression designating the number of employees on the firm payroll. Much like Barley and Kunda (2004), I heard "management by head count" as a common rationale for hiring contractors.[4] Publicly traded companies, I was told, face special scrutiny by Wall Street analysts, who track corporate performance by monitoring revenues against fixed costs for personnel. Keeping the company head count down and fixed costs low can thus bolster the price of the company stock, and because contractors do not figure in its head count, their presence can obscure actual labor costs. Unlike employees, contractors represent variable costs, usually listed as vended services, so they provide a managerial strategy for cost control even when their fees total more than employees' salaries. Indeed, many of my informants wondered whether contract employment truly achieved significant cost savings.

The Role of the Staffing Agency

In some settings, the costs of contracting include transaction costs paid to staffing agencies, which act as labor market intermediaries. Staffing agencies across the economy have contributed to the institutionalizing of flexible staffing.[5] Agencies recruit potential workers, screen them to identify their skills, sell their services to clients, and so act as brokers in a triangular employment relationship. Their profits depend on a markup, usually a percentage of a worker's hourly wage. High workforce mobility has created business opportunities for staffing agencies, which have, in turn, contributed to workforce restructuring by institutionalizing systems that match workers with employers.[6] Temporary work arrangements have thus proliferated in tandem with an expansive staffing industry. Although many staffing agencies are large enterprises (some on an international scale), others are small businesses with only one or two employees. Most of these specialize in specific occupations or sectors of the economy.

Case studies of temporary clerical and industrial employment have elaborated processes of subordination and exploitation associated with agency-mediated work. Staffing agencies submit workers to demeaning forms of testing; keep them guessing about future assignments; and threaten loss of income for infractions, real or imagined.[7] Agencies also protect the interests of their client firms, whose business they seek to maintain. With a steady supply of workers, the staffing industry retains leverage in this three-way employment relationship, and where the staffing industry controls access to the labor market, these intermediaries package and commodify low-wage work, standardizing both services and workers.

In contrast, studies of higher-wage occupations indicate variations in staffing agency practices. Agencies operating in health care intervene in response to nurses' complaints about hospital policies.[8] Agencies that place temporary attorneys assume that lawyers will follow codified standards of legal practice and rarely resort to surveillance or intimidation to exert control over individual workers.[9] Agencies that place technical contractors similarly depend on common occupational practices. Rather than supervisors, recruiters in this sector act much like sales representatives as they seek both contractors and clients for their services.[10]

The staffing agencies my informants had encountered ranged from impersonal "body shops" to more specialized service providers, which might try to meet their individual requests. Occasionally, I heard an informant speak of pressure from a recruiter, or I heard of agencies that failed to be forthcoming about the likely difficulties with a specific client or project. Contractors' responses to these unpleasant situations depended, in part, on their perceptions of labor market conditions. During boom times, when work seemed plentiful, a contractor might ask a recruiter to intercede, but a worsening economy could made contractors warier and hesitant to complain. During downturns, too, more contractors sought out staffing agencies and their recruiters in efforts to find work.

Legal Definitions and Practical Distinctions

Not all industries that hire contract professionals routinely turn to staffing agencies. In the book-publishing industry, for example, clients tend instead to hire and pay contractors directly. The BLS defines such arrangements as independent contracting.[11] Independent contractors find their own projects and forge their own agreements with clients. Many consider themselves self-employed and are also counted in the BLS census of self-employed workers.[12] Whether paid by the hour or by the project, they receive full payment without the withholding of taxes. Under regulations of the U.S. Internal Revenue Service (IRS), therefore, they must pay their own federal taxes in estimated installments. Independent contractors are sometimes called "1099 contractors"—or describe themselves as "on 1099"—because the end-of-year tax forms they receive from their clients are an IRS Form 1099 rather than a Form W-2, which reports income and withholding for employees.

Since the reform of the U.S. Social Security system in the early 1980s, independent contractors have also been required to pay a self-employment tax that includes both the portion of Social Security tax required of employees and the portion that employers otherwise contribute. This provision doubles an individual's Social Security tax, but because most independent contractors can also deduct from their taxable incomes such business expenses as supplies and equipment, they may, in effect, reduce the amount. Indeed, some of my informants considered their deductions a tax advantage that outweighed the additional tax burden of self-employment, even though they had to track expenses related to their work.

Independent contractors who are defined as self-employed in the United States may also establish and fund their own benefits. For example, in lieu of the 401(k) retirement accounts that employers commonly provide for employees, they may open similar tax-deferred accounts—self-employed 401(k)s, simplified employer pension plans (SEPs), or Keough plans, which require them to contribute a percentage of each year's income.[13] As alternatives to the mechanisms that support standard employment, these provisions suggest that independent contracting is an officially sanctioned, well-institutionalized system, fully recognized in practice and in law.

The definition of independent contractor, however, has been much contested. Although contract employment has long been a common practice in some occupations and industries, new regulations in the 1980s restricted its definition and changed the legal status of a segment of the contract workforce. The statute that impelled this change was a provision of the Tax Reform Act of 1986, Section 1706, which eliminated from the tax code a "safe harbor" clause that had protected clients from liability for tax withholding. In response, the IRS developed a set of criteria, or test, with which to define independent contracting. The IRS criteria, which some contractors call "the twenty questions," were wide-ranging. They included periodic payment, a desk at a client site, or routine status reports, which in some combination might disqualify someone as an independent contractor and indicate, instead, that a standard employment relationship exists. In practice, however, the application of the criteria has been uneven, and the

IRS has been concerned principally with monitoring large companies, especially in the technology sector.[14]

The statutory change in the mid-1980s redefined the formal status of many independent contractors, at least for tax purposes. In response, through the late 1980s, the business press warned about the legal dangers of "misclassifying" employees, and many companies sought new mechanisms for maintaining a contract workforce.[15] To accomplish this aim, they turned to the staffing industry. Its growth since the decades following World War II had itself been the result of a regulatory shift that had redefined these labor market intermediaries and made staffing agencies the employers of record for the workers they matched to clients.[16] By the 1980s, therefore, the staffing industry had an established model for flexible staffing, with agencies acting as brokers in a triangular relationship.

The staffing industry model placed workers on agency payrolls and then billed clients for each worker's wage plus a markup that covered overhead and profit.[17] As the nominal employer, a staffing agency was required to deduct payroll taxes and comply with IRS requirements for reporting wages. By withholding taxes, the staffing industry augmented its function as a labor market intermediary and redefined agencies as actual employers. By 1987, therefore, the industry was well positioned to accommodate clients seeking a "safe" business practice, to avoid legal liability for "misclassifying" a segment of the workforce as independent contractors.

Some of the contractors and managers I met contrasted agency contracting with their memories of the 1970s and 1980s, when companies had readily hired contractors "on 1099." A few even believed that this form of contracting had become illegal at some point in the late 1980s or early 1990s. By then, they recalled, many large firms had designated a few staffing agencies as "preferred vendors." With these agencies, a company might negotiate smaller markups, and hiring managers and human resource departments might establish long-term relationships with individual recruiters.[18] Yet few hiring managers, I was told, delegated staffing decisions to recruiters, no matter how well known. Recruiters might screen resumes and refer contractors, but managers retained the decision-making authority.

A hiring manager might also recruit contractors directly, turning to a staffing agency merely to act as a payroll agent, a business service that places the contractor on the agency payroll. Indeed, some of the contractors and managers I met spoke of their three-way arrangements as "payrolling." A contractor and client would agree on the terms for a contract assignment—the work involved, the likely duration, the rate of pay—and a staffing agency would then intercede as the employer of record. A few of my informants had worked for clients who had given them a choice of payroll agents among a number of preferred vendors, and a few more had, on occasion, chosen their own payroll agents, with the approval of their clients. Some staffing agencies sought to attract contractors by offering health insurance or 401(k) contributions, although these benefits, more often associated with standard employment, had limited value for contractors who moved frequently from one client—and one agency—to the next.[19]

Day to day, my informants reported, recruiters had little, if any, involvement with their work. Contractors usually submitted documentation, approved by their clients, to the agencies that were nominally their employers, and the agencies would periodically issue paychecks. Contractors working on long-term projects, which provided a steady stream of revenue for the agency, might occasionally receive some acknowledgment, perhaps an invitation to lunch or some other agency-sponsored event. Some recruiters also made site visits, checking in with contractors and, perhaps, checking up on their performance as well.

Although a few informants in each group sought to work entirely on an independent basis, most considered their legal status fluid. In any year, therefore, a contractor might have income from self-employment reported "on 1099" and wages reported by one or more staffing agencies on Form W-2. Those working for more than one client at a time might be receiving both forms of payment simultaneously as well. For most of my informants, therefore, tax status was mostly a formality that had little effect on day-to-day work. The responsibilities they assumed and the work they performed were largely the same, no matter the process for the payment and calculation of taxable income.

Contractors might also incorporate their own businesses, as four of my informants, two in each occupational group, had done. As employees of their own corporations, these contractors paid themselves salaries from the revenues their employment generated. They also underwrote much the same business expenses that contractors "on 1099" deducted from their taxable incomes. Incorporation incurred additional fees and reporting requirements, they explained, but had little to do with daily work practices.

Because it altered their legal employment status, however, contractors could find incorporation useful for avoiding staffing agencies entirely. Work relations, in both occupations, thus depended not on formal legal status but on daily interaction with colleagues and clients.

Occupational Practice across Work Sites and Industries

For clients across industries, these contract professionals draft and revise copy or code, meeting specifications for products to which they contribute individually. Indeed, some describe themselves as "contributors," connoting the complex set of integrated functions involved in the development and production of a published document or a sequence of coded commands. Harnessing their abilities to meet identified goals, few practitioners in either occupation exercise wide-ranging control over product specifications. Instead, generating copy for a document or code for a program, they conform to established systems of product development and quality assurance long established in key industries that employ a significant segment of practitioners.

Origins of Contract Work: Industry Expansion and Occupational Rationalization

Industries that established occupational practices—publications for writers and editors, computer technology for programmers and engineers—developed job structures that defined these occupations and then facilitated the process of contracting out. In the decades that followed World War II, expansion in both industries spurred employment.[20] Rapid growth promoted new bureaucratic structures, with jobs based less on the integrated craftlike enterprises of an earlier era and more on an industrial division of labor, with greater subdivision among sets of tasks. In today's terms, occupational practice became less flexible, and jobs increasingly fit standard categories with narrow scope and clear lines of authority.

In book publishing, the overarching title *editor* assumed modifiers that denoted different aspects of editorial work. Acquisitions editors, or sponsoring editors, retained the greatest authority, usually associated with management and sales. Below them in the hierarchy were those who did the hands-on editing, among them copy editors, sometimes called line editors, who reviewed and revised copy, and developmental editors, who might assume greater responsibility for substance and style. The proliferation of job titles denoted positions that marked imprecise and overlapping areas of responsibility, and they appeared in different combinations and in different segments of the industry. All, however, represented a bureaucratic system of employment newly established in the postwar period and expanded in the 1960s and 1970s. The result, to different degrees, was a greater standardization of jobs within industry segments.[21]

The expanding computer industry saw similar developments at about the same time. In this new field, growing firms established systems of employment with distinct positions for software engineers, coders, testers, systems analysts, and programmers specializing in specific computer languages or applications. Job descriptions and titles varied from one setting to the next, but most employers developed hierarchies that fragmented the more holistic skill sets that dated from the early days of computing. Some analysts of the industry saw in this bureaucratization the preconditions for deskilling and downgrading of work.[22] Others associated these same developments with multiskilling across an occupation that was growing to encompass an ever-larger knowledge base.[23] In any case, programmers and engineers who developed computer systems became employees in organizations in which managers dictated specifications and defined essential skills.[24]

Employing organizations thus shaped occupational practice, so that professional employment developed differently from such occupations as law and accounting, which began through solo practice in the service of individual clients and only later bureaucratized. Unlike attorneys or accountants, these two groups of professionals have long applied their skills in the service of corporations or state-run entities. Embedded in formal systems of work relations, their occupational practice has long been oriented toward meeting the goals of an employer, and as systems of contract work developed, they too were largely defined and controlled by employing organizations. Contract employment, therefore, developed in the wake of occupational rationalization, through which employing organizations designated functional areas with specific mixes of tasks, knowledge, and skill.

Although not a new phenomenon, contracting became increasingly common as firms restructured and adjusted employment practices to promote flexibility and accommodate frequent change. Many of the contract professionals I interviewed described a growing awareness of contract employment during the 1970s and 1980s. Book publishing, for example, witnessed a rapid expansion of editorial freelancing, beginning in the 1970s.[25] Some freelancers joined project teams at client sites, but many worked from home offices, and so, to some observers, could be largely invisible. Case studies of computer firms from the same period also document the presence of contractors, sometimes called consultants, hired occasionally to fill specific functions or augment staff during times of peak demand.[26] By the 1980s, as firms across the economy restructured, this fluid, flexible workforce had been well institutionalized. The result was a dual system of work relations.

Occupational Similarities: Tasks, Teams, and Opportunity Structures

The contractors I met described performing much the same work as their counterparts in standard jobs, but a contractor's relationship to the status hierarchy of a client remained open to change. A contractor might, for one client, provide an additional "body" needed to meet a schedule or complete a set of tasks and, for another client, might bring special expertise not represented among employees. Where contractors assumed the "scut work" that employees preferred to avoid, contract work might be associated with lower-level tasks. Where contractors, instead, engaged in more challenging work, they might enjoy higher status, which could, for some, extend to supervisory responsibilities and the oversight of employees. Indeed, several of my informants described projects for which contractors had become managers or team leaders. In both occupations, therefore, the contractors I met considered themselves the colleagues, not subordinates, of employees.

Informants in both occupations described working in project teams. These might include some mix of contractors and employees or be composed entirely of contractors. The teams might encompass a large staff or include only one or two other people. They might be tightly focused work groups, whose members concentrated solely on their collective enterprise, or they might be loosely constituted arrangements, with members working simultaneously on multiple projects with different teams. Contractors' accounts of team effort reflect an outgrowth of flexible work relations in which postbureaucratic structures promote collaboration and self-management among designated groups of workers.[27] Within client organizations, my informants explained, teams were often temporary configurations for the employees as well as the contractors. Some fluidity in working relationships, therefore, was common across both segments of these occupational labor markets.

Although they reported varying degrees of participation in planning and oversight, my informants generally described their work as collaborative and interdependent. Team work, their accounts made clear, demands some coordination of tasks, priorities, and time lines, and an effective practitioner needs to channel information appropriately, identify the needs of others, and keep them informed of changes. Formal meetings, in which contractors might participate, could facilitate this coordination, but in both occupations, the process was open-ended for all but the most circumscribed of tasks. Rather than isolating a segment of the labor market, therefore, contracting demands interactional skills.

Communication practices, however, can vary considerably. Contractors working far from a client work site, often from their own home offices, described communicating principally through e-mail, fax, and phone.[28] When working within driving distance, they might also attend face-to-face meetings or work occasionally on-site, but they were otherwise invisible to their colleagues. Contractors who worked principally on-site were more visibly integrated into project teams and had also to adapt, to some degree, to office routines. A contractor's work site most often depended on the client's preference or on industry practice. In some segments of book publishing, for example, off-site contracting has long been institutionalized. My informants who worked as technical writers and editors also described more home-working arrangements than programmers and engineers experienced. Both occupations, however, evidenced variability, and over time, a contractor might engage, to some degree, in both on-site and home-based employment. Flexibility and adaptability had thus become imperatives.

Despite talk of team work, practitioners in these two occupations spend significant time in solitary concentration. In both groups, work involves individual mental effort, with close attention to detail. Team work is thus asynchronous, and contact among team members can be sporadic, with long periods of singular effort. When communication is required, team members might convene for meetings, in person or online; they might converse or exchange messages; or they might rely more often on memos and reports. In both groups, practitioners described collaboration as an ongoing process of conveying information to others and assisting with problem solving. Occupational practice, however, also demands considerable autonomy, and individual practitioners remain responsible for managing their working time to meet deadlines and delivery dates.

Mobility across client firms makes a contractor's knowledge of occupational practices especially important. For example, knowing that an artist will be rendering drawings for an illustrated book, an editor also knows that missing specifications early in production can delay publication. Knowing that segments of code must eventually compile to produce a piece of software, a programmer knows that the interface between them needs attention well before the program is scheduled to run. Contractors in both occupations thus participate in established labor processes that define the phases of development and the flow of information. These common processes promote codification, a shared understanding about areas of expertise and associated work activities.[29] Practitioners can, thus, carry their expertise from one client to the next, assured of a basis for work requirements.

Opportunity structures, therefore, encompass divided labor markets with common occupational processes, facilitating mobility within an external labor market from one client to the next. But contractors might also move, in the course of their careers, across the boundary between the external and internal labor markets, to take standard jobs in employing organizations. Indeed, 35 percent of the contractors I interviewed had moved from contracting to standard employment and back again to contracting, indicating that in these two occupations, contractual status can change several times throughout an individual's career. With hourly rates and project fees that can net incomes equivalent to the salaries paid to employees, contractors may consider options on both sides of the labor market boundary throughout their careers.

Labor market access in both occupations depends on experience, typically understood as a marker of expertise, and on multiple connections with colleagues, clients, and, in some cases, staffing agency recruiters. Less important are formal educational credentials or certification in a specific field. In neither occupation does a single institution act as gatekeeper for either segment of the labor market. Instead, occupational practitioners are themselves gatekeepers, providing recommendations for those they consider occupationally competent. As opportunity structures span labor market boundaries, occupational connections promote mobility and sustain communities of practice[30] among both contractors and employees.

Occupational Differences: Mobility Patterns, Valuation, and Pace of Change

Patterns of mobility, however, differ somewhat between the two occupational groups. With home-based contract work more often available to writers and editors, these contractors are also more likely to work on multiple projects, often with more than one client at a time.[31] Most of the writers and editors whom I met described a diverse clientele, often including publishers of print materials and other organizations seeking expertise for internal or external communications. Programmers and engineers might also maintain a diverse clientele and could also work for more than one client simultaneously, but they more often described clients that wanted contractors on-site, frequently for a standard workweek. For contractors employed in such arrangements, moving from one client to the next usually meant a complete break between assignments. The mobility patterns in such circumstances more closely approximate the experiences of employees who frequently change jobs.

The clientele for writers and editors might also include individuals, usually authors with work in progress and a need for assistance, which might range from occasional advice to silent partnership. Although none of my informants had relied exclusively on individuals as sources of work, several described occasionally working for individual clients, with no formal organization involved. Such arrangements, they explained, depended greatly on personal affinity and effective collaboration. All of the programmers and engineers I interviewed, in contrast, described working exclusively for firms, and although small firms might comprise only a few employees, they were organizations, not individuals. Unlike the writers and editors, none of the programmers and engineers I met described labor markets comprising individuals seeking their services.

With the staffing industry especially prevalent in the technology sector, programmers and engineers, more than writers and editors, tended to involve recruiters as they moved across client firms. Indeed, two of the programmers I interviewed reported relying entirely on recruiters as sources of work. Although the intercession of a staffing agency might have a negligible effect on daily work experience, an agency agreement could severely limit a contractor's ability to seek new assignments independently and almost always restricted a contractor's access to repeat business with the same client. Here the ubiquitous noncompete clauses that agencies demanded in their contracts tied a contractor to that agency as the sole market intermediary, usually for some defined period. Programmers and engineers, who navigate these triangular arrangements more frequently, thus tend to find their options increasingly shaped by the mediation of a staffing agency.

Programmers and engineers might also be geographically mobile, with contract assignments sometimes available worldwide, typically through staffing agencies. These assignments usually involve full-time on-site work, often at premium rates for what clients consider special expertise. Geographical mobility requires frequent relocation, potentially straining relationships with families and communities, and some of my informants considered this form of employment an option to use only sparingly.[32] Among the programmers and engineers I interviewed, four had been geographically mobile, all within North America, within two years of the interview. Among writers and editors, none of my informants had encountered an equivalent form of mobility.

The population of geographically mobile programmers and engineers in the United States also includes a segment of immigrant workers, represented by only one of my informants, who had earlier worked on an H-1B visa. The terms of employment for these temporary immigrants typically tie them to a single sponsor, often a staffing agency, and bar them from other employment. Consequently, they face an opportunity structure different from the labor markets in which both employees and other contractors move more readily. Analysts contend that the terms of their employment place downward pressure on wages and working conditions.[33] Controversy over U.S. immigration policies, however, has focused principally on the supply of skilled workers rather than on employment practices related to this segment of the labor market. In policy debates, this form of immigration is thus closely connected with outsourcing, a form of contracting out beyond national borders.[34]

Fast-changing technology also disproportionately affects programmers and engineers. Constant technological innovation means a steady stream of new systems and technical tools, which require practitioners to be ever vigilant and up to date on knowledge of new developments. Writers and editors who work in technical areas must also learn about technologies and trends. They, too, may be required to invest frequently in new equipment and develop new proficiencies. Yet ongoing innovation and ever-shorter product cycles can render a programmer all but unemployable in only a few years. Programmers and engineers, therefore, face a greater risk of obsolescence and must more assiduously seek strategies that maintain their occupational viability.

Economic cycles of boom and bust also present greater opportunity—and corresponding risk—for programmers and engineers. Periods of economic expansion since the early 1980s have been marked by rapid expansion in technical employment. The dot-com boom of the 1990s, for example, produced a new media industry in which programmers and engineers were central figures. Here the high-flying rhetoric of a new economy melded, temporarily, with fast-expanding opportunity.[35]

Although my informants reported relatively few contractors employed by dot-com start-ups, their emergence did provide new venues for employment. The bust that followed, however, left a large segment of workers unemployed in a labor market with limited capacity to absorb them, either as contractors or as employees. Some of the writers and editors I met had similarly found themselves stranded in periods of economic retrenchment and, for a time, unemployed. In general, however, their range of potential clients encompassed industries less susceptible to economic cycles. The effects of both boom and bust, therefore, have been more extreme for programmers and engineers.

Writers and editors also lack the cultural cachet associated with programming. Although neither occupation is publicly visible—indeed, workers in both occupations are the invisible back end of much communications—programmers and engineers enjoy the prestige of prototype knowledge workers in a new, knowledge-based economy.[36] With esoteric skills that seem almost magical to some, they are the vanguard of a much-heralded digital age, the pioneers who have ushered it in. Writers and editors, in contrast, are more closely associated with old media, which have lost some luster in a digital economy. Although writers and editors are also knowledge workers, their skills often seem, to the public at large, more accessible and easier to learn. Indeed, a few of the writers and editors I interviewed complained of requests for assistance from acquaintances seeking access to the occupation, and several of my informants lamented the assumption that "anyone who can read" can easily acquire their skills and ply their trade successfully.

The hourly fees paid to contractors in these occupations reflect this relative valuation. Among my informants, writers and editors reported fees as low as $15 per hour and as high as $95. Higher hourly rates, many explained, were more commonly paid for project management or writing in technical areas, and then usually when they worked for clients outside the publishing industry, in which companies tended to pay fees in the lower portion of the range. The programmers and engineers I interviewed also reported a range of hourly rates, from as low as $25 to as high as $175, with different kinds of clients paying different rates for the same expertise. There, too, a hierarchy of skills placed developers, who more often described themselves as software engineers, at the top of the scale and testers and applications specialists at the bottom. The differences within each group, therefore, could be greater than the differences between the two occupations.

Occupational Demographics: Race, Class, Age, and Gender

The contractors I interviewed in both occupations are mostly white, educated, and broadly middle class, demographically similar to their counterparts in standard jobs.[37] Only five of my informants self-identified as nonwhite according to common racial and ethnic criteria, three as Asian and two as Latino. When asked, the contractors I interviewed often explained that they had encountered few, if any, African American colleagues, either as contractors or as employees. Lack of racial diversity may reflect hiring processes that depend on collegial networks, which may in turn exclude minorities, however informally.[38] Lack of educational opportunity may also limit occupational access for some racial minorities. Indeed, all of my informants had attended college, and some had advanced degrees, although not always in fields related to their occupations.

Both internal and external segments of these occupational labor markets, therefore, reflect considerable homogeneity, but contractors in both occupations tend to be past the first phase of their careers—that is, usually past age thirty and often older. Although they ranged in age from twenty-three to sixty-seven, most of my informants were in their forties and fifties. Despite my efforts to find younger and inexperienced workers, only two informants, one in each group, were simultaneously new to their occupations and to contract work at the time of the interview. Contracting, I was told over and over, is largely inaccessible to those without experience, so that aspiring practitioners can only rarely use contract employment to "learn the ropes" and enter the field. Thus, unlike employees, most contractors in these two occupations have reached at least early middle age.

The gender composition of these occupational groups, however, is markedly different. As my informants consistently acknowledged, programmers and engineers are predominately men and writers and editors predominately women. In both groups, the gender composition of the workforce does appear to be the same across internal and external labor markets, indicating that contracting is not itself a gendered phenomenon. Rather, each occupation reflects a legacy of gender typing in key industries that has contributed to developing gender-related norms and expectations. These, in turn, have affected the relative valuation and cultural representations of these two occupations.

A process of feminization in book publishing, beginning in the 1940s, transformed a male-identified occupation to one in which women predominated only a few decades later. Editorial work had long attracted an educated elite, usually men who entered the field for access to scholarship and high culture,[39] but postwar expansion brought greater commercialization and new employment practices. Employers configured new organizational hierarchies and faced contradictory economic pressures to hire more employees and also contain costs. By opening editorial work to women, employers could meet both demands.[40] Women thus entered the lower ranks of editorial work, mostly in jobs that paid less than earlier generations of employees had enjoyed.[41]

Feminization, some analysts suggest, was a precondition for expanding the practice of hiring editorial freelancers.[42] By the 1980s, in most large publishing houses, freelancers, principally women, had assumed a significant share of the concentrated hands-on work, which in some segments of the industry went "out of house" to contractors working in home offices.[43] The increasing number of women on staff as well—some of them rising to senior positions—only reinforced the image of editorial work as a women's profession. As my informants consistently noted, writers and editors in many industries are predominately women, reflecting the feminization of the occupation as a whole.

In contrast, computer programming developed first in the military as a subfield of electrical engineering, long established as a male preserve. Only as the industry expanded to the private sector in the postwar period did it see some growth in women's employment,[44] usually in the lower-status functions of computer operations or data processing.[45] But despite industry growth through the late twentieth century, the number of women in higher-level positions in computer programming has remained disproportionately low.[46] These positions are often assigned the title *software engineer,* signaling the roots of the occupation in engineering, and indeed, many programmers have been trained as engineers.[47]

Computing thus developed a gendered occupational hierarchy, with men performing higher-status work. Women did become programmers in greater numbers beginning in the 1970s, yet the occupation remained socially defined as male, sustained by a masculine occupational culture in many high-tech firms.[48] Long hours and late nights excluded those responsible for families. Occupational practice encouraged displays of technical prowess and an aggressive interactional style. Hackers and nerds symbolized an obsession with new technologies and mastery over machines. Although effective performance required negotiated decision making, success meant claiming credit for individual achievements, and to achieve organizational success, programmers might need to compete for visibility.[49]

Studying Contract Work

Embarking on this project, I sought to explain contractors' participation in a system that excludes them, structurally, from the formal organizational authority associated with standard employment. I wanted to understand the cultures that supported occupational achievement outside the career structures of organizational careers. I sought, too, to explain contractors' choices and the sources of identity that sustain their involvement in their respective fields. By specifying the occupational focus of my project, I found contract professionals willing, even eager, to share accounts of their working lives and to discuss the changing relations of employment that have affected them. I also found occupational communities in which practitioners readily identified one another, offering their understanding of criteria for occupational membership.[50] By elaborating their perspectives, therefore, my informants participated in defining the boundaries of each occupational group.

Finding Contract Professionals

I began my investigation by seeking interviews. I knew at least a few practitioners in each occupation, and so I first asked for contacts among potential informants whom I had not already met. To establish multiple points of access, I posted notices on websites directed to each occupational group, and I accepted occasional referrals when friends and acquaintances offered assistance. Most of my referrals, however, came from my informants. I systematically asked those I interviewed for referrals to colleagues who might inform my study. I explicitly sought practitioners for whom contracting was a principal source of personal, although not necessarily household, income. I also sought both demographic diversity and work experience in a variety of industries and geographical regions.

Contract professionals in these two occupations tend to cluster near the industries that employ them in large numbers, and in the United States, they are concentrated in the Northeast, the Northwest, and central California. As a researcher based in New England, I found that most of my informants were within a day's travel and that I could easily meet them in person, but I expanded my reach to meet informants working in other regions of the United States as well.[51] I also interviewed four contractors by phone. Comparing my informants' accounts, I discerned no regional differences in occupational practices, nor did contractors with work experience in different parts of the United States report region-specific distinctions. In some geographical areas, contractors do have a wider range of prospective clients, creating more opportunities and, perhaps, easier mobility from one assignment to the next. The demand for specific expertise appears to differ somewhat in some areas as well.[52]

I interviewed sixty-eight contract professionals, thirty-four in each occupational group, meeting most in their homes, some in public places, and a few at client sites. The samples I constructed reflect homogeneity both within and between these occupations. I did, however, seek to oversample among the minority gender in each occupation, and I found word-of-mouth referrals especially helpful in this regard. Many informants expressed an awareness of gender-typing and seemed especially interested in showing me a shift toward gender integration. Of the thirty-four programmers and engineers, thirteen are women; of the thirty-four editors and writers, fourteen are men. In contrast, I found few younger workers, and racial diversity proved elusive, despite my active recruiting.

Using referrals to find contractors, I soon recognized the importance of professional networks in each of these occupational groups. The contract professionals I met all appeared to be well connected, both to their clients and to various networks of colleagues. To identify differences in occupational practice, therefore, I sought practitioners who lacked connections, and I posted requests on occupation-related websites for contractors with little collegial engagement. Eventually, I interviewed six contractors who self-identified as having limited networks, four editors and two programmers. I found, however, that they, too, maintained at least a few collegial contacts. As many of my informants speculated, contracting requires connections, and a contractor in complete isolation is unlikely to remain business for long.

Most of my informants also believed themselves to be highly capable, and many were concerned that I represent contracting well. Indeed, several explicitly asked that I interview only those they deemed the best qualified or most skilled. I could not, of course, assess the quality of work that any of my informants produced, but to understand the range of contractors' experiences, I tried to find at least a few who were faring poorly, so I asked my informants for referrals to colleagues whom they considered somehow deficient. After repeated requests, I eventually interviewed six of these practitioners, three in each occupational group.[53] I found, however, that none self-identified as unsuccessful; rather, each had found a receptive clientele.

The population of contract professionals in these occupations may well include practitioners who try contracting and either quickly give it up or fail to find work. Perhaps they lack the requisite motivation to secure a series of assignments or the experience to convince clients that they can truly meet deadlines and project specifications. Perhaps they lack professional networks and so are unable to identify a clientele. Perhaps, too, as several of my informants speculated, they "just aren't good enough" as occupational practitioners. Perhaps—but they are not part of this study. The contract professionals I found were not all happy with their work or with their employment status. Although several were adamant about the advantages of contracting, some were considering a return to standard employment or the possibility of other careers. In the meantime, however, all were managing reasonably well, or so their accounts suggest, practicing their profession in an external labor market.

Talking to Contractors, Observing Their Work

When they could find the time to commit to an interview, the contract professionals I met were eager to talk about their work. Indeed, time constraints were the principal reason that some prospective informants refused my request or were ultimately unable to meet with me. Once we began the interview, their greatest concern was usually that I present contracting as legitimate employment, available to qualified practitioners. In this regard, my own experience as a contractor seemed to establish my legitimacy as a researcher, or at least the contract professionals I interviewed seemed to consider me worthy of their trust.

I asked my informants about the circumstances that had led them to become contractors, their long-term career goals, their working relationships with colleagues and clients, and their perceptions of the advantages and disadvantages of contract employment. I was most interested in the context that informed their work experience, not only their choices but also their perceptions of options, risk, and flexibility. I probed about differences across work sites and about strategies they had used to solve problems. Most responded with detailed accounts, which often included their own analyses of contract work. Some continued to stay in touch with me in the months that followed, usually through e-mail, to elaborate on a topic we had discussed or report the resolution to a situation in progress at the time of our interview.

A few informants further offered to introduce me to managers or recruiters with whom they had good working relationships. In all cases, I quickly agreed. These additional sources of data, I reasoned, might provide a different perspective on contract work, especially in programming and engineering, where I had no personal experience. Eventually,

I interviewed twelve informants who were in some way responsible for hiring contractors or overseeing their work: three recruiters, eight managers of departments employing programmers, and one editorial manager. These informants, too, were eager to describe their work practices and decision-making processes, and they provided corroborating evidence of contractors' accounts of negotiation, hiring, and work-based relationships.

I asked these managers and recruiters about staffing decisions, the use of staffing agencies, and their criteria for hiring and evaluating contractors. I probed about decision making, about who had authority and under what circumstances. I asked about both the advantages of a flexible workforce and the problems that the system of contracting could cause. Much as contractors wanted to underscore the legitimacy of contracting, the managers I met sought to explain the care they took to treat contractors fairly. Managing teams that included both contractors and employees, they seemed acutely conscious of the potential for inequality and for double standards that might undermine team cohesion or productivity. When they oversaw highly productive work groups, they considered even-handed team management an accomplishment.

I interviewed all managers at their work sites, where four invited me to stay and observe team meetings and work-site interaction.[54] In three settings, I later returned, ushered in by managerial authority and free to watch the daily routines with the promise that I would share my observations. Introduced as a research consultant, I was able to speak not only with contractors but also with employees who had experience working alongside them. I could easily tell the groups apart. In all settings, employees and contractors wore electronically coded badges of different colors, which not only denoted their contractual status but also determined their access to certain areas of the building. As a visitor at each work site, I wore a badge of yet another color, which distinguished me from all who worked there and, presumably, limited my access as well.

I spent approximately twelve weeks observing, intermittently, in two of these settings and three weeks as a participant observer in another, where I was briefly hired as a contractor to complete a set of documents. Although my observations proved useful, I analyzed the data cautiously, recognizing that I had spent relatively little time as an observer at any single site. I also make no claims that these setting represent, in some way, typical environments for on-site contracting. Rather, the ready invitations I received suggest that these work sites might better represent best practices in managing integrated groups of contractors and employees. Indeed, all seemed to be convivial settings, conducive to team effort.

A steady, and perhaps more representative, source of corroborating data was online discussions in each occupational group. Many professional organizations provide ongoing advice and online discussions for members, and informal online chat groups abound in both occupations. I joined five such groups merely by submitting my e-mail address to the manager of a Listserv, and in a sense, I observed interactions by reading e-mail exchanges. Discussions ranged from technical matters, many of them beyond my grasp, to ruminations that addressed aspects of my research. Although I mostly avoided participating, I twice used a Listserv to ask a question that an interview had raised. This "lurking" online as I proceeded with my interviews also helped validate my emerging analysis of contract employment.

2

Assessing Options, Making Choices

Contracting requires experience. Most of the contract professionals I met had invested years learning occupational skills and practices while formally employed in organizational positions. Some had risen through their employers' ranks, achieving notable organizational status as team leaders, project directors, or department managers. Leaving these jobs, when the departure was optional, had been far from a precipitous decision for the contractors I encountered. Many, however, had confronted a stark choice: find a new job elsewhere or try your hand at contracting. Indeed, my informants' accounts were morality tales of organizational change in which downsizing, restructuring, and corporate caprice figured prominently. In a period of volatile organizations, they explained, any promise of job security had come to sound hollow.

Contracting, however, represented new risks. The prospect—indeed the expectation—of short-term employment brought the specter of unemployment always a little closer. Without an employer's commitment, at least nominally, they would assume responsibility for finding contract assignments, negotiating terms with each new client, and ensuring that the work they took on would earn them adequate incomes. Outside the shelter of an internal labor market, contractors might expect to become organizational shock absorbers, hired when needed but quickly dismissed in times of rapid change. What, then, would propel an experienced professional into this form of employment?

The calculus of working time provides a significant part of the answer. Working time contributes to the construction of two distinctly different forms of employment, one on each side of the labor market boundary. When the standard job becomes a "greedy institution,"[1] immersion in work means long hours and unpaid overtime. As employees, my informants explained, they had devoted evenings, weekends, and holidays to employers with tight deadlines and last-minute demands, all for the prospect of an organizational career that had dissipated in the wake of internal change. As contractors, in contrast, they lacked organizational status and the promise of long-term employment, but with hourly rates paid for the time they worked, their compensation more closely matched their effort and investment. Working time, their accounts suggest, is a scarce commodity, often contested. The difference between a fixed salary and an hourly wage, which increases in proportion to time spent at work, can thus figure significantly in the assessment of options.

Lack of organizational position had also released the contractors I met from requisite displays of organizational loyalty. For employees, they explained, a culture of commitment demands visible identification with company goals. As members of the organization, employees are subject to the beliefs, values, and perspectives that pervade organizational life. Contractors, in contrast, can avoid such allegiances. Socially separated from employees, even when integrated into work-site routines, they stand apart from the internecine conflicts, commonly termed office politics, which can undermine expressed goals and hamper individual success. Ironically, although their status enforces distance from employing organizations, contractors claim a sense of security. Rather than organizational membership, they strive to maintain their distance, patrolling the boundary between the internal and external labor markets. Narratives of experience in employing organizations thus support the choice to work on contract.

Mobility as Security

Mobility, together with a willingness to adapt to change, had become security for the contractors I met. The ability to move on—having the skills, knowledge, and occupational connections—had become a source of stability in an external labor market. Chastened by their experience as employees, the contractors I interviewed had become wary of employers' promises. Lisa, a writer, editor, and project manager, told of her last years in standard employment, in a technical products firm that was slowly losing its share of the market: "They [her employer] were desperately trying to sell the group, and they tried to sell it to some other company, which fell through. And eventually, after over a year [another corporate employer] bought it. But by the time they bought it, the group had reduced its size way down.... So I was feeling maybe like I should get out of there. It wasn't a secure feeling."

Lisa had watched as members of her group left for other jobs or for contract assignments. Standard jobs were available, she recalled, but "things were changing.... people just keep moving from job to job... so you have to be able to do that, no matter what you do." Encouraged by a colleague, Lisa ultimately joined a team of contractors at another company. "That's how it started," she remembered. "My friend made it seem like this contract job was a good opportunity. So I went."

Job Security versus Employment Security

Accounts of organizational volatility pervaded my interviews with contractors. Mergers, acquisitions, downsizing, reengineering[2]—all had made standard jobs insecure. Images of job longevity and stability—the gold watch, the retirement party—represented a bygone era. Some of the contractors I met had begun their careers expecting to remain with one employer and, with hard work, to be promoted through processes of internal hiring that constructed career ladders for salaried employees. In some cases, this expectation had seemed, for a time, to be reasonable. Growing industries had promised ongoing opportunities. Periods of economic expansion had helped make organizations seem stable. Eventually, however, conditions had changed.

Many of the contractors I met described slowly coming to reevaluate their options. Valerie, a writer and production manager, had worked as an employee at two publishing companies for almost fifteen years and had become the managing editor in her division. Then her company merged with one of its competitors, and the newly merged corporation began a series of layoffs. As a manager, she had at first been responsible for delivering the bad news, but as the downsizing continued, she realized that her job, too, would probably be eliminated:

> At some point I became aware that I was very vulnerable, much more so than I had ever really imagined being.... so to think that I was secure by working for a publisher, working for a big company was a false idea.... And I think now that I'm going to look out for myself much better than any company would ever look out for me,... knowing that I'm the one who's responsible. I'm mean I just feel like it was such an illusion to think that you were secure.

Having weathered several waves of downsizing, Valerie considered herself a "survivor." She could manage a volatile labor market, she explained, but wanted never again to be caught unprepared in a storm of organizational change. Employment security, based on employability with multiple clients, had replaced the job security of organizational position.

Practitioners in both occupations told much the same story, distinguishing the illusion of job security in an internal labor market from their contractual relations with clients. Bennett, a software engineer, declared contracting to be "more honest" than standard employment, a difference he had experienced after eight years at a software development firm where changing priorities and reconfigured hierarchies had undermined success for much of the staff. There, he lamented, employees had to compensate for ever-shifting expectations. "One of the major reasons why I choose to be a consultant rather than a regular employee is that it frees me from the abusive relationships that many managers have with employees," he explained. "They simply can't do to me what they could do to their employees.... I'm just too free to leave." Labor market options, Bennett believed, gave him leverage to move on.

Contractors' accounts are replete with concern for a kind of honesty that standard employment had lacked. Staff positions had promised continuity. Loyalty and good performance were to be rewarded with recognition, increasing pay, and rising organizational status. With security eroding, however, any promise of a successful career in return for a job well done sounded hollow. This broader shift in employment relations rationalized choices for the contractors I met. Ben, a software engineer and project manager, had worked for two large corporations well known in the 1980s for innovation in computing. Each, however, had slowly disintegrated, selling its products to competitors, until the shell that remained finally closed:

> I went through the whole downsizing, right-sizing turmoil in the industry, and I saw some of the most unethical, abusive, usury things that any human could ever do to another human. And I went through it with a large company here that went through a huge number of layoffs, eventually went into bankruptcy.... I was never laid off. I was never fired, and most of the time during corporate buyouts or subsidiary sales, I was offered substantial bonuses and relocation packages.... But the way I saw a number of employees who in some sense could least take it, they were very abused.

Ben's sense of breached obligations exemplifies the notion of a "psychological contract" that informs attitudes toward employment.[3] Although rarely a formal agreement, a psychological contract implies an exchange between employer and employee that binds both parties to reciprocal norms. The psychological contract of the mid-twentieth century exchanged job security for demonstrated commitment. Employees could expect rewards for good performance and could expect, too, that layoffs would occur only when company finances mandated a reduction in force. When downsizing and layoffs proceeded even during boom times, the change in organizational norms represented, for many, a contractual breach. For those caught in the teeth of change, the new terms often violated a sense of justice.

Even indirect experience could generate outrage and feelings of betrayal. Janice, a writer, editor, and project manager, had been working for a large computer manufacturer when her employer began consolidating by selling some of its products to new corporate partners. With the sale of each product went a staff of employees—developers, technicians, product support staff—who were usually offered jobs with the new employer. Janice explained,

> This happened to a friend of mine. Her choice was either to go to that other company with her existing job at the existing pay—most of the benefits

were sort of the same—but it wasn't the same company. . . . I mean it's just, to me it's like immoral and unethical. I really have a big problem with it. . . . It just seems to me it's a way for business to not deal with the fact that there are people connected to projects. It's like when they first started the layoffs at [company name], we all became magically "resources," you know. We weren't human beings anymore. We were "resources."

For Janice, the sale of the product teams along with the product reduced the employment relationship itself to a commodity. A commitment to the company, as well as the product, had informed a personal investment. Watching her colleagues change employers without their consent was "one of the big reasons I became a contractor," Janice asserted.

Contracting, of course, might be no more secure than standard employment. Indeed, it was often more tenuous. When projects were cancelled, contractors could expect to cease work immediately. When budgets had to be cut on short notice, contractors might well be the first to go. Evan, a manager at a software development firm, called himself a survivor, having remained with one organization for thirty-three years, through repeated mergers and spin-offs that had made him an employee of three successive corporations that owned the plant at which he worked. Corporate restructuring or changing priorities, he explained, could quickly affect his staff:

From very high levels of management, we've had absolute edicts, I mean no exceptions. Any and all contractors within divisions—not within the entire corporate, entire whole world or whatever—but within certain divisions, all contractors must go by next Tuesday. And there we were again; this was very serious because again in some cases the contractors were doing better work and more critical work. . . . People making the decisions at the top were making balance-sheet decisions.

Integrated into project teams, the contractors Evan oversaw functioned much like employees, so that precipitous reductions in a workforce could cause serious difficulties in completing projects. Such decisions, however, rested with upper management, forcing middle managers to adjust to the new constraints.[4]

Paradoxically, some of my informants had seen similar reductions lead to layoffs of employees while the contractors remained in place, or they recalled projects that contractors had completed after a layoff had depleted the staff. Valerie recalled "rehiring" members of her own staff as editorial freelancers, when work remained to be done. These experiences run counter to much of the analysis of the core-periphery organization, in which contingent workers on the margins provide security for core workers in standard jobs.[5] Apparently, many firms employing the contractors I interviewed had instituted such a structure. Yet, in some cases, the presence of a peripheral workforce had been no guarantee of job security for employees in the core. Rather than offering a buffer against insecurity, contractors might instead provide a ready resource, especially when they could quickly assume the responsibilities of laid-off employees.

Practitioners in both occupational groups described far-reaching managerial decisions coming from unseen places, sometimes without warning. Those who had been contracting for a protracted period, therefore, tended to see contract work as more secure. Employment security meant assuming the responsibility that the external labor market imposed, but with high mobility nearly universal, they would always expect to move from job to job. Industry volatility, workplace restructuring, and managerial caprice had conditioned their expectations and constructed their choices. Contracting, which offered no implicit promises of security, could thus seem like a more "honest" arrangement.

Transitions into Contract Work

My informants' stories echo earlier studies, in each occupation, in which an external factor, often a layoff or relocation, caused an employee to leave a job and try contracting.[6] For a few, the transition had followed organizational instability so severe that they were unsure about whether they had quit or had been laid off or fired. Melanie, a writer and editor, described working for a publisher in the mid-1980s: "I was actually fired from my job, ... but I was, I guess, laid off. So both.... It was a complicated situation. It was a new office, and I wasn't really getting along with the new supervisor, ... and so they decided they didn't need me.... And I left, and I started freelancing [for the same company] right away." By the time she left, Melanie recalled, the decision had become so fraught that neither she nor her new supervisor could clearly label the cause. Yet, once removed from the organization, she found conditions tolerable and for almost a year accepted steady offers of contract work from her former employer.

Most of my informants described more straightforward departures. Noreen, a writer and editor, had arranged her own layoff: "I was downsized, but I asked to be. Of course, it was after the [severance] package was like nothing. The people that left first got the good deal. My manager, of course, hadn't really downsized anybody, so when I left, I did the exit. I ran the exit interview for him 'cause he had no clue what he had to do.... But it was a real blood bath." Like many large corporations, Noreen's employer had offered a severance package to employees who left voluntarily. The package, common in some industries, was an incentive, sometimes offered selectively, to leave. It was meant to lessen the impact, and as downsizing continued, the size of the package usually diminished. For some contractors, therefore, a former employer had eased the transition across the labor market boundary.

For others, contracting had offered an increase in pay that could cushion the change. Carl, a programmer, had left a software development firm in 1994 during a layoff that followed the recession of the early 1990s. Although standard jobs still seemed scarce, he recalled, "the demand for contractors was pretty good, and the money was about twice what they were paying full-time employees." The pay differential that Carl remembered may have been extreme, but most contractors described hourly rates higher than their salaries, calculated on an hourly basis.

Although the distinction between contractors' wages and employees' salaries make comparisons imprecise, most of my informants reported incomes at least equivalent to the salaries they had received—or believed they would receive—in comparable standard jobs. Programmers and engineers, such as Carl, more often described a wide gap between contractors' hourly rates and equivalent employees' pay. For writers and editors, the gap appeared to be smaller, but there, too, experienced contractors could expect to earn more per hour.

Seth, an editor and production manager, described taking a standard job with his principal client in 1993. Still new to print production, he had been working for two years as a freelance proofreader, and he hoped an expanding company would provide opportunities to learn more. "I took a full-time job at [company name]," he recalled. "And I went from being a freelancer averaging $15 an hour to being an on-site full-time employee for about $12.50 with benefits.... And it was the transition from freelancing,...[to] being a paid employee, not being paid for overtime because of the 'rules' that, you know, my income plummeted." As a contractor,

Seth explained, he had billed by the hour and was paid for all the time he worked, but as an employee, he had been expected to adhere to schedules despite changing specifications, which could mean especially long hours. The company's "rules" thus demanded time far beyond a forty-hour week, but for working overtime, Seth received no compensation.[7]

Positions on staff did come with benefits—insurance, paid vacations, sick days—which could matter to those who lacked access to insurance through partners or spouses. Working as a contractor meant purchasing benefits, at ever-rising prices, or taking the risk of being uninsured. Calculating the monetary difference between two forms of employment thus involved many factors, not all of which were equally important to all contractors. Despite the cost of providing his own health insurance, Seth returned to contracting after three years. The company was relocating, he explained, and his job would have required a longer commute. With more experience, he hoped to attract a larger clientele. As a project manager at the time of our interview, he was charging $40–60 per hour, and his income had almost tripled over six years.

Seth's experience exemplifies the ease with which contract professionals in both occupational groups move in both directions across the boundary between internal and external labor markets. Although only two of my informants, one in each group, were explicitly seeking standard employment at the time of our interview, most believed they could find standard jobs. Their sense of options did depend somewhat on labor market conditions. Economic downturns could hit certain industries hard, and programmers and engineers reported especially limited options during recessions. A few identified colleagues who had been unable to find work for many months or even years during sharp declines. Some also reported taking work that they found unappealing, an alternative to unwanted downtime with no income. During the boom of the late 1990s, however, clients had frequently offered standard jobs to contractors who had performed well.

In good economic times, the availability of alternatives can provide the impetus to leave a standard job.[8] Phil, a writer and project manager, had learned about contract work from a colleague as they together considered whether to "jump ship" after a wave of industry consolidations:

> I was working as a tech writer at a company that no longer exists, and I was working with a person who was also an employee at that company. And she had spent many years as a contractor and had taken a full-time job.... But

she ended up leaving, and she said, "This is how you can not have to deal
with political crap. You can make more money." To me, it was a very obvi-
ous track.... She put me in touch with a couple of agencies.

Staffing agencies, with their networks of potential clients, offered a means
of transition for some of my informants. Programmers and writers seeking work in the technology sector were especially likely to include recruiters in any transition plans. But Bennett, who described a similar "moment
of decision," had charted his own course:

> It's something that I had pondered for some time. I was unhappy with my job
> and my work situation and my bad relationship with my boss. And...I knew
> that I wanted to leave, but I didn't know where I wanted to go....I called
> people that I knew and said, "I'm becoming an independent consultant. Is
> there something that you would like me to do for you?"...About two weeks
> after I started making phone calls, I had my first contract.

Although they had developed multiple labor market connections, both
Bennett and Phil had also maintained long-term relationships with specific
clients. Their tenure as contractors, both believed, had gradually become
an asset in finding work. "I had one client for five years, Bennett explained,
"and I had another client for three years. I've been with my current client
for about three and half years, and it looks to go on for several more." Phil
described a similar arrangement, noting, "It helps that I've been out here
[in an external labor market] for eight years. Everyone knows I'm serious." Many of the contractors I met expressed the same observation: the
longer they worked as contractors, the greater their legitimacy. A move
into standard employment, therefore, required careful consideration. For
most, such changes in contractual status tended to occur many years or
even decades apart.

Yolanda, a writer and project manager, had considered such a change.
Having begun to contract after moving to a rural area, she had worked
on contract for six years when an urban advertising company that had
provided her with steady work offered to make her a telecommuting employee. "Of the maybe half dozen clients I've had in the time I've spent
self-employed, I almost ended up going to work full time for one of them,
just because they were a good company," she explained. Turning her client

down, Yolanda thought contracting would offer her greater flexibility to arrange her daily schedule and, with a track record as a contractor, she felt secure enough. "They could tell us [contractors] tomorrow that they don't want us to work," she acknowledged, "but I can find something."

Each of my informants who had been contracting for at least three years reported having received at least one unsolicited job offer, usually from a client who wanted to retain that contractor's services. In these two occupations, therefore, the boundary between external and internal labor market segments remains permeable. Having made a transition to contract employment, contractors can consider their options open. My informants may have turned job offers down, but only a few were adamant that they would never return to a standard job. Changing circumstances or an especially desirable position might shift the balance of factors that made contracting more attractive.

Time, Space, and Flexibility

The discourse of flexibility permeated contractors' accounts of their choices. In both occupational groups, the practitioners I interviewed cited the temporal flexibility of contract employment as a means for seizing control of their daily schedules. Even those working at client sites saw contracting, at least potentially, as a strategy for accommodating work with family life or other personal pursuits. Such rationales echo a well-documented shortage of time, in which standard employment demands long hours of "face time" visibly spent at the office, which for employees serves as a proxy for commitment.[9] Those who limit their working time, therefore, may appear less than fully committed and, further, might face sanctions—few raises, poor performance reviews, lack of advancement—for violating organizational time norms. As Todd, a recruiter who had worked for ten years on staff as a publications manager, reflected, "You can tell them the hours you'll be there, but then you'll pay the price."

Release from Organizational Time Norms

Outside the reward structures of standard employment, contractors face fewer sanctions for time deviance. With new terms negotiated for each

successive assignment, most are better able than employees to establish individual arrangements that meet their personal needs. Those who work
from home are rarely, if ever, visible at the office, and the schedules they
maintain may differ considerably from standard office hours. Meiksins
and Whalley (2002), in their study of reduced working time among technical professionals (job sharing and part-time employment, as well as contracting), describe flexible schedules that release workers, to some degree,
from the time constraints of a full-time standard job. Reducing work
hours, their study finds, does limit prospects for upward career mobility,
but workers avoid trading long hours for the promise of future reward.

Even when they work long hours, the contractors I met considered
their status a kind of leverage for achieving temporal flexibility. As Joseph,
a software engineer and systems analyst, explained, contracting meant that
he had no obligation to report either his schedule or his personal priorities
to his clients: "I work very hard, but I also take off maybe a month in the
summer....So nobody tells me how much vacation to have or when I take
it. And if I'd like to leave next week, I'll take off a Friday to Monday and
put together a nice long weekend for myself and my wife....I like the
freedom to set my hours even though they are horrendous." Working for
several clients at a time, Joseph was juggling multiple schedules, and when
a client wanted his presence on short notice, he had to balance the request
with other obligations to be sure he could complete the coding and systems
design that were "deliverables" for each assignment: "In this open-ended
agreement like I have now with this particular company,...they want my
time. So I say I can't give you any more than three days a week 'cause I
have other things to do. Actually, some weeks I just can't be there on Monday. Some weeks I can't be there on Wednesday....So I stick to my bargain
doing three days a week." Although they may, on occasion, be subject to
significant demands, contractors face relatively few penalties for having
other commitments.

Although completing work as promised is always imperative, contractors might arrange daily schedules to accommodate their own interests.[10]
Martin, an editor and proofreader, spent many evenings playing in a band
and often returned home well after midnight. Contracting from home allowed him to work the hours he chose without having to appear alert first
thing in the morning: "It's a very short commute, mostly me crawling from
my bed to the computer, but I don't even have to dress if I don't want to.

I can work in my bathrobe. It's actually the thing I like about it most. If I don't feel like working at nine o'clock, I don't have to work at nine o'clock. I can work at noon and just like make it up.... I've done quite a bit of work late at night." For home-based contractors, flexibility usually means determining their own work hours, subject to communication with clients and team members. Many thus arranged their time to accommodate activities incompatible with a standard schedule.

Kevin, a translator and editor, described alternating periods of intense concentration with directing an organization and participating in his local community: "How do I organize my work? I graze.... I mean basically I just cruise: get up, make myself a cup of tea, coffee, then back to where it is, and maybe I'll do some translation. Then maybe I'll do some stuff that I need to do for [organization he directed], or I'll do something else completely.... But then I'll get back to it." Seeing little need to separate the many facets of his life, Kevin made paid work an integral part of daily activities that might include various other interests and responsibilities. Melding paid employment with unpaid tasks, home-working contractors blur the boundary between work and home that divides public from private life. With home-based work more readily available to writers and editors, they emphasized this temporal flexibility more often than programmers and engineers. But any contractor who can avoid an organizational allocation of time might subvert the time norms that come with the standard job.

The obligations that make flexibility attractive, however, can also erode the billable hours that add up to a contractor's income. Bruce, a software engineer and systems analyst, described a common work-family conflict: "The kids come home from school; they need a ride here and there.... If a kid wants something, the right thing to do is drop everything and do what the kid wants. The problem [is]... getting the billable hours in." Because child care imposed its own schedule, interruptions could fragment the concentrated time that these occupations require. Parents who worked at home described routinely attenuating their working time into early mornings or late nights to compensate for inattention to paid work during the day. Rita, working at home as a programmer, described segmenting her work day while her children were young: "I would start very early in the morning, like seven in the morning, and try to get the most productive hours in while the kids were in school.... I'd get the kids, bring them, spend a little time. Then they'd go off and play, and I'd go back to work,...and then I'd stop in the late afternoon and get dinner ready....But the crunch times could be horrendous. Sometimes I'd be up most of the night."

Despite the potential for work-family conflict, the home-based contractors I interviewed consistently cited flexibility as one of the principal advantages of contracting. Managing their own time, without the expectation that they participate in organizational life, provided considerably more autonomy than standard jobs allowed. Home-based contractors also emphasized the ease with which they attended to household tasks. Brent, a programmer and project developer, explained, "It's rare that I have a day when I just code or design all day....I can do different things, like stuff in the house." He might start dinner or put in a load of laundry, Brent elaborated, and then continue programming. Contracting at home thus allowed him to attend simultaneously to two domains. Meredith similarly described software development as so "absorbing and draining" that she needed occasionally "to clear my head....I also need time to do all the things in the house," she ruminated. "I don't think I could go back to a nine-to-five job, let alone a nine-to-nine job."

For contractors working at client sites, temporal flexibility was more limited because clients required their presence at the office for at least a significant portion of their time at work. Some contractors preferred such arrangements, either because they wanted to maintain a separation between home and work or because they valued face-to-face communication. Daniel, a programmer, had recently refused a project that would have allowed him to work from home with an international team of developers. The prospect of avoiding a commute had been appealing, but he had instead taken a long-term contract assignment that placed him full time in an office environment: "It's cheaper for them if you work at home, right? But doing software development, you really need, you're working on multiple-person projects more, and you need to reach people in person. Plus I think that there's still a lot of really old-fashioned software development managers who want their people there all the time." My own observation confirms Daniel's. At three of the technology companies I observed, managers insisted that contractors remain on-site, at least until they were familiar with office norms and routines. Evan, more than anyone else I met, was adamant that contractors work exclusively in the office. Daily contact, he believed, fostered team cohesion and allowed him to monitor performance more closely.

Some managers also expected that both contractors and employees keep the same standard schedules. Anna, a programmer, had worked on-site at a telecommunications firm for seven years and only occasionally spent a day or two working at home, connected to the company's central computer. Her supervisor, however, made sure that she was logged on and available throughout the day. "She'll send me a note through the e-mail," Anna mused, "asking me small things, and I'll chuckle. She's just checking to see if I'm on." Yet Anna had seen much variation at the same work site: "Other managers that I know in that company are not like that.... As long as you get the work done, they don't care if you do it here, there, or you know. But she's very controlling."

My informants' accounts illustrate the same variable practices. Most firms had few formal policies, and decisions about working at home depended on individual managers' discretion. Industry practices, however, might determine whether contract work at home is an exception or a norm. When home-based contracting has been long institutionalized, as it is in some segments of the publishing industry,[11] neither managers nor contractors consider on-site work an option. Indeed, in some settings, office procedures presume that editorial freelancers will be working off-site. Among my informants, therefore, writers and editors tended more often to work from home offices. When home-based work is instead a matter of managerial discretion, contractors might negotiate for some measure of spatial flexibility. Programmers and engineers, therefore, described greater variability, and potentially greater contention, over the location of their work sites.

Different Calculations of Time

Unlike salaried employees, contractors receive either hourly rates or project fees, which provide either a "running meter" for time spent on paid work or a predetermined price for a "deliverable" product.[12] Many of the contractors I met believed that this equation of time and money requires greater efficiency, both for them and for their clients. Those working away from an office environment can more readily ignore the office distractions that slow productivity for employees. Sylvia, a writer and editor, worked principally at home and was sure that she produced almost twice as much work for each hour spent in concentration outside an office: "My time is a lot more productive.... You're not wasting a lot of time in meetings. You're not wasting a lot of time because someone has wandered into your office and is chatting about the weekend."

When contractors work on site, however, the differences diminish. On-site contractors are also likely to spend time in face-to-face meetings and office conversation, and they can be similarly subject to the distractions that affect staff with standard jobs. When confronted with problems that take unplanned time, they have a proximal community with which to share the frustrations of redoing work or accommodating last-minute demands. The myriad organizational inefficiencies that affect their progress—changes in direction, obstructed communication, errors left uncorrected—are frustrating for both employees and contractors, no matter their work site. On-site contractors, however, experience these difficulties in tandem with their colleagues in standard jobs.

Late on a Thursday afternoon, I attended a "large staff" meeting of software engineers, system testers, and documentation writers, all part of a team comprising employees and contractors who had been working together for well over a year. Their collective task was to upgrade a product for new release while continuing to serve a number of important customers that required ongoing technical support. The needs of these customers had made scheduling difficult as members of the group were called away to solve a problem and their absence sometimes slowed the pace of other team members dependent on them. As with any complex project, individual segments had been parceled out, but the result had to be an integrated whole in which all the pieces functioned together. This technical challenge meant that team members needed to consider one another's needs for information as they completed their segments and had to communicate about myriad minor decisions that might affect one another's progress. With the staff's attention stretched thin, the department manager had hired contractors, who were approximately one-third of the more than two dozen people working on the project.

That afternoon, the manager dropped a bomb—from corporate headquarters had come a new mandate that would alter the product specifications and require that portions of it be revised. Rather than testing and debugging, which everyone thought would constitute much of the remaining work, the task was now to incorporate the new specifications while retaining as much of the original design as possible. One imperative, however, was to avoid delaying the release. The department manager openly expressed frustration. Had he known about these changes earlier, he assured everyone, he would have proceeded differently. He had asked for more time, but upper management had been loathe to agree. Recognizing that the manager had tried to inject some rationality into the decision making, several of those in the room seemed supportive. The change in plan would require special effort. All involved would certainly spend the next few weekends at the office. Not only was the extra time itself an imposition, but the result would also, probably, be an inadequate product that failed to meet the standards that many team members appeared to share.

Despite the new pressure, the project staff seemed to accomplish little for the rest of the day. Small groups huddled in the corridor for a few minutes after the meeting, and as people dispersed to individual cubicles, they continued to congregate, complaining about the imposed change and its implications for all involved. The employees seemed most visible and vocal. As one of the engineers explained, the company had "pulled this kind of stunt" before, with close to disastrous results. Just a year earlier, he had been working on another project team, which had released a product that was late, over budget, and poorly documented. That mistake had cost the company "maybe millions" in lost sales and extra product support that could have been avoided. "People busted themselves," he explained, staying at the office all night in some cases to complete the effort. "And all they got for it was more work," made necessary by the many errors and glitches that the truncated development process had generated. Yet, despite the problems, none of "the brass" seemed to notice either the human or the hidden costs of the decisions.

The contractors, in contrast, were quieter. One of the writers rushed to her phone to arrange child care for the weekend and warn her partner that the next few weeks would be "hairy." Several returned alone to their desks. Joining a pair of test engineers, I asked what the change in plan would mean to them. Their response was simply that the extended effort would probably net them considerably more money in a relatively short period. One noted that she might try to delay the start of another contract, which she was discussing with a different client. "The thing is," she elaborated, "I don't really mind these marathon jobs. I can max out on them and then rest up." "Yeah," the other noted, "This is a bad way to go. It won't work, but we'll clean up."

The difference in responses between employees and contractors reflects, at least in part, the difference in their calculation of working time. On salary, employees would receive no additional pay for the long hours they would need to put in. Their willingness to meet the new specifications was instead an investment to be repaid later—at least ideally—in raises, bonuses, and organizational advancement. Accepting the new mandate as a "challenge" was a display of commitment, and indeed, both employees and contractors expressed much loyalty and respect for their manager, whose job it was to see the project completed on time. Despite their frustration, therefore, team members participated with camaraderie, and even the most critical appeared willing to commit the coming weeks to the effort. Yet only the contractors could be sure of a payoff. Paid by the hour, they would see their incomes rise in direct proportion to the hours they worked. In contrast, some employees complained that demonstrated commitment had, in the past, brought only more work with yet another short schedule and last-minute changes, necessitating still more long hours with little respite.

Contractors experienced different dilemmas. In the short term, they had to gauge the likely need for their services in the coming weeks. Would the demands for ongoing customer service mean that they would be needed throughout the crunch? Or would some contractors be let go as the project wound down and the volume of work diminished? How long would the effort truly take? Several noted quietly that slippage was likely. Yet they also knew that accurate predictions, at least that afternoon, would not be forthcoming. As long as the company demanded adherence to the original schedule and the manager had to rally the team, they could expect little in the way of a "reality check." Still, when the project was finally completed, each contractor would need another assignment, perhaps with this company, perhaps with one or more other clients. The test engineer who wondered aloud about delaying the start of her next contract project was already concerned about a potential scheduling conflict. So, too, were contractors who would soon be looking for new work. If they moved too quickly, they might be overbooked. If they waited too long, they might experience unwelcome downtime. The effort of looking for work could itself take time, even for well-established contractors.

Although contractors and employees shared the time crunch that the new mandate had created, the differences between contract and standard employment constructed distinctly different experiences of the problem. Employees experienced a greater short-term sacrifice, evident in their expressed frustration. The demands for additional time exacted control over the staff because their careers depended, at least to some degree, on complying with the schedules.[13] For contractors, in contrast, the demands for additional time provided a short-term opportunity to earn additional income. Many contractors apparently shared employees' concerns about product quality, but they were less likely to be dealing directly with the consequences of the forced compromises months or even years later. The managerial mandate thus revealed a cleavage in a working group that otherwise appeared cohesive.

Contracting and standard employment thus represent two distinct temporal arrangements, each of which exacts demands. A contractor's calculation of working time encompasses efforts to find work and maintain a clientele. Contractors must spend time identifying potential new clients, developing professional networks, updating their skills, and carrying out various administrative tasks that remaining in business requires. Unlike employees, they cannot depend on employing organizations to absorb the costs of ancillary activities associated with work. Their hourly rates and project fees, therefore, rarely account for all the time they spend in work-related pursuits. The contractors I interviewed rarely quantified the time these efforts required, preferring instead to see them as a necessary part of professional life. Like their counterparts in standard jobs, they too invested in working time beyond the hours they were formally paid to work. These different reward structures thus pose trade-offs, but the temporal dimensions of contract employment informed decision making among the contractors I met.

The Meaning of Membership

For employees, the standard job represents a form of membership. Employees belong to the organization in ways that contractors do not. As organizational members, employees are expected to identify with their employer. Although identity and belonging may fail to provide satisfaction and security, the standard employment relationship carries a formal affiliation that contractors lack, no matter how long they work for a single client. Although contractors may well share the work experiences of employees, their involvement in organizational life is presumably transitory. All contractors anticipate moving on, and even when integrated into a work site, they remain socially distinct.

Symbolic Boundaries

Social interaction can indicate this difference in contractual status. As I listened to employees speak about their jobs, they often spoke in plural forms that signaled identification with their employer. "*We* will be introducing the new edition at the sales meeting," I would hear, or "*We* sustained a hit last year, but this year's release should make up for it." Contractors sometimes used plural forms as well, but any identification with a client was typically limited to statements about a specific project or team of colleagues. "*We* have to meet the target date," a contractor might say, or "*We*'re still missing the following elements."

The difference usually goes unacknowledged unless a contractor seems to presume a relationship beyond the scope or duration of the current contract. At a status review meeting in a small Internet company, a half dozen team members brainstormed marketing ideas for the launch of a new product. Promising to pass the suggestions to those in charge, the team leader wrote them on a white board. Toward the end of the meeting, one of two contractors suggested, "We should track user responses" to a new feature then in development. A short but noticeable pause followed this very reasonable suggestion. No one objected. After a moment's silence, the team leader firmly endorsed the idea. The pause, however, had signaled more identification with the company, expressed in the use of *we,* than a contractor usually assumed. As everyone knew, the contractor would be gone by the time any users could respond. Had this contractor phrased the suggestion differently, perhaps by saying, "*You* should track user responses," or even "Tracking user responses would be a good idea," the suggestion might have received the group's endorsement without the hesitation.

Although inclusion in a workplace might be an advantage of standard employment, many of the contractors I met had found organizational norms intrusive. Employees, they explained, were expected to display loyalty and commitment to their employer, so much so that companies sometimes supplied the means. In one firm, I noted symbols of identification—T-shirts, coffee mugs, and banners promoting specific products—visibly displayed in most offices. "They give us this stuff," an employee noted with a broad gesture, "and we're supposed to keep it around." Although contractors' offices contained the same items, they were sparser. Sipping coffee from a mug with a company logo, one contractor noted that she would leave the mug behind when her contract ended. Some of my informants further described employers who had reached into time they considered their own. Formerly an employee at a publishing firm, Seth had felt pressured there to socialize with coworkers. "I worked with good people, and we hung out together on a limited basis, and I'm still friendly with most of them," he explained, "but I don't like being expected to hang out and go out for drinks and, you know, that it's part of what we do to keep our jobs."

Such symbols of membership represent an officially sanctioned mode of identification with the company and its products. As in many organizations, these employees were expected to be purveyors of the corporate image and clearly committed to company goals. As these dismissive remarks suggest, however, identification with the company can be less than complete. As Gideon Kunda (1992) found in a large high-tech corporation, officially sanctioned expressions of identification are both a form of control over employees and, paradoxically, a backdrop against which to define a separate self. Organizational membership may enforce a codified set of behaviors, attitudes, or beliefs, but the more prescriptive these become, the more members may detach themselves, engaging in a form of role distancing that separates the individual from the organization.[14] Employees, therefore, must actively construct boundaries that distinguish the self from the organization. Contactors, in contrast, find these boundaries already in place.

Conflict and Politics

When contractors consider the advantages of their contractual status, they often cite relief at avoiding organizational conflicts broadly termed office politics. My informants associated office politics with the arbitrary and seemingly irrational exercise of authority. Politics, they explained, too often guided the allocation of resources and rewards and too often undermined stated goals. The politics of managerial decisions could deprive them of support, misread priorities, or misdirect communication. Both contractors and employees lamented what they saw as politics trumping product quality. In their study of technical contractors, Barley and Kunda (2004) found office politics associated with accounts of managerial incompetence that seemed to plague occupational practice. My informants largely concurred. Managers, they complained, too often failed to grasp the complexity of a project or failed to adhere to processes developed to catch and correct errors.

Stories of code that had gone untested or copy unchecked could produce raw frustration. Jon, a writer and editor, had for ten months been witnessing a series of problems made worse by managerial decisions at a telecommunications firm:

> You get a fix for one thing, but then it will complicate another.... The program I was talking about before, the tool we were all grappling with and having a really hard time with, that was a fix to a problem. And it just created worse problems really in the end. And the thing is that the people that actually can institute things, the people that can make change and can have a say, they don't understand the particulars of it, right? So they'll say, "Oh, this will fix it. OK, let's do it." And they'll send it out to get done, but they don't understand how to check on it, what needs to be checked on, all the little "thises and thats" of it. That stuff just slips past them. And so you end up with a fix that leaks, basically.

Still new to his field, Jon had at first hoped that his contract assignment would lead to a position in a company well known for its innovative technology. He had found the work intriguing and was eager to learn more. After less than a year, however, he was considering whether a job with this company would ultimately prove too frustrating: "Like we can't do it any other way? This is just how it is within organizations. It's absurd. That's why a lot of people leave. People just get tired of it. [Company name] is just a terrible bureaucracy. It's absurd how slow it takes for things to get done.... It just seems to me like it's madness.... I'm really afraid about going into it, that I'll get in there and just find myself stagnant and depressed."

Despite the obstacles to success, Jon had been given increasing responsibility over segments of the work. He was enjoying the company of his coworkers and had found most willing to help him learn the internal procedures and routines. His goal, in turn, had been to facilitate the group's efforts without involving himself in the competition for recognition that employees seemed to seek. Now, having watched employees vie for a manager's approval, he wondered whether long-term contracting would be a better option: "There's a lot of personal politics that you have to deal with, you know. And that depends on how savvy you are, how savvy those around you are, and how upset they'll get at your own advancement."

On occasion, contractors reported, arbitrary decisions associated with politics could cost someone a job. Tales of supervisors threatened by a subordinate or seeking to place blame for a problem surfaced in many of my informants' accounts. Donald, an editor and production manager, had been working for almost a year as an employee at the office of a publisher, analyzing reviews of work in progress and communicating with authors. "We had three people, including myself, doing reviews," he remembered, "and all of a sudden I got an e-mail one morning from my boss telling me that she was unhappy with my work, that I had been making some sloppy editorial mistakes." Having heard no warnings about the quality of his work, Donald had been stunned by this assessment, which he later attributed to this manager's plan to replace him, along with a colleague who had assumed similar responsibilities. "She managed to bully the two of us who were doing it [handling reviews], . . . and so we both lost our jobs," he explained.

Although contractors, too, may be affected by office politics, the injuries tend to be less long-lasting or severe. Lacking affiliation with an employer, a contractor has less at stake with each project and each client. A difficult environment, therefore, may merely be something to endure. Several of my informants described relief at the completion of a project, especially one that had demanded long hours or difficult interpersonal relationships. For a moment, at least, they would be caught up, free from conflict, and able to experience a sense of accomplishment. Employees, they contended, may experience greater continuity, but they more frequently faced yet another project with similar demands, and the cycle could seem relentless, irrational, and, at times, personally threatening. For contractors, outside the organizational reward structure, the experience of conflict was more limited, and same irrationality posed less of a threat. The slights and frustrations that accumulated over time, therefore, tended to matter much less.

A contractor's mobility thus provides a mode of control over the un-predictability of organizational life. For a contractor, myriad changes—project specifications, possible relocation, pending reorganization—have a more limited impact. Members of the organization may face reconfigured hierarchies, new reporting patterns, and staff reassignment that can undermine their prospects for professional advancement. Contractors, in contrast, share these concerns only temporarily, if at all. Organizational volatility can impede progress and may even cost an assignment, but a contractor generally has less to lose. Linda, a software and database developer, characterized differences in the experience of interpersonal conflict:

> As a contractor,... personal conflicts are short-term more threatening and long-term much less threatening than, you know. Any given job is a lot less important than it used to be.... If you're a full-time employee, the bad part is you're probably going to be working with this person for years to come, and your life can be hell. But on the other hand,... you've got some kind of hierarchy to, you know, this is my job. This is why I can say this. This is why I can do this. My boss says so, and you can take it up with my boss.

Organizational affiliation, Linda remembered, had provided her with support, and when she tried to influence the direction of a project, she did so from a position that conferred authority. As a contractor, she could still exert influence, but she lacked the formal authority she had exercised as an employee.

The difference in contractual status thus shapes responses to organizational conflict. For employees, organizational position defines expectations but demands the participation that comes with membership. Contractors, in contrast, can forgo the trappings of organizational inclusion. Carol, a writer and editor, told an especially dramatic story in which she had been suddenly outsourced by a firm seeking quickly to lower its head count of employees. As she recalled, her group had been assembled and all the members told they would be "payrolled" through a staffing agency, which technically became their employer. Work was to continue as before, with no evident changes in plan, but the outsourced employees were no longer organizational members. Having hoped, at one time, to move into management, Carol had been stunned by the change in status, which now blocked her prospects for advancement within the firm. In response, she had made an equally sudden decision: she would change her wardrobe. Despite the casual dress common among the employees, she had always dressed up; from then on, she would dress down. "I used to wear two-, three-hundred-dollar suits and jewelry and high heels and stockings and all that stuff to work.... The day I was outsourced was the day I wore jeans and never looked back. And I thought, 'Why am I spending hundreds of dollars on an outfit? Why bother?'"

The casual clothes were less a statement of protest, Carol explained, than an acknowledgment of change. Her self-presentation, designed to signal her interest in a managerial career, had obviously escaped notice. Corporate management had seen her merely as a fixed cost, easily converted to a "vendor of services." Having failed to attract attention as a corporate-level player, she would redirect her energies, concentrating on her work without a symbolic display of ambition. Her casual clothes now signaled a tenuous connection to an organization in which only her services, not her expectations, had been engaged. Five years after abruptly becoming a contractor, Carol described contracting as "a different approach." No longer seeking success in more conventional terms, she cultivated a contrast between corporate affiliation and her own self-direction, reliably producing quality work. Standard employment, she had concluded, was rarely worth the investment.

3

PERFORMING EXPERTISE

Despite their disillusion with standard employment, the contract professionals I met had remained engaged in their respective occupations. External labor markets were well institutionalized, they explained, and contractors moved within a system of employment. Establishing a relationship with each new client, however, required an ongoing process of managing impressions and controlling a presentation of self. Lacking formal titles and job descriptions, contractors must negotiate working relationships with both managers and employees at client firms. Common occupational practices contribute to their understanding of the work to be done, but unlike employees, they cannot depend on organizational status to establish their authority over work-related tasks and responsibilities. For them, authority depends on expertise. How, then, do contractors establish working relationships? How do their strategies support these external labor markets?

For contractors, expertise means more than discrete and measurable skill. Expertise demands the communication of competence that facilitates ongoing employment. True, a successful contractor needs to meet a client's requirements and accomplish assigned tasks. In these occupations, accuracy, clarity, and attention to detail always underlie successful practice. But the contractors I met spoke, too, of signaling their competence and developing their clients' trust. They emphasized strategies that reinforced their authority and reassured their clients, and their accounts reveal the symbolic meanings that support an institutional logic to contract employment. Calling on a culturally mediated repertoire of strategies, practitioners in both occupations had sought discursive control over their work. By interacting with clients, they could define professional selves, anchored in systems of occupational practice.

Expertise is thus the outcome of client interaction. Without the status conferred by organizational position, contract professionals depend on the micro-processes of communication to demonstrate their command of occupational practice and commitment to a client's goals. By reducing the prospect of misunderstandings, strategic interaction helps to instill confidence and engender trust. These processes demand vigilance, attention to appearances, and often some backstage support to sustain the performance. For a contractor, then, a smooth, competent performance is an interactional accomplishment. Although contractor and client rarely negotiate as equals, a performance of expertise helps to manage uncertainty and mitigate the structural risk of the external labor market.

Making Impressions, Conveying Competence

Contractors strive to create impressions. Analyzed in the interactionist tradition of Erving Goffman (1959, 1969), sociologist, their exchanges with clients are strategies calculated to present themselves as capable. Alluding to experience, anticipating problems, suggesting solutions, they enact frontstage performances in which they seek to place their abilities in the best possible light. Before any discussion of price and payment—always priorities but rarely raised early on—the conversation between contractor and client is a kind of audition in which each party tries out the other, assessing the prospects of working together and identifying areas of concern.

With every new encounter, social interaction forms the basis for ongoing negotiation and exchange. The client, however, holds the upper hand

and makes the first and final decisions. As formal organizations, some of them large corporations, clients exercise greater social power. Hiring managers at client firms decide which contractors to engage, and the client—sometimes in conjunction with a staffing agency—has the first opportunity to define the situation, frame the discussion, and lay the groundwork for interaction. Even when the client is an individual seeking a contractor's services, as some writers and editors described, the client must decide to make an investment in the contractor's services. Discussing a project's particulars, therefore, a contractor seeks to establish an equality of competence in a relationship that remains materially unequal.

Encounters with New Clients

Responding to a client's initiative, the contractors I interviewed recounted efforts to create positive impressions, sometimes to refine the situation, and often to expand the scope of social action within the structured relations of contract employment. Ben, a software engineer and project manager, elaborated: "Especially with new clients, I try to get them to agree to some number of days to analyze their situation. A successful analysis will make or break the whole project. At the end of that analysis, I'll have something...saying this is what I understand your system to be; this is what I believe you want me to do." Seizing the initiative and defining the client's need, Ben tried to use an up-front assessment as an opportunity to demonstrate his expertise. Only then, he explained, could he estimate the time and costs required to accomplish specific tasks. Having established his domain of authority, he had found most clients willing to accept his assessment. "I've thought of putting it on a business card, you know, 'managing expectations for more than six years,'" he mused.

Gary, an editor and production manager, described managing client relations by asking questions that displayed his understanding of occupational practice. "I ask the right questions," he explained. "Do you have this? Do you have that? Are you going to be able to get this to me? When? And you want me to get this to you when? I try to make sure that there are no misunderstandings as to what the client wants, so I just make sure all the information is there.... When the people I talk to...know production, they know what I mean. Then it's kind of understood that I know what I'm doing." Asking questions, Gary had found, was especially reassuring to new clients, but the questions were also a way to verify that he would have all the necessary materials in time to ensure the quality of the final product. "I don't assume anything," he told me, "So I let them know they really don't have to be nervous.... And I have to make sure I know exactly what they want, that I have everything I need to work with." Gary's questions, like Ben's initial assessment, promoted trust in his abilities and helped to ensure his success. The purchase of trust is thus a social accomplishment, a component of expertise that establishes a contractor's authority.

Not all clients cooperate with a contractor's effort to delineate project requirements and establish expertise. Peggy, a programmer who worked principally for financial services firms, had more often found her scope of action limited at the start of a new assignment. Finding most of her work through staffing agencies, she would at first interact with a recruiter, who typically knew little about technology and could rarely answer her questions. "They call and say, 'You've got the requirements, and it pays so much,'" she complained. "I usually have to accept or reject it up front." Pay scales, Peggy had found, could vary among agencies but were rarely open to negotiation. Nor were project particulars. "The requirements are just some [programming] language or other," she explained, "and they [recruiters] know nothing about how programming gets done."

Interviews with work-site managers could be just as perfunctory, especially when hiring managers lacked a working knowledge of technology. Only after beginning an assignment, Peggy elaborated, could she finally begin to display her abilities, but by then, she had less latitude to shape the terms of the relationship. "When I get there, I have to prove I'm intelligent," she lamented, "and some of them [managers and employees], they just assume I don't know my stuff." Without the chance to signal her competence, Peggy had found her abilities recognized only after an "extended probation." Repeat business with a client might allow her to present her expertise more quickly, but the intercession of a staffing agency could otherwise be an impediment. Negotiating with recruiters, the programmers and engineers I interviewed more often cited such obstacles, but writers and editors had experienced similar difficulties. A client's close familiarity with occupational practice, my informants explained, facilitated recognition of their expertise.

Even after establishing themselves with clients, contractors may find relationships fragile. Staffing changes, for example, might require them to reaffirm their qualifications, to establish themselves anew. Myra, who worked principally as an editor, described a protracted period of negotiation with a new managing editor at a publishing company that had been one of her steadiest clients. Discussion had begun with a phone call. "She [new editor] said she'd be needing people," Myra remembered. "When I said I thought I'd be available, I was told 'send me a resume,' and I thought send a resume? But you *know* me. I've done all these books with you!" To Myra, the request was a warning that client relations were more tenuous than she had assumed. Still, acquiescing to the request, she had hoped that the new editor would soon learn of her track record and become less cautious.

The ongoing exchange, however, was far from reassuring. Soon after sending the resume, Myra was asked to edit a single chapter as a "try out," to provide an unpaid sample of her work. Myra was angry but responded with a counteroffer: "I said, 'I'm happy to give you a price, and I'm happy to look at the book, but I will not edit a piece of it. I will give you an editing sample I've already done.'" An example of completed work, she believed, would fairly represent her abilities without taking unpaid time. Along with the principle was a concern for quality. "It was also that my ideas change a lot when I'm editing, and if I did only part of something, I wouldn't get to rethink....I didn't want to get caught looking dumb."

Myra's experience underscores the tenuous nature of contractor-client relations. A change in staff, new organizational policies, or corporate restructuring can all jeopardize a long-term understanding on which the contractor had based an expectation of future work. Although she drew the line at providing free editorial services, Myra had been prepared to establish a new relationship, but only on terms that would allow her to perform without compromise: "Editing this sort of thing has to be precise. Every little change or phrase can just change what they're doing. So you can't just look at the relationship of sentences. Usually [with others involved in the project], there's a fairly detailed discussion about what's needed, and then I know and just do it." Long-standing relationships, Myra explained, rendered self-presentation less complicated. A short conversation, by phone or online, could usually verify her understanding about a new assignment with a familiar client.

Promising new clients require special care if a contractor is to create the right impression. Sylvia, a writer and editor working principally in her home office, described her response to unsolicited telephone inquiries. "I always tell the client that I'll get back to them," she explained. "Then I need to sort of think about it for a minute." Collecting her thoughts, Sylvia would list questions, usually beginning with the client's schedule, the project status, and any immediate tasks to be done. Few of the contractors I interviewed described accepting projects, even tentatively, without first asking such basic questions. Clarifying the scope of a project before agreeing to a set of terms helped them manage their schedules. By seeking information, they also avoided appearing desperate or in need. As Sylvia noted, "I have to check my calendar" is an effective first response.

Linguistic Cues and Subtle Signals

When a new project will place the contractor at a client site for at least several weeks, discussion more often involves a face-to-face interview. On-site work was more common among the programmers and engineers I met, but writers and editors might also be engaged at client sites, sometimes for months or even years. Much like interviews for standard jobs, the hiring process for these long-term assignments usually involved a series of meetings that could last the better part of a day. In such settings, hiring managers provide a backdrop for a contractor's self-presentation. Jesse, a manager charged with interviewing contractors, explained his technique for assessing a programmer's abilities:

> I describe my project, and I describe it in as much technical detail as I can squeeze into, say, ten minutes. And I will often just get up to the board and basically lecture for ten minutes. Then I listen to the questions they ask, and the level of question helps me gauge the level of technical competence this person has. You know, are they able to pick up on a key problem that I had to solve, even though I didn't talk about it? Are they able to pick up a key concept that's taken us a long time to work out?

A capable practitioner, Jesse believed, should recognize the pitfalls of a project or at least demonstrate problem-solving ability. A grasp of the labor process was for him a marker of expertise. His judgment, however, still depended somewhat on impressions. "Sometimes I'm really looking for the right words," he explained. "You pick up cues from conversation."

Interviews for prospective employees invoke different criteria. Long-term employment, which the standard job implies, encompasses some combination of formal training and informal learning on the job. Employees, therefore, enjoy greater latitude in acquiring work-related knowledge and skill. Employers, particularly those in technical fields, might expect to support this process through some mix of formal instruction and projects that offer new challenge. One mark of a competent employee, therefore, is a willingness to develop abilities over time. Contractors, in contrast, receive little or no support for professional development, and most clients expect them to bring all the requisite background to the work they take on. Unlike employees, contractors must hit the ground running, conforming quickly to the client's rhythms and routines. The managers I interviewed thus distinguished between firm-specific knowledge—office procedures, specifications for products still in development—and familiarity with the work processes that they defined as essential skills. These they sought to identify in advance.

Whether in person, by phone, or online, contractors attend to cues that signal the priorities of a client, all the while avoiding any hint of their own deficits or limitations. Interaction with managers, employees, and recruiters may require circumspection in choosing words, applying terms, and demonstrating the use of industry-specific language. Bryan, a programmer and systems engineer, described the vigilance he exercised: "I listen to people talk. I listen to their vocabulary. There's always some new buzz word going around. If you don't know what's happening, you listen until you figure it out, and when you know what's happening, then you can ask intelligent questions and enhance your position." Questions better left unasked, Bryan implied, are those that could make the contractor appear uninformed or unfamiliar with a process, product, or field. Knowing buzz words, however unnecessary to the task at hand, can generate confidence in the contractor and put a client at ease. A common language indicates a common understanding. Asking for clarification, in contrast, signals a lack of understanding, which managers and employees may well interpret as a lack of skill.

Contractors' accounts indicate special attention to the working vocabulary of a client. Bernice, an editor and indexer, described a "close call" with a potential new client, a medical publisher with a tight schedule. "They [the project manager] kept telling me to 'skip the A and P,'" Bernice explained, "because it would just take too long. I agreed. I said to them, 'Yes, A and P can be very time consuming.' But I didn't have a clue about what A and P was. I could have asked, but I thought I'd better not." Although sure that she could compile the index, Bernice lacked a grasp of shorthand usage that was common parlance for this client. Fortunately, she deciphered the code—as the book's headings suggested and another contractor confirmed, "A and P" meant "anatomy and physiology." Conscious of their audience, the contractors I interviewed similarly described monitoring their performances, hiding flaws that could mar the image they sought to convey.

Exuding Confidence, Engendering Trust

To project a confident demeanor, the contractors I met described practicing a kind of information control. They might voice doubts about aspects of an assignment—the choice of tools, the integration of project components, or the likelihood of meeting a deadline with all elements complete—but these reservations, carefully raised, are also evidence of expertise. In contrast, a contractor's self-doubts remain closely guarded. To sustain a convincing performance, most of the contractors I interviewed described some form of backstage support. Bernice, for example, had checked the likely meaning of "A and P" with another contractor, a medical editor whom she trusted not to reveal her ignorance of medical shorthand. Rather than appear less than confident, many of my informants had similarly solicited assistance. Sylvia, too, cited a few trusted colleagues to whom she could turn "on really bad days, when you can't remember the past tense of 'was.'" Online discussions in both occupational groups could raise similar questions or ask for help with specific problems.

Maintaining a Front Stage

Bernice and Sylvia worked principally in home offices, away from direct scrutiny, and so spent most of their time backstage, where they could keep their guard down. Working at home also rendered their performances less visible, so that they tried to be especially responsive to questions or requests. Home-based contractors who interact with a client's customers or suppliers may even try to pass as on-site staff, whose legitimacy seems less likely to be challenged. Phil, a writer and project manager, explained the ambiguity of his arrangement: "Here [at home] I have some sense that I have to respond to things very quickly, but I also deal with people who don't respond to things for weeks.... So even though I have the sense that I need to appear to be on-site, I know that's simply not the case."

Phil reported to a manager in the eastern United States but coordinated much of his work with colleagues and customers in Europe and Japan. Even on-site, he would have been invisible to those with whom he collaborated. His location in a home office, he believed, in no way hampered the speed or quality of his performance, but he nonetheless took care to avoid any hint of inattention. For example, he carefully kept household activities out of earshot and made sure that work-related phone calls were never interrupted. Most of the home-based contractors I interviewed described similarly separating client contact from their personal lives. Like Phil, many maintained dedicated business phones, which protected them from unguarded moments, when household responsibilities might seem to interfere with paid employment.

At client sites, too, contractors need to protect backstage areas from exposure. For Phil, occasional face-to-face meetings sometimes required care. "Not every question is fair game," he noted. "If you don't know how to make something work in Word or Framemaker, you know, you don't bother the client. You go home and figure it out." Contractors who worked together on-site might turn to one another for assistance, and in some cases the conditions of contracting might promote solidarity and support. Anna, an applications programmer, described status divisions in a large telecommunications firm, in which sharp distinctions separated groups of employees and on-site contractors, there called consultants:

> An employee can go to another employee with a lot of stupid questions. They can keep going back with questions because they're an employee. But when a consultant goes to an employee on numerous times for questions that they think stupid, they'll think *you're* stupid, so you can't do that. It's almost like a no-no. That's why we go to another consultant for help.... You have to have the camaraderie between consultants to help each other out.

Anna perceived employees not as personal threats but as a set of interests that produced a different logic of interaction. Programmers in both groups worked cooperatively, doing the same tasks, participating in the same meetings, even socializing together away from the office. After seven years at this work site, Anna could see no difference between work assigned to contractors and tasks given to employees. The two groups, however, functioned apart when a problem had to be solved, and the consultants never asked employees for help. Because standard employment offered opportunities for professional development, employees could openly learn on the job. For them, training was a corporate goal, allowing them more readily to ask questions and make mistakes. The company held them to a different standard, without the command performance expected of contractors.

Some staffing agencies have developed infrastructures that help contractors maintain a front stage. A few of the programmers I interviewed described problem-solving lunches and discussion groups that staffing agencies had sponsored. Access to agency-mediated websites and Listservs also allowed some contractors to use one another as resources. To the extent that its contractors, who are nominally its employees, appear prepared and capable, the agency benefits from providing a backstage to enhance their performance. Lauren, a programmer and systems analyst, described a website where she could post questions and engage in collaborative problem solving. When a colleague responded online, she could then present the client with an answer but avoid attributing its source:

> I'm the one who's supposed to know,...[so] I don't go to anyone on-site [for assistance]. I go to my company [the staffing agency]. That's because they have this big database thing. I can say, "Hey, I'm having this problem. Can you help me?" And if they're not too swamped at their client, they'll help you. And every so often you'll see these things where somebody got help in the middle of the night and they say, "Thank you, thank you, thank you."

Mutual support and group problem solving are normative components of many work-site cultures, especially when technical work involves up-to-date knowledge of technology and trends.[1] With a rapid pace of change, all involved recognize that no one can be completely apprised of recent innovations. Even when the work is largely nontechnical, however, team members need to communicate informally to review progress or inform one another of developments. Further, for both contractors and employees, collaboration may become a means for claiming credit, establishing authority, or developing work-related expertise. For contractors, however, these collective efforts carry additional opportunity and risk: work-based interaction provides an opportunity to display competence, but seeking assistance also risks exposing deficits.

Addressing Risk

Confidence, trust, and risk create a complex dynamic. Risk is closely related to uncertainty, and trust to predictability.[2] As theorists in many traditions have argued, trust can be a means for managing uncertainty in the face of risk.[3] Rather than an attribute of individual character, therefore, trust is a social mechanism that symbolic display may enhance. Without the risk inherent in work relations, contractors' displays of confidence would be unnecessary. Without their signals of confidence, however, working relationships would be less predictable. Contractors thus express confidence to promote trust and mitigate risk.[4]

All contractor-client agreements present risk. The contractor may fail to deliver. The client may fail to pay. Between the project start date and the final payment, any number of problems may occur. Faced with systemic risk, both the contractor and the client seek to tame uncertainty by establishing trust. They try to agree, for example, on project priorities and needed resources to establish a shared understanding that can inform the relationship over time. Employees, in contrast, can more readily depend on established lines of authority and so rely less on a carefully crafted performance.[5] Contracting may allow latitude for defining the situation, but it also requires a contractor to attend constantly to client relations. More than an employee, a contractor needs to signal reliability, diminish perceptions of risk, and enhance the development of trust.

Pat, a writer who produced marketing materials, described a particularly difficult project for which trust had proved essential. Her client was a small company for which she had long worked, and the assignment was to join a team drafting several chapters of a book that profiled prominent corporate leaders, who had already been interviewed for the project. Pat described the difficulty:

> She [the client] had the tapes transcribed, and from that, we were supposed to write up chapters.... And she asked me if I would be willing to take a few chapters, and I said, "Well, what's involved?" And she said, "Work from

the tape transcriptions and write it up." And I said, "That's it? I'm not supposed to go anywhere else for any other information?" "That's it," she said. So on the basis of that, I took three chapters. Right away I discovered there was nothing to these interviews. It was all fluff, you know. So we went back and forth a bit.

Additional research, Pat explained to her client, would require additional time, which her project fee had not included. She had agreed to a price based on trust, established over time, but the client had misrepresented the task. Eventually, they resolved the problem. Pat would complete one chapter and document the status of the project, and the client would settle for a more limited final product. Although neither party was entirely satisfied, Pat credited the relationship. "We knew each other," she mused, "and I just trusted her, you know, and I think she trusted me....I didn't make the terms clear enough up front....She realized that she had made a mistake too."

Here a long-term relationship meant that trust could withstand a challenge, but without established patterns of problems solving, client relations become riskier. When conflicts intensify, resolution may stem less from trust than from the greater power of the client. Conflict-ridden work relations may thus resemble hierarchical systems of authority, in which challenging directives may mean risking insubordination. Most of the contractors I interviewed, however, described collaboration that generated more diffuse patterns of communication, allowing them to instill confidence and establish expertise.

Richard, a programmer, described a gradual process of developing the confidence of his client. New to the field and, at age twenty-three, much younger than most contractors, he could offer little experience, and his negotiations with a small start-up firm had been tentative on both sides. With growing proficiency, however, Richard had found the scope of his responsibility expanding:

> What I had hoped for I haven't had, in terms of my working relationship with my employer....I wanted to be able to kind of conceptually determine what the product is going to be like, you know, how it will be used and what the user's experience is going to be....What's gotten me to the point where I am, more than anything, is I've shown that I can learn....And I give in response what I consider good—no, excellent—customer service. I'm completely honest with pretty much everything.

Despite the lingering doubts of his client, Richard had earned trust by demonstrating honesty, and he hoped for greater involvement in decision making over time. Growing trust in his abilities had, in turn, brought him new confidence, which helped to mitigate the risk that he and his client had at first assumed.

Navigating Informality

Even when clients seemed wary of their abilities, the contractors I interviewed reported rarely receiving detailed directions as they began new assignments. To orient a contractor to a new project, they explained, some clients do delineate specifications and identify possible pitfalls. Projects in process, however, remain hard to assess, and even discrete tasks, well defined by industry practice, leave something to the practitioner's judgment. A test engineer may find bugs in a program, necessitating more testing before functionality is achieved. A production editor may similarly find incomplete text elements, which require additional time and attention. Unforeseen problems, my informants explained, are the norm, and no contractor wants to absorb the cost of resolving them. Anticipating the unexpected, therefore, the contractors I interviewed had engaged in informal processes of clarification, through which they sought to establish channels of communication, promote trust, and display expertise.

Ted, a writer and editor, described a book publisher for which he did "light copy editing." Budgets were limited, he explained, and the managing editor had little patience with his questions. Still, Ted had learned to be persistent:

> It's always a light copy edit, so it's like I need to clarify what a light copy editing means.... This book right now is a light copy edit. It's not wonderfully written, but it's totally functional. It's a photography book. They're telling people how to do certain photography things. So second person, first person, third person, you know, it's OK. Nobody's reading and saying, "Oh, what a wonderful sentence that was."

Ted understood the client's limitations—despite the bad writing, the project budget could not absorb the expense of extensive revision. Yet, rather than simply accepting the directives of the client, he had documented his own assessment of the needs of the project to indemnify himself against blame for a deficient final product. "Don't ask me to do less than it actually needs and then wait for it to get to the final stage of production, when somebody's calling down saying, 'What the hell is this?'" he exclaimed. By clarifying his scope of responsibility, Ted and his client had developed an uneasy accommodation. He would provide minimal editing, and the client would expect no more than it had agreed.

Ted's account illustrates the interactive process through which informal negotiation can establish expertise. The client might prevent him from imposing high standards, but Ted could still show himself capable by allocating his time and attention to meet the project goals. In this case, he was listing discrepancies between the text and illustrations, identifying the corrections that would need to be completed before the final phases of the project. By clarifying client expectations, he could direct his individual effort to underscore his professional judgment. In the process, he also affirmed the client's trust.

Many of the contractors I interviewed described reaffirming expectations at key stages of a project. Joseph, a software engineer and systems analyst, considered his agreements with clients "proposals," which allowed him to define his terms but also leave open the prospect of revision: "I will set milestones, goals, you know. I'll make it quantifiable and measurable: by such and such a date and for about this amount of money, we can decide whether we're going to go forward or not. By this date, the software will be done. By this date, we'll introduce it to a customer, do testing.... But there's a lot of flexibility." Joseph's proposals provided a guide, but rarely a complete blueprint. Adjustments, changes, and even major redirection were the norm, not the exception. When agreeing to a price or a budget, therefore, he also established terms for renegotiation and protected himself from unplanned costs: "I say, you know, specification changes, normal specification changes that are going to result in no more than minor amounts of work, no problem. But if there's a major change in specification that requires a different approach or redesign, I need zero-based budgeting. We start again. At this point on, it's going to cost us. I build in red flags in my proposals."

Such a document demonstrates the mix of trust and distrust that characterizes contractors' relationships with their clients. By defining the elements of the project, Joseph sought to engender trust in his expertise, yet his "red flags" signaled his distrust of the client's good faith and reciprocal understanding. A trusting relationship, he emphasized, could be possible only after he had evidence of the client's willingness to provide essential support and prompt payment, and for each new project, the evidence took time to accumulate. For long-term clients, proposals might be less detailed, but he always made sure that the client received a written document spelling out what he would do.

Despite the deliberation that went into his proposals, Joseph avoided calling them contracts. Rather, he stressed, "all my work is done on a handshake," implying that the very informality of the arrangement promoted trust on both sides. In more than twenty years of contracting, he had only occasionally worked for "the kind of company that insisted on a contract." Such clients, in his experience, tended to demand a new document with each change in plan, requiring a multilayered approval process that discouraged negotiation. Many of the contractors I met echoed Joseph's distinction between contracts (which they understood as formal, legalistic, and rigid) and the agreements they preferred to make with clients: informal, flexible, and open-ended. Informality left them latitude for revising expectations in the light of new information. Without such informality, they feared losing the opportunity to evaluate a project and, if necessary, challenge the assessment of the client.

Contracts, as contractors tend to use the word, are standard documents written in the bureaucratic voice of the client to protect the interests of the client.[6] Formal contracts, my informants complained, are instruments of conformity that restrict performance and negate expertise. The standardization they impose can impinge on a contractor's discretion. Large corporate clients, I was told, are most likely to insist on some degree of formality, and staffing agencies routinely present contractors with formal contracts, usually written in boilerplate language. These typically specify a fee or rate of pay and a termination date, which often bear little relationship to the actual needs of the project. Some further stipulate that the contractor "will do his/her best work" or "will behave in a professional manner," directives that most contractors find demeaning. Like the "bad temp stories" told by agencies that place clerical temps,[7] these terms are subtle threats that can serve as mechanisms of control. Not only are the expectations for "best work" and "professional manner" never spelled out but such caveats imply surveillance to ensure conformity to unspecified demands.

Formal contract language may provide legal leverage if an agency or its client firm wishes to dismiss a contractor, but none of my informants could recall hearing of any contractor let go for failing to meet the vague requirements of a written contract. The forms and regulations were instead an annoyance that tended to reduce their expertise to a series of tasks and almost always failed to describe their work adequately. Informality, most maintained, allows a contractor to define the needs of a project as it unfolds. Ongoing informal negotiation thus sustains a contractor's performance and supports greater equality in client relations.

Asserting Control

The processes that constitute an expert performance—identifying expectations, assessing materials, drafting specifications—are also, for contractors, an assertion of control. Many of my informants spoke passionately about the sense of control that their work arrangement gave them, especially when comparing it with standard employment. As a newcomer to contract work, Emily, an editor and proofreader, described the difference: "I'm finding it very liberating because in the past, or in any situation where there was a definite authority figure and the rest of us were definitely on a different level, you were part of that structure. I guess I always found it a little bit intimidating.... There's something about freelancing that makes me feel like I'm in charge more." Even when assigned editorial "scut work," checking proofs and marking minor corrections, Emily considered herself less of a subordinate than the employees who performed the same tasks. For them, organizational membership so rigidly defined relationships that they would have to "pay their dues" in low-level jobs for at least two years. In contrast, Emily believed, contracting left her more options, which she hoped to exercise sooner.

Brent, a programmer specializing in computer animation, described a similar sense of options as he negotiated his role in each new project: "When I present myself, I start out with the creative stuff because I know my technical stuff is solid enough, and it'll come out. But if I start with the creative stuff, it lets them know, first of all. It lets me be sure they've seen it, and it also lets them know that's what I'm invested in." Confident in his technical abilities, Brent was seeking projects that would engage him creatively.

Increasingly, he described his work as "part programming, part artistic," and he described his concerted effort to integrate these two domains. Although he, too, was willing to do "scut work," reading and checking code, he tried to use client negotiations to assert the scope of his expertise: "I try to make it very clear that I'm not just going to be a programmer. I'm going to help them think about the whole thing and try to come up with the whole whatever they want.... I'm going to take a big role."

Still relatively new to contracting, Brent seemed a little surprised at his success in finding clients who appreciated his mix of knowledge and skill. One reason, he speculated, was his refusal to work though staffing agencies, which would probably have limited his control: "I don't want to go through agencies because it's, I guess I fear that they wouldn't get it right. They would want to, 'Oh, OK, we got this programmer.... Here's a job writing a web page for a banking company.' You know, no." Control over the assignments he took, Brent believed, had allowed him to create his own options. "I got into contract work originally because I was at a job and I wasn't happy there," he ruminated. "Why should I take contract jobs that won't get me where I want to be?"

How are we to understand this sense of freedom? None of the contractors I interviewed, in either occupational group, proclaimed the rhetoric of free agency and limitless opportunity so audible during the economic boom at the turn of the twenty-first century. Rather, all identified numerous constraints and trade-offs. Like Emily and Brent, however, the great majority did consider themselves somehow "liberated." Over and over, they described contracting as an experience of control unavailable to employees. Those who worked principally at home emphasized control over their working time. Those who believed they had reaped the benefits of tight labor markets described choosing their clients and projects among many available options. Most, however, described control through a process of interaction in which they shaped client relations by exhibiting expertise.

Setting Limits

The exercise of control in some settings may generate conflict between professional standards and organizational constraints. When upper-level managers cut costs or shorten schedules, for example, both contractors and employees must adjust to limited resources. Thomas, a writer and trainer, described a common dilemma for writers working in firms that develop technology: the technical documentation for which the writer is responsible can remain incomplete, even after a deadline has passed, as Thomas lamented:

> Organizations are notorious for not having time for course developers and technical writers. I mean they're too busy writing the product. I mean that kind of in quotes.... Willing access, instead of mandated access [to needed information or people who possess it] is very hard to come by. So you have to set that up, up front. You could have a formal project meeting where the boss of all those, you know, the bosses of all the bosses of all the departments says *x* amount of resources is formally announced. And then I make darn sure that when it's my time, I'm there, and I'm getting the information I need.

Not bound by the hierarchy, Thomas readily jumped many levels of management, even "going over all their heads" to find what he needed to complete a segment of work. Not fettered by structures that constrained employees, he sought to ensure his success by circumventing formal organizational procedures.

Thomas's efforts reflect a concern for expert performance that pervades contractors' accounts. Although the contractors I interviewed described ignoring the politics that sometimes surrounded them, they remained acutely aware of organizational obstacles that might impede their own progress. Clients with tight deadlines and changing specifications might make unreasonable demands, they explained, but failure to adapt could nonetheless reflect badly on a contractor. Attentive to tasks, time lines, and project goals, contractors in both occupational groups described strategies to protect themselves from expectations that they might not be able to meet.

Many accepted new assignments only tentatively and tried to forestall any commitment until they were assured of client cooperation. Pete, a software developer, expressed a typical concern:

> There are some projects where they're throwing in the contractor or looking for contractors to save their bacon because the project is running late, and they're hoping that if they toss more bodies at it, that will meet some deadline. That rarely happens. And then it's frustrating for everyone, because

I know a couple of times I've agreed to a contract in that situation. But I wasn't quite aware up front that it really was a project so desperately missing the deadline already. And then you realize that there's four or five times more work to be done.

When hired to bail out projects long overdue or way over budget, Pete elaborated, he tried to avoid responsibility for the problem he was hired to solve. Although seeking full disclosure and a promise of resources could make him the bearer of bad news, he had learned to persevere. "I've had to tell some pretty important people that their project wasn't going to make it," he lamented. "I had to wonder if they'd shoot the messenger."

Setting limits can also protect the contractor's income when significant changes require time-consuming revisions. Although no contractor wants to absorb unplanned costs, those who accept project fees rather than hourly rates exercise special care. Grant, an editor and indexer, related a particularly troublesome episode:

They wanted me to index the book. OK, so I quoted them a price. And they kept sending me these page proofs and then calling me up. "Oh, we've changed materials, so stop doing it." So finally, I said, "When you have the page proofs set, then give them to me, and I'll start the index." Well, I did the index, and even after I did, they started changing the pages on me. And it just turned into a big nightmare. So, you know, I've become very careful about not starting work until actually, you know, the page numbers are set in stone.

Grant knew established processes for indexing any document and was sure that his demands were reasonable. Had the client approached another indexer, he noted, the same difficulty would have developed. Asserting control of the process, he had tried firmly to set limits—rather than revising the index with each new set of proofs, he would work only from final pages.

Janice, a writer, editor, and project manager, described a similar series of exchanges with a client who seemed unable to complete a website:

I just did this really big website for somebody, and it's her own company....she's very collaborative, which is great, but...this was constant talking, and at one point she started making things worse. She would just take things that were already well written, that we had both agreed upon, and then she'd change them again. And I finally said, "We're at that deadly point in the project, which I call the fuss-with-it, where things are already good and you start monkeying with them because you either don't want to face the next part or you just don't know what to do with yourself. This is the point you're at, and you have to stop."

Janice suspected that her client's inability to let go of the project was "some kind of syndrome," a common problem that she had learned to manage by limiting the revisions she would do. Unlike Grant, she had received an hourly rate for implementing changes, which her client had willingly paid. Yet acquiescing to ongoing changes could compromise both the product and the relationship. Her success thus depended on asserting that the work was complete.

Contractors' latitude to set limits may vary with labor market demand. During boom times, when offers of work more often come unsolicited, a contractor might feel emboldened to challenge a client. Roland, a programmer and project manager, described a particularly intransigent client with a project he had ultimately left unfinished: "One of the things... marketing wanted, basically, they wanted all sorts of things on the website for one project that just were not technologically possible.... And basically they're like, well, what do you know? And I'm like I know a lot. I don't know anything about marketing. I'm not telling you how to do your job. Don't tell me how to do mine. If I say it can't be done, it can't be done." Faced with unreasonable expectations, Roland had quickly moved on, but a year later, after economic conditions had worsened, he speculated about his own precipitous response. Perhaps in a downturn he would instead have bided his time while looking for work elsewhere. He still, emphatically, deemed the client intractable, but a slackening market, which had hit programmers especially hard, might have made him more circumspect until he found another assignment.

Setting limits can thus range from pushing back against the requirements of a client to insisting on access to resources or compliance with common practice. Most of my informants described these strategies as forms of leverage that offered greater control than they had experienced as employees. In standard jobs, they explained, employees can less often negotiate the terms of the work at hand. In contrast, after having established trust in their abilities, contractors could assert authority, even when they identified restrictions and articulated the scope of their responsibility. Setting limits, they assured me, need not necessarily mean losing a project. Rather, the process provided an opportunity for them to define the conditions for their employment and simultaneously display their expertise.

Negotiating Collaboration

In both occupations, my informants cited discursive processes—analyzing projects, revising plans, articulating alternatives—through which they might offer direction to their clients. Although theses strategies were indirect assertions of control, they provided points of leverage for influencing relationships. Ellie, an editor who rewrote manuscripts and collaborated closely with authors, described an iterative process of communication:

> Some people have a clear-cut task that they want somebody else to do. Some people like to do it much more collaboratively. Some people get better at it. They take a look at one chapter that I've worked on, and they think, "Ah ha. Now I get this," and they decide they want to do it themselves, which is fine with me. Or they decide they want to try it, and then they send it back to me and say, "What else can I do now?"

Ellie's collaborative strategy emphasized her clients' prerogatives, yet she sought to control the substance and process of her work. She might begin by editing a short passage or might critique the project before revising. By determining the options, she sought to shape the collaboration.

Brenda, a programmer and systems analyst, described collaboration as an effort to "add value" to a client's operation. Geographically mobile, with "the all-American cardboard box as my décor," she was for most of her clients a technical specialist. "I introduce some new practices at spots where I think they'll be helpful," she noted. "I may come into a firm that has never done a project big enough to need source code control before, and I can tell them, well, there are some wonderful tools out there that control this kind of a mess, and here's what they're called and here's what they do." At the time of our interview, Brenda was assessing her client's systems to identify possible upgrades. "Every time I leave a client, they have more information…than they had before I got there," she noted. Like Ellie, however,

Brenda acknowledged the limits of a contractor's control. "I don't try to get my clients to adopt the best practices," she elaborated. "I know I don't have the leverage."

When a project requires close collaboration, control may stem from iterative exchange. Among team members, for example, an understanding of the labor process—with its standard sequence of stages for development, review, and revision—can inform negotiation for specific project needs. Organizational procedures, such as standard transmittal forms, might provide formal mechanisms for coordination among practitioners or departments, but these systems rarely prove adequate for the complexities of integrated tasks. Teams of practitioners, both contractors and employees, must instead augment organizational protocols with informal interaction.

Sherry, an editor, translator, and project manager, described negotiating with team members over the allocation of responsibilities:

> If I turn in something with the understanding that this is where my job ends and this is where someone else's job begins, and then I find out that my job should have ended at a little bit different point than it did, then they'll come back and say, "Well, why wasn't that done?" And I say, "I just had no idea that was part of my job."...Or sometimes I show them how much more efficient it would be for me to do something instead, or I find out why they do it one way, so I learn their system.

Sherry used minor discrepancies between her expectations and those of her client to demonstrate her expertise. By negotiating the details of her work, she could display both a grasp of the overall process and a willingness to adapt to work-site protocols. By facilitating the work of her colleagues, she could also, on occasion, control the scope of her own involvement and thus the content of her work.

Paradoxically, Sherry asserted control by embedding herself in a client organization, even as she acknowledged her independence from direct managerial oversight. Like Ellie, she depended on a discursive process of collaboration, conforming to client procedures and expectations even as she proposed alternatives. Sherry monitored her own performance, but she also appropriated managerial practices. "The goal setting for yourself is important," she explained. "Give yourself your own performance review every year and ask, 'Did I do it well? Did I do it not well? What do I need to work on?'" Lacking formal supervision, Sherry reviewed her own progress and set the terms of her own success.

By appropriating the tools of organizational control—goals, deadlines, directives—contractors subsume managerial oversight and experience control over day-to-day work. This performance of control further constitutes the contractor as an active agent—confident, capable, and willing to meet the needs of a client. Outside the imperatives of the organization, apart from its system of sanctions, incentives, and rewards, the contractors I interviewed had developed identities as trusted, capable practitioners. Their identification with work and occupation—rather than with employer and affiliation—thus provided them a means for asserting an authority based principally on expertise.

In one sense, this strong identification with work provides the means by which clients harness a contractor's concern for expert performance to organizational needs. Depending on a contractor's willingness to meet expectations—and on the prerogative to dismiss a contractor quickly—clients retain control over directives and priorities and rarely cede major decisions. Yet a contractor's identity as an expert also supports control over the quality of the performance. As participants in a system of work relations, contractors channel their efforts, negotiating expectations and identifying the limits of their responsibility. More than a series of tenuous arrangements, contract employment is a form of occupational practice in which the performance of expertise becomes a source of stability and control. A contractor's success thus depends on an expert performance, conveyed through social interaction and applied to the goals of the client.

4

Managing Marginality

Contracting circumscribes contractors' involvement in employing organizations. Hired for specific expertise, contractors are often valued contributors to the goals of their clients, and they can and do influence work-related decisions. Rarely, however, do they assume a significant role in long-term decision making. Rather, they remain marginal actors, occupying a social location that allows little latitude for engaging in conflict or voicing dissent. Despite expert performance and productive client relations, they participate in a work arrangement that limits their involvement and enforces status distinctions.

In relations with clients, contractors navigate a set of contradictions that they can never fully resolve. They stand ready to contribute to client goals but assume a detachment from organizational life. They participate in charting the progress of a project but avoid internal disputes and organizational politics. High mobility in an external labor market supports their autonomy, but they practice careful accountability to sustain a performance of expertise. Unlike salaried employees, contractors must account for their time and the cost of their services, tracking billable hours and verifying client approval for the progress of their work. On the margins of employing organizations, they take part in labor market practices that maintain their separation from employees with standard jobs. Their marginality, then, becomes evident in the interactional processes through which they communicate with clients.

Communication practices reinforce the structural distinction between contracting and standard employment. Contractors working from home typically use telecommunications to keep apprised of developments at client sites, even as the spatial distance provides a buffer from organizational culture. Contractors working at client sites find organizational boundaries marking contractual difference and requiring careful attention to the interactional cues. Whatever the work site, the terms of a contractor's participation are never firmly fixed, never given formal organizational status. Yet, even as an outsider, a contractor must contend with internal systems and hierarchies of control. How, then, do these contract professionals navigate the contradictions of their social location on the margins of client firms? How do their strategies maintain a system of contract employment?

Autonomy and Accountability

Contractors must navigate between autonomy and constraint, assuming responsibility for conforming to organizational norms, even as they also negotiate some latitude for deviance. Two accounts illustrate this tension. Jeffrey, a software engineer, had been working full-time, on-site at a large computer firm many hours from home. Tired of the commute, he had proposed working instead from a home office, and despite official policy, his client had ultimately agreed. "They [the client] say they don't allow it,...[but] they knew who I was," he explained, "and typically I was there [in the office] before seven. There was nobody before seven. And they know I'm good." Having displayed his commitment, Jeffrey had renegotiated his work arrangement, exercising a prerogative largely unavailable to employees. "It takes a little bit of time to generate 'the fuzzies' with people," he reflected. "You have what's needed to get the job done, but, yeah, it takes more....My job as a contractor is to make the client happy, whatever it takes."

In contrast, Melanie, a writer and editor, related an incident that had sorely strained client relations. Hired to write chapters for a textbook, she had submitted draft copy for review. Months had passed without a response, which she interpreted as approval. Then the client balked. "I guess nobody was really looking at the manuscript for a couple of months," Melanie remembered, "and then all of a sudden I started getting a lot of feedback like 'Why aren't you doing this? This is in the guidelines.'" Eventually, Melanie traced the problem to a miscommunication—she had failed to check for new specifications, which her client had failed to transmit. "I pretty much know what I'm doing," she noted, "so...it didn't really bother me that he [the project manager] didn't say anything....[But] I suppose I should have checked for updates." Although not entirely at fault, Melanie offered to revise her work and to absorb the cost of the error.

Lapses in communication, like the renegotiation of an agreement, reveal the related processes of autonomy and accountability. Autonomy allows a contractor to manage information and chart the direction of work in progress. A contractor achieves some measure of autonomy through a performance of expertise. Accountability, however, supports the performance and sustains client relations over time. Believing she had been accountable by submitting a draft for review, Melanie had nonetheless been charged with failing to adhere to updated guidelines that she had never received. Here her strategy to be accountable had proved inadequate, costing her unpaid hours compensating for the missed information. Jeffrey, in contrast, had successfully proved his accountability—a process he called "generating fuzzies"—and so purchased a greater measure of autonomy with the option to work from home.

The contractors I interviewed described practicing accountability through frequent communication: acknowledging receipt of information, answering questions, and documenting results. Contracting, they explained, demands an accountability that differs from the standard job. Unlike employees, contractors are never on the payroll and do not routinely receive paychecks. Instead, they must act to be paid. Those who are formally self-employed or employees of their own businesses usually submit invoices, often with a status report or project summary that tells the client what the payment has purchased. Those working through staffing agencies may also submit forms that list the number of hours worked during a given pay period. Requiring a supervisor's signature, these forms are a periodic reminder of accountability and an additional measure of oversight. Although only one of my informants told of a client's challenging the number of hours billed, most were aware of client scrutiny for their time spent and work accomplished.

Tracking Billable Time

The notion of billable time can provide a strong incentive for practicing accountability. Although some contractors receive project fees, which provide payment either at specific benchmarks or at the completion of the project, contract work in these occupations more often pays an hourly rate, which requires contractors to track their time spent and bill the client accordingly. A contractor working at a client site can usually bill the client for all time spent there, and although seldom closely monitored, the contractors I met described trying to be scrupulous about their use of time.[1] Several, for example, reported deducting any time spent in lengthy personal phone calls. In much the same way, those who worked from home offices distinguished billable from nonbillable time. Out of the sight of their clients, home-based contractors described logging, day by day, the hours they devoted to paid work.

Many of the contractors I met also described reviewing their billable time against a subjective sense of the service provided.[2] Bruce, a software engineer and systems analyst, related questions he often asked himself before submitting an invoice: "I think OK, the client agreed to pay me for three days of consulting. Well, let's see, that's $4,500. Oh, my God, am I really going to charge them $4,500? I know I put in the hours; that's not the question. But did I get $4,500 worth of value for them? ... That sort of dilemma comes up a lot.... So I end up submitting bills that I think reflect the value of the work done." Although Bruce charged $150 per hour and had "learned not to negotiate about that," he sometimes spent time that he considered unproductive. Inefficiency, he feared, could undermine his status as an expert practitioner and compromise his relationship with the client. "I'm writing a computer program for them [a client] now," he explained. "I'm not happy with the progress I'm making on it. I think I've bitten off a little bit larger chunk than I could chew. I didn't understand how to organize it properly before I started, so I've been spinning my wheels a lot. It just doesn't feel appropriate to charge them for all that spinning-wheel time." Maintaining a high hourly rate, Bruce believed, garnered the respect of his clients, yet it also rendered him accountable for using his time efficiently. Although confident that he was giving his clients their money's worth, he also tried to avoid suspicion that he might have overcharged. "Can I submit a bill of this magnitude and keep the client?" he wondered, and when in doubt, he compensated by "chiseling" the hours he billed.

Many of my informants described further excluding from their bills any time spent in backstage efforts to find information or update a skill. Unlike employees, they could expect no on-the-job training or client investment in their skills. Sherry, an editor, translator, and project manager, explained, "If I feel like I was hired to do a job and I had actually to do some extra work in order to get caught up to a certain level, I'm not going to charge them for that." Such self-imposed guidelines, she reasoned, should extend to occasional "extra" time spent on tasks she found especially engaging. Developing market analyses, for example, allowed her to read in areas of personal interest. Yet she sometimes worried that her painstaking reviews could cost her client too much. "I'm not going to charge for time that I'm spending reading something because I find it interesting rather than it's really helping their product at all," she noted. Concerned with an appearance of efficiency, she occasionally "shaved" her hours to be sure that she was meeting unspoken expectations.

Experience as employees had taught most of the contractors I met about practices related to billing and payment, and most felt they knew whether their billable hours fell within a reasonable range. Many described making "seat-of-the-pants" judgments about the hours they logged, subtracting inefficiencies but sometimes adding time they had spent on work while otherwise occupied. Bennett, a software engineer, explained his rationale:

> Every day at the end of the day, I write down how many hours I worked.... But I can't keep track of the time I spend thinking about a problem or trying to solve a problem when I'm doing other things. I mean I can be reading a book, and suddenly an idea will pop into my head: Oh, if I do this and this, then.... And I'll start sketching out a design idea. If I do that, then I'll start charging for it, but other than that, I don't.

When they found themselves attending to work off the clock, some of my informants deemed the time compensation for lapses in attention while logging billable hours. As Bennett rationalized the practice, "The total pretty much evens out."

Many also distinguished between their careful calculations from the practice of "bill padding," which they decried as illegitimate. As Sherry lamented, "I've been really working on keeping careful track of hours I spend,...but I know some freelancers pad, and I just find that padding doesn't work in the long run." Sherry was one of several informants who suspected that other contractors were dishonestly inflating the number of hours they billed. Although she assured me that she would never "rat" on a colleague who overcharged in this way, she found the practice worse than distasteful.[3] Inflated hours, she pointed out, ultimately justified lower rates, which in turn devalued her expertise and penalized those who scrupulously monitored their time.

Contractors' scruples can lead some to monitor their colleagues. At a software development company, as I joined three contract engineers for lunch, a discussion was underway about another contractor—not present at the table—who appeared to be attending to personal business while at his desk. As in many technology firms, both contractors and employees worked in cubicles that formed a honeycomb of offices in a large open space. With only partial walls between them, these individual spaces were far from soundproof, and the contractors at lunch had overheard their delinquent colleague discussing the start-up firm he had recently founded. All present agreed that he was "walking a fine line" and "should really be careful." One speculated that he might also be appropriating company equipment; another noted that the company phone system would automatically log his calls. His behavior, they feared, could reflect badly on contractors in general and lead to greater scrutiny and less autonomy for everyone.

Although payment by the hour demands a contractor's careful use of time, the same hourly wage can also be an incentive for a client to use a contractor's time efficiently. For a client, a contractor represents a cost that rises proportionately to the time spent. The employee who arrives late for a meeting, for example, can expect the contractor to be "running the meter." The manager who brings a contractor on-site pays for an unused resource when essential materials are unavailable. Bennett contrasted these managerial imperatives with the conditions he had experienced in standard employment:

> When a company has something that they need done by a certain date, they don't really care how many hours their engineers need to work on it. They feel perfectly free to impose deadlines and then consume the engineers with a lot of unproductive overhead. But when they pay me by the hour, they try to minimize the overhead, and they don't give me, they don't distract me with a lot of crap.... Because they pay me by the hour, clients do not feel free to waste my time with unproductive meetings.

With contract services usually treated as a separate budget item, calculated apart from the salaries paid to employees, the cost accounting of a firm reflects the distinction between the fixed costs of payroll and the variable costs of contract work. Internal systems thus contribute to the structural demarcation between contractors and employees. Although contractors' careful monitoring of time does serve the interests of clients who depend on them to track their billable hours sparingly, effective cost control also requires clients to provide contractors with the resources necessary to conduct their work efficiently. Tracking time, therefore, operates as a mechanism for enforcing accountability for both contractors and clients.

Assuring Client Consent

Successful accountability contributes to client consent. When work goes well and all involved are pleased with its progress, a contractor may exercise considerable control over its daily rhythms. Yet without the structural authority that comes, even in limited form, with organizational membership, a contractor's scope of influence rarely expands beyond a single project. Long-range planning usually remains outside a contractor's purview, and ultimate authority always lies with the client. Contractors describe a process of assessment through which they identify organizational structures and key decision makers whose approval they may need.[4] For those working on-site, frequent informal interaction may render formal processes of accountability less necessary. For contractors working from a distance, however, consent more often requires ongoing attention.

Katherine, a programmer and database manager, described a multilayered approval process she had developed with a research institution, where she provided technical support and website development:

> I need to get sign-off or co-opt the approval of a number of different people either in the team or the researchers that are actually gathering the information to be delivered on the web. So it gets complicated. And you have to get, to put it in everybody's face:... "If you don't sign off, then I'm going to assume that it's approved." And often a lot of my work is kind of going in these feedback loops where you have to say, "No, you didn't sign off, so approval is assumed."

With this client, Katherine had learned, specifications were subject to change without notice, leaving her responsible for meeting schedules without adequate time. She had therefore learned to cover herself by making the approval procedure explicit—each person had an opportunity either to approve her work or to ask for revisions, but if her deadline passed without a response, she would consider the latest version final. If subsequent changes required more time and greater costs, she could then justify the expense. Consent, she explained, protected her from compensating after the fact for others' inattention.

For projects involving many people and conflicting directives, Katherine needed also to identify who was in charge and then have that person approve the final version. Characterizing the arrangement, she explained, "Supervising my work is something I actually have to go hunt out from people." Most of the contractors I interviewed similarly preferred taking responsibility for oversight and review. Close supervision, they explained, was an unwelcome form of micromanagement, which could undermine their self-presentation as expert practitioners. By taking steps to assure approval for a plan or set of specifications, however, they could seize the initiative and assume a measure of managerial decision making. Katherine thus characterized her requests for feedback as "managing up."

Close collaboration, especially when at a client site, can mitigate some of the effort required to keep a client apprised of progress, but there, too, contractors cited mechanisms that assured consent for the trajectory of their work. Jackie, a software engineer, described the strategy she used when beginning a long-term project: "I hand in weekly status reports, and I do it every week when I first start, and then I skip a week here and there, and then I skip a lot of weeks, and pretty soon it doesn't matter. Basically, they want to see results. But if you can't show them results, you can tell them what you're doing." When unable to deliver a segment of work, Jackie always explained the steps she was taking to learn the project requirements and technical specifications. Without evident progress to show, she accounted for her time, submitting written status reports at regular intervals and documenting her understanding of longer-term client goals. Only by proving herself accountable, she emphasized, could she avoid closer scrutiny of her performance.

Not all contractors I met were so comfortable seeking approval, and a few had found that the effort contributed to unwelcome oversight. Martin, an editor and proofreader who had been a contractor for only six months, described a review of a document in progress as "a big contrast" and "more stressful" than anything he had experienced as an employee. "Pretty much everything I do is subject to almost immediate supervision," he complained. "They'll get back to you in like five seconds with a criticism of what you did." In the standard job he had held for three years, Martin had been left alone to draft copy and manage data retrieval, and he had rarely needed to justify his decisions. As a contractor, however, he had to seek the approval of his client and continue to account for his time, only to have others quibble over details. Lack of internal consensus by the client had apparently made consent fleeting and illusory, but for Martin, the experience also undermined his autonomy and so subordinated his expertise.

Success for any contractor can thus mean assuring, at identifiable intervals, that a client has consented to goals, plans, deliverables, or constraints. Having identified expectations, my informants explained, a contractor needs to ascertain more frequently than an employee that consent remains intact. Last-minute changes and redirection of effort can prove frustrating for anyone, but for a contractor, late revisions will also incur additional time and expense, for which someone must ultimately pay. Marks of a capable contractor, therefore, are identifying problems that will cost time or money and assuring client consent for a plan of action that allocates the available resources.

Meredith, a programmer, trainer, and database developer, described an unhappy client for which she had assumed too much consent. She had drafted a detailed proposal and believed she had delineated specifications, yet when she presented a close-to-completed project, her client had found the database inadequate. "There was a piece I think they were expecting," Meredith recalled, "and it's possibly something that had been talked about in the bigger picture. But then when we pared it down to this is what I can provide, it wasn't there." Meredith remained unsure about the cause of the misunderstanding. Perhaps her explanation had been too technical. Perhaps she should have divided the project into smaller phases and delivered each one separately. The client had paid in full, she noted, but "they weren't happy about it."

Reflecting on the experience, Meredith had developed new strategies for assuring consent as her work progressed. Frequent e-mail exchanges, she found, generated a record that both phone calls and face-to-face meetings lacked. The informality of online exchange maintained a tone of conversation but still kept track of the decisions made and questions still pending, as Meredith explained:

> I try to do a lot from e-mail. Not that I'm paranoid, but people don't remember that they said it by phone. And when I've had an e-mail relationship with a client,...and then I say "Well, I asked you this in an e-mail, and you said no. I brought up that these are three open issues, and we haven't resolved them yet,"...I mean they're paying you to anticipate any of the issues, and so you don't want their surprises. You want to say, "This is an open issue, and we don't have a solution for it." That's OK, but not as a surprise.

With the expansion of e-mail during the 1990s, many of my informants had come to document decisions through online exchange. Frequent communication, they explained, could avoid misunderstandings and so enhance accountability.

Although these strategies of accountability might help avoid overt conflict, contractors do encounter areas of dispute. Noreen, a writer and editor, described an exchange with a manager who had at first seemed ambivalent about the drafts of a brochure she had submitted: "I said, 'Be straight with me,'" she recalled. "They should give me feedback for something they don't like. I say, 'Tell me, and I'll change it.' I mean I'm really working to try to do what it is that they need to have done in the best, most efficient way that I can figure out how to do it." Despite her willingness to revise, Noreen disagreed with her client, who had insisted on technical jargon that customers might not understand, and she anticipated complaints after the product was on the market. Knowing that client prerogatives would prevail, she expressed frustration common to contractors who find their advice ignored. "You figure they're hiring you and paying you for your expertise, and then they don't want your expertise," she complained. "So it's sort of like arrrrgh! You know, the client is 'always right.'" With her objections overruled, Noreen had acquiesced, hoping not to be too closely linked with the client's decision.

As an employee, Noreen believed, she would have felt less threatened. From an organizational position she had been able to "spread responsibility" for questionable directives. Faced with the same dilemma, she would consult key players, seek upper-managerial review, or express her objections in writing, to be on record in case of adverse consequences. As a contractor, in contrast, she felt exposed, with only the quality of her work as evidence of her expertise. A fundamental disagreement with a client, she speculated, might even be a reason to step aside or suggest that the client replace her. Noreen had never parted company with a client in this way, but she mused, "Sometimes, when you contract, there might be no other choice."

Dissent and Disengagement

Noreen's experience represents a common quandary for contractors. When challenging a decision, employees may have a greater formal claim, but they also have more at stake. Subject to the politics of organizational life, employees risk their long-term viability in the organization. For them, an approved definition of reality can become a condition of membership, and organizational culture may thus mediate their behavior.[5] To challenge organizational norms—perhaps by naming problems, questioning priorities, or negating product claims—may well invite sanctions. Contractors, of course, may also incur risk for overt dissent, but without a long-term investment, the consequences are usually less severe. The contractors I interviewed, therefore, described opting to take risks that, as employees, they might have chosen to avoid.

Taking Risks

Charles, a writer, editor, and trainer, offered an extreme case. He had been working as an employee, and his group had been charged with solving the company's marketing problem, which had become all but intractable after recent bad publicity. At work, however, any mention of the cause of the publicity was considered a breach of loyalty, and employees, including Charles, avoided discussing it. But then he challenged the norm:

> The company had a meeting where they brought in all the executives, and I gave this report in front of all the executives, and after talking to my boss extensively about this—and he'd given me permission—I told them among other things that one of the major obstacles was something…that had been in the news. And somebody immediately jumped out of their seat and said,"I have to go talk to the president." And sure enough, I was fired not too long after that.

Charles and his boss had both recognized the risk of naming the newsworthy event, but neither had predicted the outcome. The terms of organizational membership had maintained a code of silence, and those who breached the code, Charles learned, could not be tolerated.

More often, violations carry subtler sanctions. They might, for example, impede an employee's mobility, especially when timely promotions or choice work assignments depend on a willingness to conform. Employees learn where disagreement may be tolerated and where they are better off remaining silent. Contractors immersed in client organizations typically learn the same norms, but located on the margins, they assume a paradoxical position: presenting themselves as experts, they may find their views welcomed as a fresh perspective, but lacking structural authority, they may also find their expertise ignored or their contributions easily dismissed. Employees may experience similar frustrations. Contractors, however, can more readily choose to leave.

Many of my informants expressed great frustration with decisions they perceived to be poorly conceived or executed, and a few had indeed hesitated to remain with projects that they considered compromised. Blaine, a programmer and test engineer, recalled a particularly difficult project in which upper management had decided, well into development, to cut corners and patch an outdated system rather than build a new product. As Blaine remembered, the new plan was announced at a meeting, which he dubbed "the emperor's new clothes meeting," at which contractors and employees split into factions, with the two groups reacting differently:

Management wound up doing something that six months previously they had said they would never do, rehashing some old code instead of rearchitecting this project.... Some of the contractors spoke up and basically said, "I'm not going to work on this. We signed on agreeing that this old thing that you're now saying you're going to rehash was a piece of junk, and now because you won't listen to what we're telling you,... you're going to rehash it."

Blaine remembered seeing a few employees nod, indicating that they at least understood the contractors' objections, but all had remained silent, evidently preferring to let the contractors carry the protest: "They didn't voice their opinion on this.... Employees knew that the stuff was junk,... and yet they wouldn't say, basically. Maybe they were worried about their jobs.... There was a clear difference between how some of the regular employees—one or two in particular who were very senior at the time—how they reacted as opposed to how some of the contractors reacted." Blaine described team members huddling together a few hours later and several employees expressing hope that the project would be cancelled. They knew they were expected to go along, he surmised, but were unwilling to risk the consequences of dissent. In contrast, several contractors saw the redirection of the project as a change in the terms of their agreements. Some publicly insisted that the managers reconsider. When the decision remained firm, these contractors resigned, citing an impasse in the substance of their work.

Blaine stayed for personal reasons. "I was in a precarious financial situation," he explained. But eventually the pressure to compromise intensified, and he too objected: "I kind of said to them, 'I don't agree with what you're doing,... but if you need someone to help you transition... I'll stay around for it.' And they sort of like terminated me. They kind of just said, 'OK, we don't need you anymore.'" For Blaine, the experience was a stark reminder of hierarchical control. To disagree is not necessarily proscribed, especially in organizations that reward participation, but those in charge can still determine what will be tolerated. By making clear his position, Blaine knew that he was pushing against the boundaries of acceptable dissent. His abrupt dismissal was thus hardly a surprise.

Contractors may find that their marginality allows for greater voice, but those who actively dissent might consider their options carefully. Financial imperatives and labor market conditions can exert considerable control, determining the context in which a contractor attempts to exert influence. Most of my informants described trying to avoid direct confrontation, even when options seemed plentiful. Instead, they sought to frame dissent indirectly, as clarification or suggestion. Melanie described challenging a client by identifying "a particular situation or particular example" that seemed inappropriate for an elementary school textbook and offering an alternative: "If... this isn't something I would want to do if I were a kid.... or it just doesn't make sense, I might say, 'This doesn't work in this particular situation, and this is why.' And then they'll say, 'In this particular situation, why don't you do blah-de-blah.' Or they'll say, 'No, you're right. These specs aren't working.'"

Most of the contractors I interviewed raised similar, project-specific concerns. Several described a process that Sylvia, a writer and editor, called "keeping the client honest."[6] Honesty might mean a clear assessment of the project status or an insistence that the client meet the stated goals or product claims. Working for individual authors, Sylvia sometimes cited the successful books she had planned and developed: "There was one author whom I worked with who's very well respected and has accomplished amazing things in his life and deserves all the credit in the world, but he wanted to put all this stuff in his book that just didn't belong there. And I fought a lot of battles with him and won ultimately," she explained. "If they're not going to let you do your job, then the game is over." With her own success at stake, Sylvia had learned to insist that her client hold fast to agreed-on goals. Acquiescing by including content she knew to be extraneous would have reflected especially badly on her.

Dissent for a contractor is typically a comparable act of small-scale resistance. When challenging a decision or redefining a situation, a contractor encourages a client to reconsider options, revise plans, or redirect resources. Such a challenge may reframe the shared understanding that otherwise guides organizational life, but it also helps to render the contractor blameless for the consequences of a client's actions. To risk dissent, therefore, is to readjust the relationship and reinforce the distance between the contractor and client. Voicing objections, offering suggestions, and reframing assumptions can define the dimensions of a contractor's marginality and so maintain the distinction that keeps contractors and employees apart, even when they appear indistinguishable.

Maintaining Distance

A marginal position also allows a contractor to disengage deliberately from an employing organization. Avoiding the much maligned office politics with which employees must contend, my informants described holding themselves apart by limiting their involvement in conflict. Many contended that their marginality fostered clear-headed judgment and so underscored their credibility. Terry, a programmer and project manager, described presenting his clients with options but avoiding any suspicion of a hidden agenda:

> I have no axe to grind. I'm not looking to build an empire, and I don't want to make, I don't necessarily want to make you look good. I'm going to tell you this is what it is.... I'll do it diplomatically. I'll do it in such a way that I will present you with half a dozen possibilities with a cost-benefit analysis for each and say, "You pick. If it were me, knowing what I know now, I'd pick that one, but you pick because I don't know what your internal agenda is."

Unlike an employee, Terry continued, "I already know I'm not going to be there forever, so it doesn't matter." With no need to enhance his standing in the organization, he could provide "the honest answer, not the politically correct answer," and if the client vehemently objected, the consequences were seldom long-lasting.

Many of my informants similarly characterized their client relations as dispassionate. Those who worked at home found that spatial distance might reinforce their social distance, but even those who worked on-site described a sense of disengagement and little investment in organizational outcomes.[7] Some spoke of greater perspective, sometimes gained through exposure to multiple work sites, but most attributed their detachment to their contractual status and compared it with their experiences in standard jobs. There they had more often been affiliated with internal factions or alliances that made them appear biased. As contractors, in contrast, they could focus their attention more narrowly, on the issues that affected their work, and ignore talk about pending changes or individual maneuvering that so often buzzed around them. Their marginality had become a protective shield.

Carol, an editor and technical and marketing writer, described a change in her approach to work when she became a contractor. Years before, as an employee, she had sought challenging assignments to enhance her chance for promotion. Now, as a contractor, she sought only to produce quality work, without regard for her position in the organization:

> Now I don't even care what [specific project] I write. As long as the client is happy, that's all I care about. And I think the other thing I really care about is, through all this [organizational change], if I had not kept my personal inner sense of integrity about the work I do. I will never do bad work, no matter where I am or what I do.... So even though I may be completely unhappy with the people, with managers, for whatever reason, that's not going to affect the job that I do.

A good performance had, for Carol, become a mark of professional pride that her contractual status made ever-more important. She would compromise when necessary but would still maintain her own standards. Distinguishing herself through the quality of her work, rather than her status in an organization, she could maintain her distance. Active disengagement from organizational life can thus reinforce the structural conditions that differentiate contract from standard employment.

Carol's experience echoes the accounts of most of my informants. To avoid office politics, they actively assumed an alternative posture: concerned about the quality of their work and willing to contribute to client goals but otherwise uninvolved. Such a stance could demand an extra measure of self-monitoring, which some described as a balancing act. Most tried to keep their balance by gauging the extent to which clients wanted their participation, to determine whether to intervene in any given situation. Some projects, they explained, required only a straightforward application of knowledge and skill and little attention to internal decision making. Others provided an opportunity to contribute new ideas, promote efficiency, or enhance product quality.

The flip side of opportunity, however, could be frustration when managers and employees thwarted their stated aims. Karen, a software developer and trainer, described a "rule of three," which she had learned to apply when dealing with recalcitrant clients:

> If I think there's a problem with the design or I think people are making a bad decision, I have a three rule. I just tell them three times that I

think they're wrong, and then, if they decide to go ahead with it, I just say OK.... I'll tell them, technically, why I think they're wrong, and if they choose not to make use of my experience, then it's their decision, and, you know, the customer is always right. And I try not go get frustrated by that.

Karen paid special attention to her tone and demeanor and actively tried to convey calm. Her credibility, she believed, was more fragile than an employee's. An employee, in contrast, might overtly express frustration, even outright anger. For employees, organizational membership meant caring about their positions and, by extension, the enterprise as a whole. When their tempers flared, those involved could attribute the altercation to work-related stress exacerbated by high commitment.

Contractors enjoy no such latitude. For them, expressions of anger, however justified, are always unacceptable. Applying a common notion of customer service, Karen reminded herself that "the customer is always right"—that is, her client would always have the final say. She had learned, she explained, to keep her frustrations from showing and, when rebuffed, she withdrew to avoid confrontation:

> I don't try to directly fight them. I tend to be very nice. I try to be willing to share information because that helps. But they will pick up on your body language cues, and...if you are angry and they perceive that, they will discount you and just think that you're mad or there's a personality conflict or something like that. So I'm a little more aware of how, of the audience that I'm trying to [influence].

Karen described abstaining as well from criticizing colleagues, no matter how difficult their behavior. Instead, she tried to frame complaints as work-related problems. Still, when team members compromised her performance, problems could become intractable: "It was one project when there was all these dependencies, and the people that I had dependencies on were not meeting them. I would just go in and say that, you know, we should have been at this point. I haven't got this information. I really need it. And I did it far enough in advance that the manager would have some kind of, should have been able to do something about it. I didn't wait until the last minute." Although truly concerned for the slipping schedule, Karen also sought to avoid blame for the delay. She took care, however, to avoid even the appearance of an attack.

Most of the contractors I met described similar efforts to limit complaints to project-specific imperatives. Most tried to differentiate between organizational obstacles, decisions, and processes that might reflect badly on them and difficulties they could endure without hindrance or compromise. Knowing that frustrations end with the assignment, they could look forward to a graceful exit and, in the meantime, avoid recriminations. Grant, an editor and indexer, described a conscious effort at detachment as he struggled with a managing editor who was demanding frequent changes and refusing to allow additional time. The editor had lashed out, he recalled, accusing him of inefficiency, but Grant had kept his composure: "The way I approached it is that I said to myself, 'OK, you've got to remain calm and professional about this and don't blow your stack off with him. Just don't blow your cool with him and, you know, just go along with what he, with what he wants, and that's how you kind of see it through.' Eventually, you know, they were happy with the index."

Grant's perseverance, like Karen's efforts to be nice, reinforced the contractor's status as outsider. Even when gritting their teeth or aiming to please, my informants' accounts underscored their detachment from organizational conflict. In interactions with clients and colleagues, they monitored their responses, avoiding accusations and attending closely to the stated expectations and project needs. Their efforts thus resemble the "emotional labor" common to many kinds of service work—assuming a deferential posture, enacting accommodation, promoting goodwill, even when seething with frustration.[8] Aiming to keep relations intact, they described staying out of the fray, keeping their anger bounded and in check.

Yet, unlike the "feeling rules" to which many service workers adhere, a contractor's detachment is more self-imposed than scripted. Deference for a contractor is a strategy for maintaining social distance through constructive disengagement. Such guarded detachment, however, also serves the interests of the clients, who can depend on contractors to withhold complaint. By accommodating their clients, contractors help to manage internal dissension by minimizing their involvement in disputes. Their disengagement can then absorb conflict that might otherwise require formal resolution. Active disengagement, therefore, supports contractors' marginality and reinforces a dual system of work relations.

Participation and Exclusion

Contractors' distance from client organizations is not always evident to a casual observer. Integrated into on-site teams, contractors may function much like employees. They might participate in project meetings, communicate regularly with colleagues and managers, and, in some cases, assume titles comparable to formal organizational positions. A contractor might, for example, oversee the work of employees and other contractors. Although they rarely, if ever, have sole authority to hire and fire, contractors do, with some clients, assume considerable managerial responsibility. The allocation of tasks and titles, therefore, is not necessarily an indicator of contractual status.

Nor are spatial arrangements, which vary considerably, even within settings. In one software development company, I observed rows of cubicles made of moveable partitions reaching halfway to the ceiling. These malleable work spaces formed offices of roughly equal size and housed everyone, from administrative assistants to corporate vice presidents. The cubicles had been assigned haphazardly, I was told, without regard to rank or position. Interspersed among the employees, in the labyrinth of partitions, contractors occupied some of these malleable work spaces. Inside most were family photos, children's artwork, and other evidence of ownership. Most also had name plates visibly posted on an outer wall facing the hallway formed by the rows of partitions. None of these marks of occupancy distinguished contractors from employees.

Only the few unmarked and undecorated cubicles provided any indication that the occupants were transients, present for too short a time to personalize the space. These offices, I learned, were left available for the few contractors who worked principally off-site, usually from home, or for employees from other plants who occasionally made site visits and needed a temporary work space and connection to the internal network. Tucked away at the edges, far from the windows that provided natural light to only a fraction of the building, these marginal areas saw little traffic and allowed few opportunities to make casual contacts with colleagues. The contractors relegated to these spaces, therefore, were less likely to establish working relationships derived from informal, face-to-face interactions. Indeed, neither contractors nor employees knew who might be occupying these spaces from one week to the next.

Participating from a Distance

Contractors working from off-site offices, too, can depend little on informal interactions. For them, patterns of communication, some of them formally established, channel participation in decision making and shape client relations. With local clients, home-based contractors might occasionally meet face to face, perhaps for lunches or on-site meetings, and some move fluidly in and out of a client office as their work requires. Most, however, depend on designated employees whose jobs include responsibility for providing them with essential information. These employees, then, become their principal points of connection, and these working relationships become especially important.

Seth, an editor and production manager, much preferred such arrangements. "While I might meet the two or three people I deal with out of say the [company name] office, it's not like I'm expected to attend meetings," he explained. "They just tell me what I need to know.... I can still stay in all the necessary loops." Formal systems meant controlled channels of communication, through which Seth could offer suggestions or request resources. Employees who provided him with updates, together with an online database that tracked his projects, could keep him adequately informed. Maintaining boundaries with clients and colleagues, he tried to limit his participation to work-related exchanges.

When systems are less established, however, participation can be haphazard, and some contractors complained angrily about clients who made decisions without their input. Thomas, a writer and trainer, had missed project meetings convened without notice, but he was still subject to the decisions that affected his work. "They'll change the schedule, or they'll make decisions about what you're doing," he lamented. "And pretty much what happens is you're told at the last minute about those changes, as opposed to being involved." Thomas had objected to his exclusion, but his pleas for participation had produced no effect. "It's kind of like, OK," he had heard in response."You choose. You can either leave or do this new thing that we want you to do." Thomas attributed his difficulties with this client to his invisibility working off-site. Unless someone remembered to confer with him, he was "out of the loop" through which information flowed.

Despite his complaints, Thomas had gradually witnessed greater inclusion through e-mail and teleconferencing, which could, in some instances, obviate the need for face-to-face contact. The same technology, he noted, was also promoting more telecommuting among employees, who in some firms also worked at home on a regular basis. When employees worked off-site, Thomas believed, managers more often made an effort to solicit input from all involved, and contractors were then more likely to be included. Yolanda, also a writer, made a similar observation about team members: "We communicate most often by e-mail. We occasionally have real-time chat sessions if there's something several of us need to work on. We conference call when that's necessary.... You just have to be on the list."

Many of my informants had seen electronic technology enhance their role in decision making, especially when team members routinely interacted through e-mail exchange. Off-site but online, a contractor can stay apprised of progress and involved in decisions. Yet, even at firms that developed computer technology, face-to-face meetings could remain the norm. Seth mused about this paradox: "When I worked at [company name], you'd think they'd have figured out how to move information. They move it for everyone else.... But when it comes to planning and scheduling, you know, they have to have meetings." Several of my informants similarly identified the uneven adoption of cyberpractices; some managers, they noted, readily relied on e-mail, whereas others were unwilling to let cyberspace substitute for face-to-face exchange.

Identifying Organizational Boundaries

On-site, contractors face internal organizational boundaries that may also hinder their progress. Vincent, a programmer, lamented his lack of access to resources:

> Getting into the library, if you have to get a book, you have to ask an employee, and they will get it for you. Technical knowledge should be utilized by everyone working on a product,... but you have to lean on somebody else to get what you need. And the supervisor may not be free always. He may have lots of meetings and conference calls, and I have to find out when he's free just to ask. Until that time, I have to hold things up to get that book.

Vincent's experience is far from unique. Requisitions of all kinds—technical tools, office supplies, even basic equipment—may be unavailable to contractors. Although common practice across industries is to provide essential tools for anyone working at a client site, many of my informants spoke of using employees as proxies for meeting work-related needs. Others complained of cramped quarters, with contractors crowded into in small, sometimes poorly equipped work spaces, which made productivity difficult. A few had compensated by bringing their own equipment. Martin, for example, had purchased a laptop computer to bring on-site. "This way, I can move around and find a quiet place to work," he explained.

Under such conditions, a contractor might well experience a sense of subordination, even stigma, as an organizational outsider. For most of my informants, however, professional identity had little to do with the trappings of a client site. Rather, their most common complaint was constraints to their abilities to accomplish tasks and meet goals efficiently, and their singular focus on the work at hand overshadowed any concern for symbols of contractual difference. Tony, a software engineer and systems designer, had spent almost two years at a software development company, where he enjoyed the camaraderie. His work had been well respected, he thought, yet at the corporate level, he remained invisible. The company had recently distributed T-shirts to mark the launch of a product, he pointed out, but he had been overlooked:

> For example, they give these shirts out to everybody who worked on this team. Well, I worked on the [product name] team, but I didn't get a shirt because I'm not an employee....I don't always get all the T-shirts and all that little nuisance stuff. And it's just a way to separate. There's a health club downstairs. I don't get access to that. The entire institution will go off for a picnic, and [company name] will pay for the food. But for me it's a very expensive meal, 'cause I lose a day's pay.

Small perks, amenities, and social events are rarely accessible to contractors. Health and recreation facilities, for example, are almost always defined as part of a package of benefits and so are reserved for employees. At two of the work sites I observed, both contractors and employees speculated that these facilities had been installed to encourage longer hours at work. Although they might have participated if given access to on-site facilities, most of my informants expressed little interest in work-site recreation. Because they are paid by the hour, one noted, contractors tried to avoid extended breaks, which were always off the clock but might nonetheless convey the appearance of slacking off.

Organizational boundaries similarly exclude contractors from long-term planning. As a programmer for seven years at a telecommunications firm, Anna sometimes acted as the team leader for her group, yet she was systematically excluded from information about corporate plans. When executives convened meetings to explain large-scale decisions, her client invited only its employees. At such times, contractors usually stayed at their desks. To compensate for missing the formal presentation, Anna made special efforts to review the summaries posted online:

> You have to almost force yourself to keep up with things, you know. Any memos that come through, you make sure you read them all. Now see they're on the Internet for [company name], so they have their own Internet for corporate people. So I go in there and read up on what's going on, just to keep up with what's happening at [company name]. And I would do that with any company, just so when someone is in a conversation, you'll understand what they're talking about.

When exclusion could substantively affect their work, my informants explained, contractors needed to find ways to compensate for their marginality. Symbolic exclusion might seem insignificant but could still compromise their self-presentation.

By effectively mapping organizational boundaries, contractors can avoid violating norms that define the terms of their participation in organizational life. Darla, an editor and proofreader, had been working for a few weeks on-site at a small publishing company before she ventured into the kitchen that served employees. "I feel uncomfortable because they have tea," she explained. "They have all these mugs there, and they've got tea. And the production coordinator never particularly said, 'Why don't you? Here's the tea. You can go have some.' ... But this woman who was there, who is a graphic designer, she said, 'Oh, here's tea, and here are the mugs, and why don't you have some tea?' There's something a little self-conscious like, OK, I'm drinking their tea. Is this OK?" Although a cup of tea was itself insignificant, Darla knew that consuming the company tea in a company mug might well have been a prerogative of organizational membership. Encountering the production coordinator, mug in hand, she had felt relieved when he seemed unconcerned. Still, she watched his response: "Is he like tisk-tisking? ... Who does she think she is to have some tea, to take our mug?"

My own experience echoes Darla's. As a contract writer for a small nonprofit agency, I had been hired for a few days to complete and compile a large grant proposal. Working against the clock, the day before the deadline, I joined a half dozen staff members who had agreed to stay late and complete the project. Despite the last-minute stress, the staff was convivial, and the project director expressed much gratitude at my willingness to help. Late in the afternoon, one of the staff began collecting preferences for pizza. No one asked me to state a choice. Still, when pizzas arrived, another staff member poked his head into the office I was using and noted, "Dinner's here." Sensing that I had not truly been invited to dinner, I hesitated, but the alternative was to leave the building and find dinner elsewhere. Although unsure, I walked across the hall, stood in line for pizza, and briefly joined employees at one of the nearby tables. A moment after I returned to my desk, the project director appeared silently in the doorway and, about ten minutes later, returned to tell me that I could go home. As I gathered my things, two staff members expressed surprise, noting that my departure would add hours to what already promised to be a late night.

Did helping myself to pizza hasten my departure? No one ever said so, and I never determined that staying for dinner had made me unwelcome. Like Darla, I had watched for indicators that marked the boundaries of organizational membership, but confused by the signals, I might well have misstepped. Although aware of the contractual differences that made me an outsider, I had tried to fit in, and like the contractors I interviewed, I had gauged my success with interactional cues, which may have signaled only acceptance of my work. I knew my contribution to the project had been welcome, but I also knew that I was still a guest, and perhaps I had presumed too many prerogatives, too much inclusion.

Several informants applied this guest metaphor to the experience of working at a client site. Even on long-term projects, they explained, a contractor should adjust to the preferences and routines of the host. As guests of their clients, they, too, tried to fit in, to integrate themselves as seamlessly as possible into a client organization. Remaining on the margins, however, contractors are never full participants. As expert practitioners in their respective fields, they may function like employees and may well be full contributors to the larger goals of the client. Their marginal status, however, demands strategic disengagement, evident in their interactions, which keeps them apart.

5

Collegial Networking, Occupational Control

For a contractor, formal feedback—an assessment of individual performance—is unusual. Most clients expect contractors to be low maintenance, to begin work with the necessary expertise and to move on quietly when their work is finished. My informants could cite few managers who had invested time or trouble in formally evaluating their performance, and as contractors, they had rarely requested evaluations. To ask a client for feedback might undermine a contractor's display of confidence. Yet without organizational mechanisms to gauge their success, contractors must depend on informal indicators and interactional cues.

In chapter 4, I identified the dynamics through which contract professionals distance themselves from intra-organizational conflict and so reinforce their exclusion from organizational membership. Lacking formal positions, they remain marginal, outside the systems that confer status and authority. In their respective occupations, however, they are far

Portions of chapter 5 have been previously published in *Work and Occupations* 33(1) February 2006, by Sage Publications, Inc.; http://online.sagepub.com. All rights reserved.

from marginal. Rather than outsiders, the contractors I met considered themselves full occupational participants. All had developed connections with colleagues. Most maintained ties to occupational communities, whose members might share a set of skills or a clientele.[1] Through these connections, which often spanned the boundary between internal and external labor markets, they had established networks that provided an infrastructure for communication and exchange.

Anticipating frequent mobility, these contractors maintained networks as potential sources of information about industry trends, work-related practice, and potential new clients. By mobilizing their networks, my informants explained, they could more easily find work when they needed it most. Networks—which might include colleagues, managers, and recruiters—provided conduits for information and a buffer from the isolation a contractor might otherwise experience. The processes associated with networking, in turn, reinforced a common understanding of occupational practice. What, then, are the processes through which these practitioners sustain their occupational connections? How do their networks promote long-term employability outside the standard organization-based job?

For contract professionals, networking means more than seeking work. Network exchange is also a vehicle for displaying knowledge, reliability, and commitment to high standards. Communication through networks develops contractors' reputations for capable occupational practice, which then enhances their prospects of referrals for future work. Referrals depend, in part, on reputation as well as expertise. Because contractors refer one another with care, they attend to their colleagues' performance, monitoring adherence to occupational norms and standards of practice. Through the processes associated with networking, contract professionals engage in a form of workforce regulation, an informal system of governance that sustains an external labor market. Occupational regulation, however, remains decentralized, dependent not on a representative professional body but on the informal sanctions of normative control.

Forging Connections, Finding Work

Networking is a word I heard used by contractors, employees, managers, and recruiters—indeed, by virtually everyone I met. Networking, I was told, could involve contact with former clients, discussions with other contractors, or membership in professional associations. By maintaining these occupational connections, the contractors I interviewed sought to enhance their access to information and to referrals for sources of work. Knowing that each contract assignment would end, they remained acutely aware of their labor market prospects. The processes associated with networking located them within boundary-spanning communities, where interaction—in person, by phone, or online—could keep them apprised of work-based developments.

Referrals can connect a contractor to a network of potential clients. Meredith, a programmer, trainer, and database developer, recounted a series of contract assignments that had come her way as one client after another learned of her specialized services. "I develop databases for small organizations," she elaborated. "Most of those organizations are nonprofits, and they're networked, and they kind of say, 'Oh, we need a programmer to, you know, a database person.' ... My first one I got through somebody that I knew, and then after that I either got repeat work from the same organization, or they, you know, people gave my name out." By tapping a preexisting network, Meredith received a series of unsolicited referrals, which then expanded her clientele. Phil, a writer and project manager, had found a similar network within a large corporation. "I've been there a long time," he explained, "and I got to know people all over the company.... So when [a specific product group] disbanded, they found me something else." Treating a client firm as a set of connections had provided Phil with a network within one organization, which had paid off when he needed to move on.

Both Meredith and Phil had positioned themselves in their respective occupational labor markets. Both had sought to remain steadily employed, sometimes for several clients simultaneously, sometimes with a single client for months or even years. Productive relationships with managers and colleagues, they believed, might always lead to new client connections. Employees, for example, might move from one employer to the next and in a new setting link them to additional sources of work. Like most of the contractors I interviewed, they had consciously forged connections that could serve as conduits for information and referral.

Networks as Communities

Some of the contractors I met described networking as an instrumental aspect of working life, something they considered part of doing business.

Others had melded work-based ties with more personal communities, as colleagues also became friends. Phil, for example, emphatically stated that he had "stopped really networking long ago," yet he acknowledged that he had met "a lot of interesting people in this field" and saw some of them for reasons unrelated to work. Bryan, a programmer and systems engineer, expressed similar sentiments. "I'll get together, but talking about work,... it's not a planned thing," he explained, "I don't go just for that [work-related connections], but if I need something, I have people to call." For many contractors, long-term relationships with colleagues might evolve from a range of common interests.

Pat, a writer, more actively cultivated work-based relationships through a group of colleagues that scheduled regular lunchtime meetings: "There are a bunch of people who meet... once a month for lunch—we call it our networking lunch—that are involved in contracting in all different areas. If everybody came at once, there'd be about fifteen or so.... We meet at a particular restaurant, and we just talk, you know. There are lots of little conversations going on, but we're all in the contracting business." The lunches were informal gatherings, Pat explained, but all the participants knew that they would eventually be seeking work. Exchanging information and keeping one another informed of developments, participants expanded the scope of these connections, any of which might some day prove useful.

Casting a wider net, Joseph, a software engineer and systems analyst, described a more diverse network: "I have, you know, besides other consultants like myself and what people I know, employees and managers in companies I've worked with. I have a big network of suppliers and businessmen and venture capitalists and headhunters and God knows what else," he explained. "I keep them in the Rolodex. I stay in touch,... or they do.... So I'm always busy." With a clientele that encompassed large corporations and small start-up firms, Joseph had established ties with many people who could let him know about corporate plans, new developments, and possible contract work.[2]

As loosely structured communities, contractors' networks serve as reference groups, reinforcing occupational identities as members exchange information about work-related developments. Criteria for membership may remain informal, but most of the contractors I interviewed reported at least one instance in which a colleague had provided some form of occupational support. Collegial contact—lunches, phone calls, e-mail messages, participation on a Listserv, and attendance at professional meetings—eases a contractor's way in the workforce. For many contractors, these forms of collegial exchange become a principal source of professional identity outside the performance of their work.

Brent, a programmer and project developer, described meetings of technical professionals, both contractors and employees, in the emerging field of computer-based design: "I'm still pretty casual about it, you know. I don't go there and sell myself. I go there, and I talk to people, and if something comes out, it comes out," he explained. "There is this bit of a community I have with other folks doing what I'm doing,... we're all trying to define ourselves as folks who do this sort of creative, technical stuff." Still new to contracting, Brent had found meetings with colleagues an especially valuable resource. Working principally at home, he had come to depend on these occasional face-to-face exchanges to mitigate the solitude and validate his identity as a capable practitioner.

Some of my informants belonged to Listservs on which similar discussions took place. Others had joined professional associations where members discussed work-related practices. Technical writers, for example, reported networking through the Society of Technical Communications, which has chapters in many locales. Medical writers might instead belong to the American Medical Writers Association. With membership encompassing employees and managers, such organizations can expose contractors to clients as well as colleagues in a specific field of practice.

Contractors might also count staffing agency recruiters among the members of their networks. For programmers and engineers, as well as writers and editors in technical fields, recruiters could be especially useful sources of information about industries with rapidly changing demands. Although some of my informants avoided staffing agencies entirely, a few felt that an agency might be a point of entry for an inexperienced contractor. Remembering her first transition to contracting sixteen years earlier, Carla, a writer and editor, considered the advice she would give someone in similar circumstances: "I think I would tell them to get with an agency to begin with. There's some fairly good ones around that really go to bat for you.... They take an active interest in finding you a job. I haven't really taken advantage of this, but I've talked to friends who have felt that way.... A good person at an agency can help you get started." Like most of my informants, however, Carla sounded a note of caution. "You don't want to just depend on them," she elaborated. "You also need to get out there and meet people in your field."

Hiring managers also turn to staffing agencies for assistance. Some develop networks of recruiters, who in turn seek out managers who might provide them with business. Maxine, a recruiter with a small staff, had founded her own agency in the late 1980s by identifying a growing clientele of high-tech firms that were then converting direct hiring of contractors to third-party arrangements with an agency as intermediary. Networking, Maxine explained, had established her business. "I'm very much in a niche market," she explained. "Anybody in the northwest technical corridor knows me.... I limited myself to an area of specialization, to a geographical area.... I know everyone, but I'm always on the lookout for new business...and also contractors."

Although the managers I met gave recruiters, in general, mixed reviews, their observations confirm the wisdom of Maxine's business strategy. Hank, a manager at a small Internet firm, differentiated recruiters who had proved themselves "well educated in my space, in particular, so they understand what I'm talking about and screen resumes reasonably well" from those who "clearly don't have a clue as to what I'm doing." A recruiter's knowledge in many areas—industry trends, labor processes, occupational practice—can be important for managers, employees, and contractors alike. As many of my informants noted, recruiters make dozens of contacts each week, sometimes have early notice of pending change, and could be valuable resources. As Carla reiterated, "You can almost, after you've done a few contracts, be your own manager.... but for an inexperienced person,...an agency would maybe tell you what's selling, what's hot. You need to learn, you know, what big changes they've been hearing about."

Former employers had also been especially valuable connections for some of the contractors I met. Many of my informants had eased the transition to contract employment by working first for a former employer, and the relationship could remain intact for some time. Marta, a software developer specializing in computer animation, recounted, "When I moved from Los Angeles to Boston, my company asked me to continue working for them.... We weren't able to set up a relationship so it would be a full-time job, so it was a freelance one." A year and a half after the move, Marta was actively seeking new clients, hoping to augment the dwindling stream of work that her former employer now supplied. She had attended user meetings and trade shows, which she thought might better lodge her in the local labor market. "If I can meet people,... if people really know my work," she believed, "I can get different kinds of projects."

The contractors I interviewed repeatedly spoke of salvaging collegial relationships from their experiences in standard jobs. Darrell, a programmer and project manager who had begun contracting in the early 1970s, had first established a clientele as an employee in a computing services firm. Having left to start his own software business, however, he had encountered difficulties: "I was finding that it wasn't going to work out when one of my ex-clients called me, a company who had been a client at my previous place of employment. And he said, 'I hear you're in business for yourself.' I said yes. He said, 'Do you want to come out here and do some work?' I said sure. And I've been in the contracting business ever since." Darrell's story is typical of a self-perpetuating process by which new clients come from old contacts, often from former colleagues who have moved on themselves. My informants thus spoke of "keeping up the Rolodex" or strategically "staying in touch" with colleagues and former clients. Networking, they explained, maintains the connections that structure opportunities in an occupational labor market.

Reciprocity and Respect

All but a few of my informants recounted instances in which colleagues had assisted one another. Answering questions, directing colleagues to resources, or problem solving about a difficult client had all been part of occupational exchange. Many also relied on colleagues to address technical or business concerns: which software to buy, where to find a tax accountant, how to approach a specific new client. A few informants did bemoan a lack of adequate assistance, and a few more complained of unequal exchange, in which a colleague made repeated demands for time and attention. Most, however, considered the donated time a favor, which might later be repaid. As Holly, an editor and project manager, noted, "It's like people in your neighborhood. If someone's house is burning, you let them use your phone. Next time, it might be you who needs the phone."

The anticipation of future need guides contractors' responses to requests for assistance. Some informants cited a generalized reciprocity, in which a return favor might appear far in the future, perhaps from another source. Heather, an editor and trainer who reported spending "maybe five or six hours a week just networking," explained, "I've been working on my own for about twenty years.... I've seen a lot of people come and go, and sometimes doing something for someone pays you back years later, in ways you don't expect." Reciprocal interactions had provided Heather with a steady stream of potential new clients, many of which she referred to colleagues. But Patrick, a programmer and systems analyst, had little patience for "tech people, who become professional networkers." After three years of contracting, he was planning to build a staffing business by subcontracting work to other contractors. Networking had become "focused," he explained, "because too many people just want to make it a cocktail party.... There was a lot of that when I started out, but they don't do it with the end in mind of how we can work together to do something."

Although both Heather and Patrick saw networking as an investment, they differed in their calculus of exchange. With many hours devoted to networking, Heather sought to enhance her labor market position by expanding her options. Apprised of new developments and prospective new assignments, she could use the information she gleaned, sometimes passing it along to others and so further maintaining her work-based connections. In contrast, Patrick sought to capitalize quickly on his connections by converting more of his networking directly to economic gain. Shifting his status from "individual contributor" to subcontracting client, he hoped to become a third-party intermediary, managing large projects and recruiting other contractors. Successful networking, for him, required faster, more tangible results.

Between these two extremes, all my informants described some form of strategically guided networking. They established relationships, exchanged information, and calculated the value of the support they gave and received. When they volunteered assistance and a colleague responded in kind, they noticed. When someone repeatedly asked for help or seemed too needy, they might pull back. Most, however, reported extending themselves with small favors, despite an alternative logic that might inform a culture of competition in a market for their services. Although none of my informants characterized collegial relationships as competitive, contractors are, in some sense, competing for a finite number of assignments. A rational response to a colleague, therefore, might be to guard information and withhold assistance. Yet the contractors I interviewed consistently viewed colleagues not as competitors but as resources for reciprocal exchange.[3]

The online discussions I monitored provided further evidence of gratuitous help. On one Listserv composed of editorial freelancers, participants traded tips about computer repair, stylistic conventions, and leads for potential new clients. On a list of contract programmers, participants discussed industry trends, staffing agency practices, and software recently introduced. Electronic Listservs might also, occasionally, post a client's request for a contractor, sometimes from a participant who had turned the project down. Like their accounts of networking, contractors' interactions online reflected a norm of reciprocity and an expectation of mutual support.

Almost all of my informants cited the respect that exchange could convey. As much as reciprocity, they explained, signals of respect maintained occupational connections. Many of the contractors I interviewed described respect as a sense of recognition or an acknowledgment of their expertise, which requests for assistance implied. Rita, a programmer and trainer, believed herself respected "when someone will ask for your advice.... They will seek you out." In contrast, disrespect meant being ignored, especially when colleagues presumably knew her work, as Rita elaborated:

> When people don't want to hear your opinion or when you almost have to beat down the door to get them to listen to your opinion. That's one. When people are more concerned about the petty things than the work that's getting done.... You know it when you see it, when they're going to other people and asking their advice when you know that those people don't know anywhere near as much about that particular thing as you do.

The contractors I interviewed noticed respect most often in the breach, and when overlooked or treated dismissively, they experienced disrespect acutely. For Sam, an editor and proofreader, signals from colleagues and clients had been mixed. In his two years of contracting, Sam had been relying for occasional assistance on the few practitioners he knew. "I can go and ask questions, and they're friendly, and they're helpful and collaborative, and I sometimes get the feeling that I'm an equal," he elaborated, "but then they ignore me, and I get the feeling that I'm some subordinate thing or other." Impatience had, to Sam, conveyed a disrespect that he had been unable to counteract. His inexperience, he thought, might have contributed to a sense of subordination, and his colleagues may have indeed considered him less than equal. Respect, in contrast, conveys equality and invites reciprocity.

Like trust, respect can carry special salience when work relations depend on horizontal rather than hierarchical communication. Melinda, a programmer who also called herself a business consultant, explained:

> The way I'm treated by most companies when I'm brought in to solve a particular project is I'm treated as the talent, and it's really a good feeling....I've worked in the field a long time, and I really understand testing, and I really understand customer support, and I'm seen as a valued resource....They go out of their way to show me, treat me with respect, and I really, like I say, it's a really good ego boost.

When clients expressed gratitude, Melinda knew her work had been recognized. Without her contributions, she was sure, any number of projects and routine functions would have taken longer or cost more. The recognition signaled respect. So, too, did the frequent questions she fielded from colleagues. Marks of respect, my informants explained, indicate a competent performance and help to maintain connections in a constantly changing labor market.

Analyses suggest that, across social contexts, respect gains importance in situations of structural inequality.[4] Respect matters most to those who might otherwise feel the effects of inherently unequal relationships: students thus seek respect from teachers, workers from bosses, and welfare recipients from case workers. Subordinates, these comparisons suggest, experience a heightened awareness of respect. So, too, do contractors, whose informal status in employing organizations depends on constructive relationships. Contractors thus seek evidence of respect in social interaction. As Charles, a writer, editor, and trainer, reflected, "I think it's about human relationships, about helping people and symbiosis....That's why I'm not very hierarchically oriented. It's great, because I think I receive a lot of respect for what I do. I'm treated on a level, as an equal, for the most part."

Referrals and Reputations

If reciprocity and respect are terms of network participation, referrals are a currency of exchange. Clients, on occasion, turn to contractors for recommendations, and a contractor who rejects an assignment may, in turn, send the client to a colleague. A few of my informants in both occupational groups spoke of receiving such a steady stream of referrals that they had never explicitly looked for work. With frequent unsolicited offers, they could accept those that fit their schedules and refer the rest elsewhere. For both contractors and clients, therefore, referrals are important sources for job matching, a process that helps maintain occupational labor markets.

Managers seeking contractors may also depend, at least to some degree, on referral networks. As I observed in a "staffing up" meeting at one software development firm, informal selection processes augmented a more formal system of hiring. The manager responsible for the new release of a product had contacted a number of staffing agencies preapproved as vendors for contract services. Each had responded with a slew of resumes, which covered a conference table in overlapping piles.[5] As a half dozen employees reviewed the resumes, discarding those that seemed not to fit and flagging those that seemed like possible matches, the discussion centered on whom they knew well, whom they had heard of, and what channels might provide additional information. Those who knew a prospective contractor might volunteer an assessment of the person's track record, as both a competent programmer and a congenial team member. Discussion then led those at the table to suggest other contractors, not represented among the resumes, who might soon be available and interested in the upcoming project.

The resumes and referrals represent complementary processes of formal and informal hiring in which occupational networks expand an applicant pool and supplement more systematic means of recruiting, such as advertising openings, with information that employers deem reliable.[6] Although augmenting formal searches is far from unusual, hiring in these occupations occurs without broadly accepted systems of training or certification and without uniform job titles that might designate experience. Managers, therefore, seldom rely solely on credentials as markers of expertise. Instead, most described supplementing searches with informal inquiries, and some reported depending entirely on the advice of employees and contractors whose connections had proved especially valuable. For a contractor, therefore, a track record of quality work and a corresponding reputation can contribute significantly to a stream of referrals.

Reputations depend on many factors—meticulous performance, assistance to colleagues, flexibility in response to change—but a key component is a willingness to meet commitments, even if a more interesting or lucrative offer comes along. Commitment to finish what one begins—or at least to find a graceful or justifiable point of exit—constitutes an occupational norm that few contractors feel they can violate. On this point, Joseph was especially emphatic: "I wouldn't start a project for a company and then find, oh, I've got a more interesting job. I would never, *ever* do that. I would *never* leave a project high and dry." Keenly aware that future work may depend on a solid reputation, many of my informants could not imagine circumstances that would cause them to walk away, without notice, from a project in progress, and some expressed outright dismay at the suggestion. Contractors do, apparently, move on, especially after an impasse in client relations, but the managers I met echoed similar objections. Evan, who hired contractors at a computer technology firm, was explicit: "No one wants to hire a contractor who won't buckle down and stay the course. They don't have to love the job, but they have to do it."

A contractor's commitment can, in some instances, demand more tenacity than an employee's. Unlike a contractor, hired only for a defined period or the term of a project, an employee has an open-ended relationship that in principle forges a closer connection with an employer. Yet an employee faces few sanctions for accepting a more attractive offer and can usually leave a job without violating a norm. An employee, therefore, may reasonably move on to a new position, even if the timing adversely affects a critical segment of work. In contrast, a concern for their reputation constrains most contractors from leaving precipitously. Walking away risks a tarnished reputation and with it the prospect of future referrals. Despite contractors' independence, the norm of commitment constrains their mobility.

A concern for competence, often equated with technical proficiency, further informs the process of referral. Among my informants, reports of "spaghetti code" in a program or a manuscript "riddled with errors" was always enough to prevent someone from receiving an unreserved recommendation. A colleague's performance reflects the judgment of the referring party, and a poorly considered referral can indicate poor judgment. In contrast, referring a competent colleague can underscore a commitment to high standards while simultaneously assisting a client. When asked, the contractors I interviewed described readily offering referrals but qualifying them carefully, considering whether a colleague could truly be trusted to perform well.

Yet contractors, like their clients, have few clear indicators of the colleagues' expertise. Detail work, like editing copy or writing code, rarely receives a close evaluation line by line, and in both occupations, much of the work receives only cursory oversight. Problems with a practitioner's performance may then come to light months, or even years, after work is complete. Daniel, a programmer, ruefully described his experience with a colleague: "This contractor talked a good game, could sling out lots of code, had something up and running quickly, and then a few months later we find all these problems, and that contractor isn't around anymore.... At least he won't work for [company name] again." Many of my informants spoke with similar contempt about colleagues who had disappointed them, necessitating last-minute revisions and risking errors. Lacking high enough standards, they emphasized, these practitioners would never receive their recommendations.

Even worse were referrals that had gone awry. Noreen, a writer and editor, described an incident in which she had recommended a colleague, only to have the client call back to complain: "This person didn't work out. I mean she *really* didn't work out, screwed up the whole project with the mess she made, didn't put anything in order.... And now it's *my* fault for recommending her. *I'm* the one who's to blame. I will never do that again." Chastened by the experience, Noreen had determined to reserve her personal recommendations for well-trusted colleagues whose work she knew. She knew three or four people, she explained, whom she could "rubber stamp." Otherwise, she "really didn't know for sure" and could not vouch for the quality of work that someone else might produce. When unsolicited offers came at inopportune times, when she could take on nothing else, she referred these few people, so that she could avoid merely turning the client away.

Again and again, the contractors I interviewed explained the caution they applied when making referrals. Gary, an editor and production manager, described a common line of reasoning: "I don't refer somebody

I don't know, and I don't really know that many people. I mean I do know people who work in the field and have a good reputation. I can pass their name along. But to really recommend them, I also have to feel comfortable enough. I need to really know their work so I can refer them." Gary's distinction is typical—a good reputation is reason enough to suggest a name, but only direct experience provides the solid foundation for a personal recommendation. The contractors I met consistently distinguished between colleagues they knew only casually and those whose work and reliability they knew well. Referrals based solely on reputation were gingerly dispensed with a *caveat emptor;* personal recommendations, in contrast, had to be delivered with assurance.

Networks of contractors do, on occasion, send clients in circles, as groups of trusted colleagues yield the same referrals many times over. Yet managers promote caution by seeking personal assurance of a contractor's competence. As the managers I interviewed explained, the right referral can save the costs of extensive searching and close supervision. For a client, collegial networks produce efficiencies that can reduce uncertainty in hiring. For a contractor, adherence to normative practice builds a reputation on which to base future labor market exchange. Concern for reputation and potential referrals thus acts as a strong deterrent against shirking obligations or even allowing expectations to remain unclear. As collegial connections provide opportunities, the need to guard one's reputation promotes discipline and exerts control.

Self-Regulation: The Logic of Occupational Norms

Unlike employees, contractors are rarely subject to the sanctions of hierarchical control that reward employees for capable performance and demonstrated loyalty. Raises, promotions, and periodic performance reviews, for example, come exclusively with standard jobs. To enhance employees' commitment to organizational goals, employers have historically provided an "implicit contract" that promises mobility along a career path in return for good performance.[7] For contractors, in contrast, the prospect of repeat business and referrals for future work provides an incentive for meeting client needs, and the imperative of a good reputation becomes a mechanism of regulation.

Experience on staff had taught most of my informants that shoddy work and late delivery are problems that clients notice and recall. Sherry, an editor, translator, and project manager, underscored these concerns:

> I do really good work 'cause it's my reputation, and I value my name. My name is in it. I don't take any project lightly. I don't care if it's a proofreading project. I don't care what kind of thing it is.... If I'm late, there's a reason I'm late. They know why I'm going to be late, and I've cleared it with them.... When I was working as a production manager and [as an employee], you know, I would every now and then get projects turned in to me three or four days late, and it's like how do you stay in business? If you say you're going to do this on time, you do it on time.

Proofreading, Sherry noted, paid less than editing or translating and provided her with fewer professional challenges. Yet these projects, too, received her best effort once she had committed herself to the job. Because her good name depended on a consistent, reliable performance, she assured me, she would "never blow anyone off."

Sherry was one of many contractors I interviewed who decried the standards of some of their colleagues, both specified and unnamed. Jon, a writer and editor working on-site at a telecommunications firm, echoed Sherry's assessment: "I think a professional doesn't let their work get by with flaws in it, really. If your name's on it and you're supposed to be a pro at it, then that's what you'd better be.... There are some people who slack off, and one of them, well, I'm still in the position where I'm doing someone else's work for them." For many months, Jon had been quietly correcting a colleague's work and, after considerable effort, was concerned that he might be held accountable for the time and expense. "I kind of had to let someone know about the mess," he explained. Alerting the project manager, he had hoped to protect his reputation if errors remained. "The only way that they would actually get my name is if they somehow filtered down and made enough complaints," he reflected, "but the way I look at it, it's my personal relationships or the way I'm looked at. That's my name on it, basically." Although individual names are seldom attached to finished products,[8] Jon sought to be associated with quality work. Establishing a reputation meant adhering to high standards.

Maintaining Self-Control

As they considered standards of performance, the contractors I met described balancing a need to act professionally and avoid conflict with their concern for product quality. To many, acting professionally meant a measured form of self-control, even when they disagreed with the plans or procedures of a client. Linda, a software and database developer, characterized professional demeanor:

> Essentially, it would be somebody acting in the sense that they know what their job is. They do it competently, are able to work within the system that's set up, and then know when you shouldn't do that and should challenge things. You need to have a level of maturity about how you handle the circumstances around you and where you draw the lines, and you need to know how you're supposed to comport yourself in different situations.

To maintain a reputation for capable performance, Linda emphasized, a contractor must avoid intra-organizational problems, remain unaffiliated in factional disputes, and be productive, even when surrounded by conflict. Lack of organizational membership, she emphasized, demands an extra measure of self-control.

Ted, a writer and editor, was especially conscious of his performance with a new client, found through a colleague who had assured the manager that Ted was good at handling "difficult personalities." Hired to revise a set of documents, Ted described intra-organizational disputes that had challenged the professional stance he tried to maintain as he masked his frustration with ever-changing demands. "You can't be easily flappable," he explained, "I mean these are things that I try to hold fast to, you know.... I don't want stress or aggravation or annoyance or anger or any of those things coming into play." Asked to accommodate the contradictory requirements of his client, Ted had produced a series of drafts, each revised to reflect new specifications. Completing the project successfully meant reconciling conflicts while upholding a reputation for calm: "So it was sort of touchy. It was fine, but that's the kind of reputation I have that they would feel comfortable giving me something like that to work on.... I'm not somebody that sort of just throws things around and seems to have no handle on anything.... I don't, well, I can't, have my own agenda."

Terry, a programmer and project manager, similarly equated self-control with adaptation, despite what he believed was the ill-considered choice of a client:

> I just sat through a meeting on Wednesday, with one of the permanent—well, they're all so-called permanent—staff, with one of the people complaining about the new procedures that they set up here for migrating a change from the development side to the production side. And the manager sat there listening to their complaints.... Do I think the system, the way they've set it up is the most efficient or the most user-friendly or the best? It doesn't matter whether I do or not.... You may be right that some particular way one shop does something is stupid, but you'd better keep your mouth shut. That's the way they do it.

Had he been asked to express his view of the system, Terry assured me he would have been careful not to assert too strong a position. He had little respect for the managers directing the operations, but cognizant of his limited responsibilities, he had kept quiet. "I was lucky that this one came along when it did," he reminded himself; "every job can't use everything you know." Self-control had, in this case, silenced any offer of expertise.

Across settings, I found employees and managers who considered adaptability an important asset for a contractor. Even when time and money might be saved, they explained, a prudent contractor would know when to remain unobtrusive. As one editorial manager commented as I arrived to meet an informant at a work site, "With the right person, I can just depend on them to do the right thing.... I don't have to explain about author relations and things like that.... They know the job, and they know they have to keep their opinions out of it." Self-control and adherence to the norms of contract employment can thus relieve managers of the need for close supervision.

The normative demands of contracting further represent a broader pattern, in which managerial control within the hierarchical organization has shifted downward to lower levels of the organizational hierarchy. Mechanisms of control in the flatter postbureaucratic organization are decentered, more fluid, and less formal.[9] This shift in the locus of control is consistent with a trend toward organizational culture as a means of assuring workers' consent with managerial goals.[10] Lacking organizational membership, however, contractors stand apart from work-site cultures and depend instead on collegial networks to communicate work-related norms. Although they exercise considerable autonomy, most are recruited with the assurance that they will meet the needs of the client. Collegial exchange promotes a mode of regulation based on social interaction and normative self-control.

Enforcing Professional Standards

Many of the contractors I interviewed equated self-control with professionalism,[11] which to them connoted reliability, high-quality work, and accountability to clients. Professionalism, they emphasized, demands vigilance in meeting commitments and the rigorous execution of skill. But professional standards should also be tempered with a willingness to acquiesce when organizational imperatives override a practitioner's judgment. Michael, an editor and proofreader, explained a dilemma he sometimes faced: "An editor should also be pretty steadfast but flexible. In other words, steadfast as far as what you've done in the way of corrections but maybe give a little on, if a writer really, *really* complains.... I'll change 'impact' to 'affect' as a verb, but certain things I'll give on." Basic editorial standards, Michael emphasized, were always essential, but in some contexts, he allowed latitude in usage, especially when congenial relations mattered more than precise grammar or exacting typography. Occasional compromise, he believed, promoted long-term relationships.

Ben, a software engineer and project manager, described similar compromises when technical problems demanded short-term solutions, even though a more comprehensive fix seemed preferable. "Our job is to make our clients successful," he explained. "That will make us successful in an indirect manner, and that's professionalism, to say that we have to sacrifice our own immediate goals, which could make something better... our standards...for what they want us to do." Professional standards, my informants elaborated, meant applying their expertise and insisting on quality, but only to a point. Client constraints also governed the many decisions their work involved. With experience in standard jobs, they were familiar with the limits that schedules and budgets could impose, and despite complaints about compromised standards, most had come to define compromise itself as a professional skill.

Daniel related an incident in which he had lost a contract assignment because, he believed, his response to a question had signaled an inability to work within this client's constraints:

> I interviewed at [company name].... The reason that I flopped was that this guy asked me, he said, "How do you feel about having schedules imposed from above?" And I said, "I don't like it," and then I said, "But what I really meant to say was I can work that way because if I think it's going to take this long and we don't have that long, then we cannot do as many features." But it didn't matter because the minute I said that, the guy had thought "doesn't like to take orders."

Although Daniel looked back nostalgically to an earlier phase in his career, when "we would put in every bell and whistle you can possibly think of in a product," shorter product cycles, with frequent upgrades, now meant that "it's always a trade-off" between an imposed schedule and detailed attention to quality. He tried, however, to articulate the trade-offs and could sometimes make a case for attenuating a schedule in the interests of quality. Still, he lamented, "Most managers aren't open to the argument that we should do it the way that takes a little bit longer because it's better.... It encourages doing things quick and dirty, but you need to know how quick and dirty.... You should know what you're giving up."

An expert practitioner, Daniel suggested, should recognize both quality and compromise, even when unable to alter project goals or specifications. Martin, an editor and proofreader, expressed the same concerns: "Being a professional means you're dedicated to having high quality in lieu of comfort.... It's knowing what you should be doing, even when you can't do it completely right." Compromise, Martin felt, rests uneasily with professional standards, which should at least inform occupational practice. Standards remained important, he insisted, even when other imperatives prevailed.

A contractor might, on occasion, intervene when a colleague appeared to be in error. Considering compromise, Michael recounted an incident in which he had reminded a colleague about the need to remain flexible in applying editorial judgment. Working collaboratively, he had become concerned when several encounters with their client seemed confrontational. "I remember mentioning it to [contractor's name], letting him know,"

Michael explained. "Maybe I was premature that he was being inflexible, but it would cause him trouble,...and he was overlooking some details." Seeing his own professional standards in jeopardy, Michael had issued a warning. His standards thus extended to a colleague whose actions might reflect badly on him.

When they recognized a colleague's inadequate performance, many of my informants had at least considered a response, sometimes speaking to a delinquent colleague, occasionally appealing to the manager responsible for meeting project goals. Ezra, a software developer, described one of his first contract assignments, a project that had been slowed by a colleague's lack of attention to detail. Approached by the team leader for his assessment of the problem, Ezra had felt impelled to be forthcoming: "He [the team leader] was the first one to really open my eyes to, you know, staying temporary does not avoid the question of sitting in judgment on people....I mean this guy needed a major attitude change....I consider unprofessional a person who just throws something together and doesn't pay attention to how it's going to impact other people who might be using it." Phil similarly described his frustration with another contractor, apparently unable to meet even basic standards of practice:

> You'd give her an existing document and everything you needed changed in it....I really had to feed her every word. And then it would still come back with half of it not done, grammar that was actually worse than the marketing people had done,...and she didn't know how to do tables. I mean all these weird things would come back....That's when you get very resentful, and you're like this person should not be here.

Forced to compensate for the mistakes, Phil believed he was exercising greater scrutiny than most managers typically provided, even to employees.

Managerial oversight does, of course, enforce client requirements, and managers do, occasionally, dismiss contractors who fail to meet expectations. Contractors themselves, however, hold one another to professional standards. For those who join work-site teams, face-to-face contact can facilitate occupational scrutiny, but outside the work site, network interaction becomes a means for evaluating expertise. As contractors monitor one another's performance, collegial interaction promotes adherence to professional standards. Through networks of similarly situated practitioners, they communicate norms and values. Through referrals, they influence hiring. Occupational oversight is thus relegated to the informal processes of collegial exchange.

The Prospect of Formal Governance

The micro-processes that promote professionalism are distinctly different from the mechanisms more typically associated with professionalization.[12] Professions that exercise formal governance—most notably medicine and law—have established control over training and certification, codified occupational standards, and achieved state sanction for a labor market shelter and oversight of practitioners' qualifications. Professional governance typically extends collective control to both the principles of occupational practice and the supply of certified practitioners. Professionalization thus centralizes control of an occupation, so that its practices are subject to scrutiny and its practitioners subject to internal sanction.

Although the contractors I interviewed considered themselves professionals, few had ever considered the prospect of formal professional governance. Like their counterparts in standard jobs, they were familiar principally with the direct control of an organizational hierarchy, and many had found contract work appealing by comparison. They tended, therefore, to equate centralized governance with greater supervision, which might in some way interfere with their autonomy. Perhaps a professional organization might be useful in some situations, but few of my informants were themselves willing to cede the control they exercised to a formal system of occupational gatekeeping.

Reflecting on their status as professionals, however, some suggested that a professional organization might raise the profile of contract employment and perhaps enhance its legitimacy. Noreen ruminated on this prospect:

> If there were some organization or some group of people that had some influence, that could help to change the paradigm, ... because I really do think it's a win-win situation. I think the company that's doing the hiring can get more for their dollar, and it gives the contractor the opportunity to be able to interweave jobs and stay challenged.... I want to be intellectually

challenged. I don't want to be sitting in an office twiddling my thumbs.... If there was some influential organization that was trying to encourage businesses to kind of look at things that way, that would probably help.

Professionalization, Noreen implied, might loosen the bonds of managerial control that she had found most frustrating during her twenty years in standard employment and so promote the aspects of contracting that she most valued. The "paradigm change" that she envisioned, however, would reconstruct the standard job, to make it more like contract work. "You can trust contractors to do what you hire them to do," she elaborated. "You don't have to watch them and have them sit in your office to prove that they're spending their time working on your project."

Many of my informants further believed that the autonomy contractors exercised would inhibit any effort to centralize control of their respective occupations. Yolanda, a writer, editor, and project manager, thought the most successful contractors would be least likely to be interested in professionalization: "I think the people who thrive in this don't necessarily join things, or I mean one of the things that we really like is the independence," she reflected. "I think we're by and large not joiners, so I don't know. I mean I'm sure the right association could probably do a lot for people who are self-employed, but I'm not sure what kind of organization that would be."

Others suggested that the pace of change, especially in technical areas, would render any formally defined standards quickly outdated. Brenda, a programmer and systems analyst, reflected, "This is a profession and an art and a craft. It's not a science yet. It's not something where the skills that you need to be good at it are easy to define. By the time you devise a certification test, whatever you're certifying people for is obsolete." Even more than standard employment, she asserted, contracting "is too wild west," resistant to the order and uniformity that formal governance would likely impose.

Many of the programmers and engineers I met echoed Brenda's assessment of professional certification; the credentials that formal training conferred, they felt, were an insufficient indicator of ability. Although several informants described taking occasional courses, most decried the certification programs developed by training companies or technology firms. Such programs, they had found, were usually perfunctory. Darrell, who had begun his career as an employee in the mid-1960s, remembered becoming a certified data processor in 1967: "It was a joke. I did no studying for it. I went and took the test, and I was the second person done. My boss was the first person done, and he was so confident that I would be right behind him when I walked out of the room, he was standing there with two cups of coffee." Thirty-five years later, Darrell still "had little use" for any credentials, even the computer science degrees conferred by institutions of higher education. "I believe in general that computer science courses do not teach people to be good programmers," he complained. "The best people learn on the job."

In contrast, occupations that have fully professionalized are accessible only to those who have completed professionally sanctioned educational requirements. Formal education not only confers credentials but also socializes practitioners to occupational practice. Katherine, a programmer and database manager, speculated that formal education might eventually become a prerequisite for employment in her field, but it was a prospect that she lamented: "More and more, increasingly, people, especially the young kids, are getting actual degrees, and computer science departments have started to specialize. . . . [But] as it stands right now, the self-taught method still stands as credentials." Professional status, Katherine had found, still had little correlation with formal education.

Writers and editors expressed similar observations; additional training could be useful, perhaps as a way to develop a facility related to specific industries or new media, but formal credentials were unnecessary. Several of the writers and editors I interviewed had at one time attended postgraduate training programs, some conducted by major universities, where they had learned basic publications skills. When they were new to the field, these programs had provided access to the occupation and for some had been the route to a first job in their fields. As experienced practitioners, however, they deemed such degree-granting programs redundant. After fourteen years of contracting, Rebecca, a writer and editor, had considered a graduate program in communications but had decided against applying: "I said to myself why would I want to get a master's when I'm already doing it, and I know that my practical experience and my English skills with English grammar are what's important, and that's why I think I'm hired. . . . It's 'cause I know how to put things down on paper, to make sense for different audiences."

The managers I interviewed echoed a similar skepticism. Fred, who had established his own software development firm, explained, "When somebody says they have a bachelor of science degree in computer science, then that can range from one end of the spectrum to the other.... I'd like to know that they have a good base of some of the fundamentals, so I will go through a technical exercise with them." Winifred, a managing editor at a small publisher, described a comparable process: "The people we hire have to be educated, but they can have degrees in lots of things." To screen potential contractors, she had devised a "take-home test" that "shows people what we do and what we need.... It's a difficult thing for us to try someone completely cold." When she needed to find a contractor, Winifred explained, she turned both to the test and to practitioners, both employees and trusted contractors, who had provided reliable referrals. She had found the test especially useful for initial screenings, but she also depended on recommendations for "a big project, when we really need people who fit."

Managers' efforts to establish their own firm-specific screening mechanisms suggest that they, too, value control over standards of practice and are unlikely to cede control to a system of formal certification. Just as they rarely allow recruiters to make hiring decisions, managers ultimately retain oversight of both contractors and employees. None of the managers I interviewed expressed a willingness to allow a third party to confer credentials or intercede significantly in their working relationships with contractors. The institutionalizing of contracting, their accounts suggest, has devolved control of work relations without compromising employers' prerogatives. The informal mechanisms of collegial networking are thus compatible with employers' needs and pose little threat to managerial authority.

A decentralized system of control, supported by occupational networks and practitioners' referrals, exerts a centrifugal force that resists centralization and formal professional governance. Although some contractors, managers, and employees expressed a desire for clearer occupational standards, decentralization also allows them the latitude to determine and adjust the standards they impose. The processes associated with networking—active construction of collegial connections, normative requirements for occupational practice, and reciprocal patterns of communication and exchange—represent instead a distinctive system of regulation that offers both contractors and clients some advantages over either hierarchical administrative control or unfettered impersonal market transaction.

Walter Powell (1990) characterizes network organization as an alternative form of governance that can counter the disadvantages of both markets and hierarchies by promoting long-term reciprocal exchanges. In occupational networks, these contract professionals can indeed develop deeper reciprocal obligations than short-term market relations generate. The processes associated with networking, however, also exert control over occupational practice, as contract professionals adhere to norms and codes of behavior while individually exercising expertise. Networking supports an institutional arrangement that contributes to decentralized governance among occupational practitioners. The professionalism that contractors demand of themselves and one another, in turn, contributes to a self-regulation that undergirds relations with clients.

6

EXTRA-ORGANIZATIONAL CAREERS

Can contracting constitute a career? Career connotes direction, but contracting demands flexibility. A career demands investment, but contractors can depend little on their clients to invest in their professional progress. Contractors may use their employment status as leverage to control daily schedules, but what of the longer-term demands of their careers? Contracting lacks the institutional benchmarks that chart progress within employing organizations; formal promotions, with increasing authority, for example, are always reserved for employees. Nor can contractors expect their clients to provide them with opportunities to learn on the job or develop new skills. Rather than expectations for advancement, they assume individual responsibility for charting their course and remaining employable over time.

Instead of organizational structures, contractors' careers depend on occupational logics, which inform their strategies to remain both employed and employable. Long-term connections with clients, colleagues, and recruiters might facilitate work on multiple projects and minimize downtime between them. Seeking assignments that offer new experience or update specific skills might expand the possibilities for finding future work. Developing a broad mix of skills, learning different functional areas, and offering a range of services can further enhance labor market options. Some contractors use their employment status to accelerate professional growth. Others decelerate their careers by limiting working time enough to accommodate family obligations or other pursuits outside paid employment. Extra-organizational careers thus allow variable trajectories, without the organizational contexts that define achievement for employees.

As an alternative opportunity structure, contract employment provides fewer scripted stages than an organization-based career. As options unfold outside the fixed positions of an internal labor market, professional development depends on a series of projects that provide, ideally, both ongoing professional challenge and increasing financial reward. A contractor's trajectory, however, always lacks the formal markers of organizational accomplishment. A career might parallel patterns of organizational progress, but it nonetheless remains a tenuously connected sequence of short-term assignments on which the contractor must impose coherence. Occupational success thus depends on negotiated processes through which contractors seek to leverage their demonstrated expertise to achieve professional advancement.

How then, do contractors make sense of the temporal sequences that constitute extra-organizational careers? Without formal status or internal organizational cues, the contractors I interviewed had fashioned their own criteria for achievement and had shaped their aspirations accordingly. Most emphasized having more options or facing fewer obstacles than they had found in standard jobs. Chastened by the violations of implicit contracts in employing organizations, some considered their careers no less predictable than standard employment in their respective occupations. Seizing on the notion of flexibility (much valorized in the new economy), they had reframed their accomplishments to encompass resourcefulness and adaptability in the wake of constant change. Lacking formal affiliation and job titles to mark their progress, they looked to broader cultural themes to claim individual success.

The Imperative of Employability

Contractors' careers demand vigilance. Clients' schedules can be erratic, leaving contractors overcommitted or underemployed. Lacking the support and investment afforded employees, contractors must acquire knowledge and skills on their own. In technical fields in particular, those who fail to stay current can find themselves all but unemployable, and for programmers and engineers, employability means frequently updating their facility with the latest technologies and tools. Remaining employed, however, is a priority for contractors in both occupational groups. Although some of my informants had relished occasional periods of downtime or actively sought time away from paid work to attend to other areas of life, all had developed strategies to maintain their careers over time.

Scheduling Work, Juggling Projects

For Noreen, a writer and editor, one client had over three years had become "a long-term relationship" and a steady source of short assignments. Noreen considered the arrangement "good, 'cause I'm not out looking for new work every other week," but gradually she had come to feel constrained. "I'm kind of getting drawn into doing some of the things that I'm really not that interested in doing anymore," she reported. "I'm just working on brochures and user information." To expand her reach, Noreen had contacted a colleague, who then referred her to a new client in business to develop educational materials. The work had been intermittent, not enough to depend on, but she elaborated, "it's been enough lead time that I would kind of manage things, so [with multiple projects for more than one client]...I just kept all the balls in the air....It's good to have different clients."

Several informants similarly spoke of scheduling work as "juggling." When one project took longer than anticipated, they might put another on hold. More often, however, they worked extra-long hours, trying to meet all their commitments, and for the duration, daily life allowed little flexibility. Janice, a writer, editor, and project manager, described juggling work for two clients, one a large company for which she worked close to full-time hours on-site, the other a small firm for which she produced newsletters and website copy. "I got really flattened right before Christmas; I had so much," she remembered. "I had a big deadline, and then I'd been doing this other part....So I had to really rethink what I was doing." Despite the time crunch, Janice believed, multiple clients created more options, which might become useful at some future date.

In both occupational groups, the contractors I met cited variety and versatility as strategies for remaining employed. The result could be overcommitment, with several projects needing attention at once, but overlapping schedules could also provide a transition, so that as one wound down, another could be ramping up. A few spoke of taking "filler work" or "back-burner projects," sometimes for a reduced fee, so that they could remain fully employed when the pace of a large project slackened. Multiple clients in different industries might also provide a hedge against macroeconomic cycles, which could affect industries and employment sectors differently. To stay in work, I was told, a contractor tries to diversify.

Diversification can be especially important when specific expertise is slated for obsolescence. Patrick, a programmer and systems analyst, described "doing a lot of Y2K work" for several years, as the millennium approached: "I had become a Y2K expert, absolutely trying not to be, so...how am I going to reinvent myself?...I poked my head up in time and looked at the web.... It amazed me how much it'd changed, so what I saw really set the tone for what I did next and what I invested in." Anticipating a labor market shift in the late 1990s, Patrick began to seek a new clientele, to be prepared after the century turned. As he had expected, the "Y2K crunch" had been lucrative but necessarily short-lived. Concerned about staying employable, he had looked to the area of greatest growth and positioned himself accordingly. "You do get opportunities to do that employed [in a standard job] in a large organization," he reflected, "but then I would have to wait three years to get another position.... There, you can't change your essence of being on a dime."

Patrick's account echoes analyses of "boundaryless careers" that provide challenge and opportunity for those who make their own strategic choices.[1] Mobility and individual agency, this concept suggests, allow individuals to enact careers through constant learning and innovation. For boundary spanners in many fields, occupations, rather than organizations, structure career trajectories.[2] Yet Patrick's strategy underscores the risks for contractors, whose choices are also investments. If a contractor invests in an area soon to be obsolete or about to be glutted with new entrants, the effort might net few returns. Hedging their bets, therefore, many of my informants described seeking a variety of clients or projects that could keep them employed, even if their careers failed to take a charted direction.

Scheduling work from multiple sources is also a judgment call. Too much can mean long hours, but too little can short-change potential income. For those with little experience or few connections, turning down work can itself seem risky. Michael, an editor and proofreader, had felt this quandary acutely, early in his career: "You cannot say no. You can have a lot of stuff on your plate, and you get a call saying can you do this, and you're really afraid to say no. You're really afraid to say, 'I have too much to do right now,' so you take it on.... The life of a freelancer can be very difficult that way." Experience had only partly mitigated Michael's concerns. Even after more than two decades of experience, he tended to "take it as it comes," rarely refusing a project because of lack of interest or the prospect of better options. Concerned about losing his clients, he wryly described himself as a "dependent contractor a lot of the time" and, unlike Patrick, described responding to the market rather than actively navigating a chosen course.

Contractors whose schedules are full, of course, do turn away work. Many of my informants reported offering referrals when turning a client down, and most also encouraged their clients to keep them in mind for the future. Sherry, an editor, translator, and project manager, explained her strategy: "I always say no, I'm sorry, but this just isn't going to fit my schedule. I really appreciate the offer, but keep me in mind for work after this date. This is when my schedule will loosen up. I say it even if it's a fictional date." Such a response not only invites future inquiries but also signals that she is in demand, can gauge expectations, and, having made a commitment, will reliably follow through. Even when turning away work, therefore, contractors can perform expertise. Presenting themselves as skilled managers, in charge of their own schedules—even implying that they are busier than they truly are—contractors signal their employability.

Dealing with Downtime

When working full-time for a single client, however, a contractor's options are more constrained. Clients that want contractors on-site often expect them to be present throughout a workweek and to allocate their time as if they were employees. Taking other projects for different clients is then roughly equivalent to "moonlighting" with a second job. Although clients cannot practically prohibit contractors from engaging in this practice, some do try to prevent it.[3] Erik, a hiring manager at a software firm, seemed sympathetic to his contractors' needs for long-term options but nonetheless wanted them working exclusively for him:

> A lot of the contractors I'm seeing will be doing more than one contract simultaneously. They've learned to cover their tail as far as making sure that if one contract ends abruptly or whatever, that they've got something else going on.... I mean one of the questions that will come up is what other things do you have going on? Do you have any other contracts? Are you finishing up any other kind of work from a previous contract? I'll ask them point blank, and most of the contractors I've dealt with are very up front, very honest.... We'll talk about it for a while, but if it sounds like it's ongoing, it's pretty much the end of the interview right there.

A contractor's hourly rate, Erik believed, justified this demand. "When I'm paying, you know, $70, $90, $100 an hour, or more in some cases, I can expect one hundred percent of a person's attention," he insisted. High fees, his reasoning suggests, should cover the time spent looking for work after a contract has ended.

Such conditions make contracting cyclical, with downtime, as most contractors call a period without work, a cost of doing business. Programmers and engineers, who more often take on-site assignments requiring full-time hours, are also more often subject to schedules governed by project cycles. For Jeffrey, a software engineer, exclusive attention to one client at a time informed his calculations of hourly rates:

> You have to figure that you're gonna have at least a month or two of downtime. So then I say OK, what I really need to do then, is say how much do I want to earn? Realizing that I have to... leave myself three months a year, on average, that I'm going to have to use to go look for work,... you take that number, nine months, just calculate four weeks a month. So you say OK, in thirty-six weeks, that's how much money I have to earn. Divide that down by the magic number of forty hours per week. You come up with a number.

Three months a year might seem long, Jeffrey elaborated, but the calculation was an average that spanned economic cycles. In practice, his schedule had been uneven, with long periods of forty-hour weeks, crunch times with heavier demands, and occasional episodes approximating unemployment.

Each long-term assignment, however, was an "immersion experience" from which he needed a short break before he could move on. "My usual process is to, first of all, just take a couple of days off, get this one out of my head," he explained.

Jeffrey's greatest concern was an economic downturn so severe that he would remain unemployed for many months, or even years. He had experienced long periods of downtime during the recession of the early 1990s, and more than a decade later the memory still evoked anxiety. "I'm afraid it could be happening again," he told me, recalling the paucity of work for programmers. "The worst period of time that I've had was '90—I want to say '92 through '94—the absolute worst period. I only worked one year out of two. It took me seven months to find one job. Worked there a year. It took five months to find another job." Long stretches of downtime pose several related risks for programmers and engineers. Beyond loss of income, these contractors might also lose opportunities to keep their experience current, and a few worried that prolonged downtime could make them ever-less attractive to the clients they hoped to attract. The prospect of competing with recent college graduates, some of them immigrants on temporary visas, could augment these concerns. "I could age out of this business," Jeffrey reflected, "if they decide that cheap new recruits are better than experience."

Jackie, also a software engineer, reported trying to avoid downtime by second-guessing her clients. "I've never been on a contract that, at the end, lasted as long as the contract was for," she explained. "You can usually tell that things are sort of winding down, and then you ask whether there's anything else that they want you to do." Despite written agreements specifying a period of employment, neither managers nor staffing agencies considered these "paper dates" binding. When the end was in sight, therefore, Jackie mobilized her network by contacting colleagues, recruiters, and prospective clients. Yet, like other contractors I interviewed, she had found staffing agencies largely unwilling to offer new projects to contractors currently on the payroll,[4] so until the project was formally over, she contacted different recruiters. "I look for jobs through many agencies," she explained, "I tell them what I want;...I tell them my availability, so they start looking a few weeks ahead of time."

Both Jeffrey and Jackie considered themselves full-time contractors. Contracting was neither a stopgap measure nor a means of reducing working time. Project schedules, however, guaranteed at least a few brief periods of downtime, and macroeconomic cycles meant that, when the market turned down, they might spend months looking for work. In their study of technical contractors, James Evans, Gideon Kunda, and Stephen Barley (2004) characterize these fallow periods as "bridge time" and argue that contractors' efforts to minimize these episodes subvert the flexibility that many claim to exercise. Exposed to an external labor market, they assert, contractors experience significant constraints.[5] In contrast, Meiksins and Whalley (2002) find that contract work defined as part-time allowed practitioners greater temporal flexibility than most standard full-time jobs.[6] For contractors seeking to reduce their hours spent in paid employment, these researchers suggest, downtime may be less a problem than an opportunity.

The differences between these studies may stem, in part, from the populations of contractors they address. At least as significant, however, is the comparative context in which contractors understand their experience. Whereas standard employment demands exceedingly long hours with little respite and limited reward, contracting might indeed seem flexible, despite the constraints of an external labor market or the demands of specific clients. A contractor who wants steady work will thus experience at least occasional limits to the choice of assignments and control of daily schedules. Few can enjoy unfettered flexibility, and in both occupations, the contractors I interviewed reported limits to the latitude they enjoyed. For most, contracting offered greater control over their work schedules than they had found in standard jobs.

Maxine, a recruiter who placed writers and editors, articulated her own limits and implied that a contractor might need to make trade-offs:

> If they get to the point where they say, "I don't do more than twenty. I don't do Wednesdays. I need ten weeks off a year," I say, "You're a freelancer. These are your things to decide....Just tell me you're unavailable."...But this is the type of business or agency that provides people on an ad hoc basis, and you have to be able to go with the flow, you know. So people who have an awful lot of restrictions on the time they can give, I mentally say OK, don't use them so often....They immediately limit themselves.

Market demands thus impose constraints. Self-imposed limits may be difficult to maintain when project needs expand, and although payment by the hour can make these "crisis periods" lucrative, accommodating a client can also mean ceding control of working time. Contractors may, in principle, agree to only a specified number of hours or weeks per year, but such stipulations can also render them less employable. A contractor who needs income, therefore, will likely acquiesce, at least occasionally, and allow the client needs to prevail. Downtime, otherwise, can become a protracted problem.

Contractors who can tolerate erratic incomes might use downtime to pursue other activities. Pat, a writer, reported intermittent periods of steady work: "It's varied considerably," she explained. "But when I've done part time, it's been between ten and, at the top, I'd say thirty hours a week.... Then some years there seem to be off periods and then periods when I've always got something.... always working... [but] I've always got other projects going on, so I can keep busy and fit it all in this way." Pat's major "other project" had been refurbishing her house, which could proceed without adhering to a rigid time line, so paid work could take precedence when a client demanded full-time attention. Other informants cited fiction writing, music lessons, skiing, and meditation retreats made possible because of the flexibility that contracting allowed. Some had found clients that limited contractors to forty-hour weeks, which had left them more discretionary time than they had experienced as employees. Contractors, they explained, need not always be available, and like employees, they do celebrate holidays and take vacations, albeit unpaid. But staying employed meant responsiveness to clients, who also exerted control.

Keeping Current, Expanding Skill Sets

Short segments of downtime, even when unwanted, can be an opportunity to expand areas of expertise. Accepting occasional downtime as a cost of doing business, many of my informants equated its judicious use with professional commitment. Myra, an editor and project manager, recalled advising a colleague who had been complaining in an online exchange: "I remember writing at one point, 'OK, if you don't have work and you want more editing, these are the things you can do: (a) temp, (b) read in your field, (c) take anything that comes your way. But if you're not willing to make yourself a better editor when you don't have editing, what are you doing here? You know, read *The Chicago Manual* if you haven't read it.' I don't know, but to me that's important." Myra's career reflected her own advice. Working first for book publishers in the humanities, she had expanded her clientele to include research institutes that produced reports. "It's this constant [learning] curve," she explained. "This is why I have to keep moving on....I don't know if it will mean more writing or finding a new editing niche." Again seeking new clients, Myra had become involved with a community organization where she could learn environmental science: "When they send me fact sheets, I'm just so happy, and I really do my best on them, and it's a good way for me to start learning how to edit science, because you want it to be readable. But it has to be so precise. And every little change or phrase can just totally change what they're doing."

Several of my informants similarly described taking projects that extended their reach. A few, like Myra, had found clients with small budgets, unable to pay market rates, and had gained experience by working for less. A very few reported volunteering, usually for nonprofits for which volunteering was a norm. Producing a newsletter or developing a database could provide a work sample or perhaps a referral later on.

Far more common, however, were concerted efforts to learn on the job. The challenge was making the effort invisible. For Bryan, a programmer and systems engineer, this strategy created a short-lived sense of insecurity:

> You go into some company where you figure you're going to only know about fifty to seventy percent. That's a learning curve. You look around, and you say, "Oh, they're not going to keep me. I don't know what the hell I'm doing over here." Then the next thing you know, you say, "Oh, yeah, I can do this." All of sudden it's bing, bang, boom. They're coming to you for advice, and you say to yourself, "Hmm, advice, I'm the expert all of a sudden."

Acknowledging inexperience or lack of familiarity, Bryan knew, would interfere with an expert performance. "They always say they want people with the experience," he noted. "You have to get it quickly."

Many of my informants echoed Bryan's observation—clients and recruiters tend to be wary of contractors who seek assignments to expand their expertise. Rather than an ability to learn, they want evidence that a contractor has accomplished the assignment elsewhere and will merely be repeating the performance. Such hiring practices pose dilemmas for contractors, who need to maintain their currency and so must find ways to learn new areas and skills. Charles, a writer, editor, and trainer, articulated the problem: "Somebody who hired me once told me that he didn't want to pay for people to get their education.... He didn't want to pay to get them up to speed, when in fact I feel like...that's exactly what people do....If I do my work well in a new area, I've learned something new that can open me up to other people who need that kind of thing." Peggy, a programmer, had similarly used current clients to develop new skills. "Sometimes the company you're working at, it might let you do something new," she noted. "You have to get into a place and negotiate, make them think you already know....But sometimes changing jobs, that's the only way to get current."

In both occupations, my informants described leveraging contract assignments to establish new areas of expertise. Most sought to develop a mix of skills and familiarity with functional areas, fields of knowledge, and industries in which firms might engage their services. Comparing technical contractors and film production workers, Siobhan O'Mahony and Beth Bechky (2006) term such strategies *stretchwork*, defined as assignments that offer the chance to learn on the job.[7] Stretchwork, they suggest, allows a contractor to progress in an external labor market without resorting to formal training. My informants similarly described stretching their claims to competence when seeking new clients or new professional challenges. The alternative was a series of repetitive projects, which could too readily constrain a career.

Even with skills in high demand, my informants explained, a contractor risks becoming pigeon-holed and limited to only one service or type of project. Kevin, an editor and translator, had established two separate groups of clients, one for translating and the other for editing, and neither group had been willing to acknowledge the range of his abilities and "take a chance" on engaging him for more than one kind of work. Kevin experienced this restriction as a form of control. "It's the desire of power to simplify everything so that it becomes quantifiable and easy for them to understand," he reflected. Erik's account of hiring programmers exemplifies the same practice. "When I look for contractors for a very specific technology, we might not have another project for them again," he explained. "I have one who did a great job. Name's on file. If I ever need that technology again, I'll call him." Asked whether this programmer might know different technologies, Erik responded, "I don't know. I guess not."

Contractors in technical fields must be especially cognizant of trends, tools, and technologies. Tony, a software engineer and systems designer, emphasized the risks of obsolescence. "In the computer business, the whole world gets reinvented within two years," he explained. "So if you're working with older equipment, you quite easily find yourself obsolete." Employees, in contrast, can expect employer-sponsored training, sometimes through formal courses, which some employers conduct on-site. Yet only one of my informants reported access to a client's on-site course, and then only after he had agreed to accept half his hourly fee for the time spent there.[8] Formal training for most contractors is doubly expensive because they pay directly for courses and indirectly in working time for which they cannot bill.[9]

Staffing agencies do sometimes fill the breach, and a few of my informants cited agency-sponsored courses. The training, they noted, was promoted as an incentive to stay employed through the agency, which typically required some number of months, or even years, on the payroll before providing training resources. Anna, a programmer who had been seven years with the same client and agency, had found the training program helpful. "They [the staffing agency] have a catalog of self-taught courses," she explained. "They give you the books,...even software that goes into your computer and steps you through it. They offer that to you, and you can take it any time....And they'll pay for my courses to keep up to date there [with the client firm]." Such support, however, would not assist Anna in "retooling" in another area. For that, she would have to look elsewhere. She explained:

> I'm a mainframe programmer. We handle the big volumes, which is the big machines, but the money there is less than the money if I took more courses in PC knowledge. There's different types of PC languages that you can learn....And there's less demand for me now....So what I was planning on doing is taking some courses....I was thinking of [name of college] just to take courses, not really for a degree, just to get my expertise in it, so if I need to, I can use it.

Like many programmers, Anna had learned a functional area and, during the boom of the late 1990s, had felt secure in her occupation.

Gradually, however, the technology she knew best had become a "legacy system," and although legacy work was still available, learning newer technologies would give her more options. Several of the programmers I met while observing at one work site voiced corollary concerns about "maintaining the legacy systems." These projects, they suspected, would soon be outsourced overseas. Their manager later confirmed the prediction. "It's the legacy work that's going to Asia," he noted, "they have people with the skills."

The development of a global workforce thus poses new questions for both contractors and employees, all of whom must increasingly consider their employability in a global context.[10] Legacy work may pose risks, but so, too, does the cutting edge of innovation, as Ezra, a software developer, explained, "People who want to be on the leading—also referred to as the bleeding—edge of technology, well, that's where you get cut. I mean if you want to stay on the leading edge, it's sharp. That's the metaphor. The bleeding would be working with untested software.... So things tend to take longer, to be less stable, harder to predict,...faster to disappear sometimes.... so you spend time that doesn't pay off."

In their study of technical contractors, Barley and Kunda (2004) describe learning new technologies as an all-consuming commitment that shaped the lives of the contractors they studied. In contrast, most of the contractors I interviewed sought to stay current but tried principally to learn on the job. As Ezra stated, "I want to maintain my skills sufficiently that I can find interesting work without having to work constantly." Rebecca, a writer and editor, expressed a similar sentiment: "I don't want to think of updating all the time. I have other things to do." Unpaid hours learning the latest tools seemed, to her, ever-more costly. So was the expense of purchasing software. "I'll be damned if I'm going to spend a thousand dollars on an application," she complained. Over time, these accounts suggest, contractors seek to balance an investment in their employability with the prerogatives of self-direction.

Flexible Trajectories

Contractors' career trajectories evidence much variation. Some spend most of their careers in an external labor market. Others move back into standard employment, sometimes more than once. In these occupations, external and internal labor markets are both parallel and symbiotic, connected through the boundary-spanning processes that constitute careers. Although the contractors I interviewed tended to express a certain wariness about the stability of any employing organization, some described feeling tempted by offers of standard jobs that might expose them to an emerging field, new responsibilities, or special challenges. At the time of our interview, Darrell, a programmer and project manager, announced that he would soon take a job as director of technology at a small start-up firm. He knew the principals, he explained, having worked with them a few years earlier, and the company had a product with an expanding market. Still, contracting remained an "exit option" if the new job failed to meet his expectations. "Times are OK there now," he assured me, "[but] if things go south, I'll be making those calls again...looking for work."

Mobility across labor market boundaries, in both directions, may thus segment a career into alternating periods of contracting and standard employment. The contractors I interviewed reported different reasons for having taken standard jobs at some point in the past: a lucrative offer, a chance to learn, a compatible work environment. After first becoming a contractor in the early 1970s, Darrell had moved back into standard employment fifteen years later, as "VP for engineering, just to help a friend get his company straightened out." When his friend then sold the company, Darrell declared his mission over, "made a few phone calls," and returned to contracting. The alternative, at the time, was to remain a manager in a newly merged company, increasingly removed from technical challenge. Standard employment, he feared, would eventually limit his options.

Although, as contractors, they rarely received formal titles, many of my informants described significant professional growth, measured in pay levels and project responsibilities, which might approximate a series of promotions in an internal labor market. Melinda, a programmer, described a trajectory common to both occupational groups. "When I saw I wasn't advancing in my career, I decided to go freelance," she explained. "When I showed what I could do, I was suddenly managing a project." In contrast, some of the contractors I interviewed had used their contractual status to minimize professional development. Lori, also a programmer, described her work as less and less rewarding. "I just do my job and go home," she explained. "I don't want to learn the latest gizmo. Some people are really into this technology, but I find it mostly boring now." Using downtime to develop new options, Lori hoped to move out of a technical career that for her had lost its luster. Contracting, these accounts suggest, can fit very different career strategies.

Among my informants, both patterns are evident. A contactor might seek greater opportunity for growth. Another might want to limit professional involvement or even ease into a new occupation. At both extremes, my informants described standard employment as an impediment. Standard jobs, they emphasized, demand conformity. They trade time at work for only the promise of professional progress, and for many, the promise had gone unfulfilled for far too long. Contracting, in contrast, could offer higher fees for the hours they worked and broader experience at a faster pace. For those trying to limit their working time, fewer billable hours meant lower incomes and less accumulating experience, but unlike part-time employees in other occupations, their status need not foreclose different choices later on.[11] Contracting might thus provide a balance between paid employment and other pursuits.

Accommodating Work and Family

Contractual status, combined with temporal flexibility, may thus be a strategy for accommodating work with family responsibilities. Sherry considered plans for parenthood: "I feel as if I have a lot more options as a freelancer.... If I want to be a mom, I can be a mom, and I can have a job at the same time and have it on my own terms." To manage child care, Sherry thought she might solicit work that she could intersperse with household tasks. She might confine herself to small projects while her children were young, she speculated, without compromising her credibility as a professional. As long as she met commitments, she believed, she would remain professionally viable, and as her children grew older, she could again seek projects that she found more demanding.

Organizational careers, in contrast, more often require professional development to proceed according to normative time lines, and when organizational logic equates success with rising formal status, those who deviate can face penalties.[12] Linda, a software and database developer, described almost ten years as an employee in a financial services firm as "a slow path up but a lot of stability." She had felt secure in a "very high-tech career path," but each successive position had demanded the same long days and nights on call, with little time for her family. "This is a company that was, that lands every year on family-friendly lists as having all these wonderful programs," she lamented, "but you can't take advantage of them." Even symbols of appreciation failed to acknowledge her needs: "On a project to thank people for putting in insane hours under high pressure, they'd want to give you tickets to a ball game that night, and it was, well, what am I going to do? We've got two kids at home that I haven't seen. No, what I need is to be able to leave on time tomorrow. How about that one? Can I have a night without phone calls? And that was, you know, it was an ongoing thing, and it was a constant thing."

When she attempted to redefine her job, Linda elaborated, the only alternative had been a "mommy-track job," in which she could "quietly do systems maintenance" but expect few, if any, promotions. Todd, a recruiter who had spent twelve years as an editor in a series of standard jobs, recalled similar trade-offs. "Any job comes with an understanding: work comes first," he reflected. "It's not that you're fired if you put family first, but they find ways to make it harder for you." Such accounts illustrate the normative expectations of standard employment, the spoken and unspoken requirements that signal commitment to an organization and make an employee eligible for increasing recognition and reward. Such demands may disproportionately penalize women but can affect men as well.[13] As Linda noted, "for anyone, mothers, fathers,...the mommy track is not for slow movers but for nonmovers." Too much time in one position, she implied, can limit opportunities or mark a practitioner as less than capable. When temporal norms govern professional progress, accommodating other obligations may well compromise a career.

Contractors who work from home can sometimes use their temporal flexibility to adapt their careers during periods of family transition. When the careers of partners or spouses require relocation, for example, a contractor might move and continue working for the same clients. Myra had even found that relocating brought an advantage as she sought new clients. "I think partly moving gave me a real caché," she mused. "The fact that I was in demand from far away meant I was good." Working from her home office, Myra had retained most of her clientele, whose repeat business had eased the transition. Their willingness to continue using her services, in turn, underscored her abilities. Geographical mobility had thus facilitated her performance of expertise.

For women, however, paid work performed at home has long appeared gender appropriate,[14] closely associated with a gendered division of labor and women's unpaid domestic work. Women in home offices, therefore, may seem to be adhering to gender norms by subordinating their careers to family obligations. Yet among the contractors I interviewed, men as well as women reported adjusting their career trajectories to accommodate paid work with family needs. Michael described an abrupt transition, which in the early 1970s had precipitated a period of contracting. "I was laid off in June. My daughter was born in May," he remembered, "so I was able to be a full-time father and do freelance work at the same time." Although the layoff had at first seemed like a setback, his availability had been a boon to his family. Concerned about his long-term prospects, however, Michael had learned enough about computer systems to find work as a technical editor, first in a standard job and then, after another layoff, as a contractor. Describing his career as a "see-saw," he reflected, "My wife and I kind of traded off earning the benefits for a while."

In some dual-career families, a contractor's career can absorb the shock of change more readily than a career shaped by a standard sequence of stages. Max, a programmer, planned to develop a technical support business. Comparing his plans with his wife's, he explained, "My wife got a tenure-track job, and we're talking about starting a family. . . . It doesn't hurt for me to hold off." Considering the inflexibility of his wife's academic career, with its high-stakes tenure decision, Max expected to assume a disproportionate share of child care, "for at least a few years," while his wife established herself. For her, the career path was predetermined and the sanctions for deviance potentially severe. For him, in contrast, career structures were less rigid, and short-term compromises carried lower costs.

Diversification: Multiple Skills, Simultaneous Paths

Max was one of several informants considering an expanded business, beyond the individual projects that constituted contract work. Some of the contractors I interviewed had considered becoming recruiters, and a few noted the ease with which colleagues had begun subcontracting projects.

A staffing business might be an attractive possibility, especially during periods of economic expansion, when the needs of clients seemed most acute. Todd, whose small business specialized in writing and document production, had begun contracting as an "individual contributor" before recruiting other contractors to do much of the hands-on work. After ten years, he had an office staff and an established niche: "We have a stable of editorial freelancers. Last year I think we worked with thirty to thirty-five people during the course of the year. Some people may have worked for us for two months, some people for two weeks, some people for the entire year. So it really depends. So I talk about 'we' because the company is more than myself."

Other informants had applied their expertise to developing their own products. When Ben, a software engineer and project manager, first left standard employment, he had intended to develop products for medical research. He had incorporated, sought investors, and developed a business plan. But after amassing considerable debt, he decided also to pursue contract work, to generate a steady income that could more reliably pay the bills. Product development had been successful, he explained, but not enough to sustain him. Like Todd, however, Ben spoke of his business as an ongoing collective effort:

> We do have a product that's been selling for about two years worldwide. And we're exploring possibilities of bringing in somebody to help grow that and possibly some new venture tied up with that....So instead of clients we have customers and investors....But looking forward, we don't know how to grow....Maybe we can grow the consulting aspect, and that could get into employee hiring, more management of employees rather than working on the technology. But I don't know.

Contracting project by project had been the steadiest source of income, but Ben continued to keep his other options open.

Ben's quandary represents a possibility that has especially engaged programmers and engineers.[15] Applying their abilities to new markets at the right moment, they might capitalize their own enterprises, form start-up companies, and become entrepreneurs. Some of my informants cited colleagues who had launched successful start-up firms. A few, however, had discovered that a good idea, well timed for the market, is only part of a formula for success. Joseph, an experienced software engineer, ruefully recalled an attempt to market his own product:

> A lot of people said to me, geez, you know, you design products for many different companies. Why don't you design one for yourself? Well, the basic problem is that I'm a very good engineer, but I'm a very poor businessman.... One of the people I worked with in the last year, we've been working together to design our own product, which we've done very successfully.... [But] the product very, very seriously threatened a competitor, and that competitor, because of my partner's previous employment, it gave them some excuse to pester us.... They've hired a killer law firm.

With the profits from his venture undermined by a legal challenge,[16] Joseph had again turned his attention to contracting and to expanding his clientele.

In contrast, Bill had expanded his career to start a training business, applying the skills he had learned as a writer and document manager. As companies of all kinds implemented new information technology, he explained, the market for training workshops had become lucrative. "At one point I had thirteen employees," he recalled. "And that was nuts.... When I added up all the time that was spent at either managing the other folks and/or making sure that the product delivered was a good one, the net return was horrendous. Now I'm by myself." With the ebb of an economic boom, Bill had downsized his business and simplified its management. Ruminating about his next steps, he was considering a return to school or perhaps a move into standard employment, where he might apply his administrative experience.

Bill was one of seven contractors I interviewed who had made training and course development one of the services they could offer clients. Teaching work-related skills was for them both an additional source of income and a marker of expertise. Training also provided variety and, in some cases, the chance to travel. Thomas, a writer and trainer, had begun augmenting contract projects with training workshops that he designed himself but had then found work with a company that dispatched him to deliver courses. "I like the variety from the people perspective," he explained. "The money's not too bad, so the money and the travel. I like to go to different places and see different groups.... It's different kinds of people from different countries, different organizations."

Extra-Organizational Progress

For some contractors, therefore, an extra-organizational career path offers greater variety than most standard jobs provide. For others, contracting can accommodate personal choices or family needs. For still others, years of experience and demonstrated expertise can lead to greater responsibility and higher fees, approximating an ascending path in an organizational hierarchy. Even when a contractor carries a title corresponding to an organizational position, however, the designation is always temporary. With only marginal status in the employing organization, the contractors I interviewed cared little for formal titles but instead sought equivalent occupational recognition, which gave them leverage in an external labor market.

Seth, an editor and production manager, had begun his editorial career with freelance proofreading, an "entry-level function" through which he had learned print production. Although finding contract work from a "standing start" had been difficult, the experience had led to a standard job as an editorial assistant, which had taught him the labor process with print production and its conventions. Again working as a contractor, he had been able to market a book-packaging service that included project management for some of his clients. "You use their freelancers," he explained. "The people that they use become available to you to package their book. What you do is you acquire a per-page management fee for doing all of the administrative work in terms of coordinating author, copy editor, tech, design, references. You become a freelance project manager." At his former employer, Seth noted, these responsibilities were assigned to first-level managers, whose positions were "at least a rung or two up the ladder" from the job he had held. "I wasn't a manager in house," he noted, "but here I am." As a contractor, he had, in effect, accomplished his own promotion.

Holly's trajectory had been similar. Having expanded her menu of editorial services to encompass project management, she had become the acting managing editor for several months at a client firm. Pleased with her work, the client had asked her to apply, and presumably be hired, as the "permanent" manager. Holly explained her reasons for rejecting the offer: "I just didn't want it. I want my independence, my office [at home]. I want to pick up [daughter's name] on the days she doesn't have after-school [activities], and I couldn't do that reliably....I can't expect them [her prospective employer] to make it all fit....I guess I have to keep explaining to people. I can do the same work on my own and make the same money." Holly had offered to stay in her acting capacity long enough to assist her client in hiring someone else. But with a "permanent" manager in place, she had returned to her home office, where she continued to oversee projects for the same client, now represented by the manager she had helped to hire.

Because career success, generally understood, means advancement in an organizational hierarchy, most contractors are acutely conscious of eschewing a standard path. Asked about their choices, most of my informants offered carefully considered rationales for turning down offers of standard employment. Many shared Holly's need for flexibility. Most common, however, was a desire to stay close to the hands-on work of occupational practice. To many, this was the "real work" that had attracted them in the first place. In contrast, administrative responsibilities that came with many promotions held much less appeal. Karen, a software developer and trainer, described her decision. "People kept wanting to push me into management because if you have any kind, the least amount of people skills, they want you to be a manager," she explained. "So I didn't want to do management,...I wanted to be technical."

Karen's decision represents a common dilemma, well documented in studies of engineering work: organizational careers, with hierarchical advancement, represent a cultural definition of success but, paradoxically, take some of the most capable practitioners away from engineering.[17] To address this dilemma, some organizations have established dual career ladders that reward practitioners for "staying technical." Yet, like Karen, many of my informants had found the technical track truncated. Karen explained, "I realized that there's very few upper technical jobs within a company, and they're very competitive to get them. Like there'd probably only be one chief architect per company, so in order to stay technical, I figured I would go into consulting." Without formal status, Karen had redefined success, not as vertical mobility in an organizational hierarchy but as lateral mobility and professional development over time.

Writers and editors face similar dilemmas, although the possibilities for organizational advancement tend to be fewer and less well marked. Some segments of the book-publishing industry, for example, offer few career ladders for hands-on editors,[18] and in other industries that produce documents, downsizing and restructuring have similarly turned to contractors for publications and communications support. Pat compared her recent experience to corporate communications in the early 1980s: "They'd train you....I had a degree in English. I mean at the time there were people who had degrees in anything and everything....And then you could move, you know, maybe into management," she recalled. "A lot of people did that....Now they've gotten rid of almost all their writers. The writing groups, the people I know who are still there, the numbers have been reduced to almost nothing." Periods of retrenchment, Pat speculated, had diminished the investment in training. So, too, had a growing reliance on networks of suppliers that reached far beyond the firm.[19] Writers and editors, like programmers and engineers, may thus find professional development more readily available outside the boundaries of a single organization.

Without a fixed position, a contractor's status remains malleable. Working as a manager may bring responsibilities equivalent to a managerial job in an organization, but the next project may correspond to a different position with a substantially different status. A systems architect might thus become a test engineer, or a developmental editor might next work as a proofreader. In an internal labor market, these changes in function would signal a demotion, or at least a loss of status in a hierarchy of skills. For a contractor, however, a shift in skills applied to given projects signals instead a measured response to the defined needs of a client. Contractors tend, therefore, to define their occupations with broad functional areas rather than specific tasks or titles.

For hiring managers, this functional range can facilitate the allocation of tasks and responsibilities. Erik, who at the time of our interview was managing "about a seventy-thirty mix" of employees and contractors, remarked on the effects of a contractor's temporary status. "I can just tell them what I need," he mused. "I don't have to worry about where it will get them next year, when the project ends." Further reflecting on the contrast with the employees he supervised, he continued, "When I ask them to do something that's—let's face it—not too desirable, contractors are almost always willing....They'd sweep the floor if I asked them to. Maybe you can tell me why." Phil, a writer and project manager working long term for a single client, answered Erik's question. "I also don't routinely turn down work unless I'm overloaded," he explained. "In-house people routinely turn down work.... They just say no to something if they don't think it's good for their careers.... But for me, I can say yes, and they like that I can adapt."

Phil's reasoning is typical. With no aspirations to rise in the organization, he had no need position himself for promotion and no desire to seize choice assignments merely to enhance his status. Nor did he feel any need to compete with peers for formal acknowledgment or individual credit. Unlike an employee, he willingly took on what the client needed done. His career depended not on vertical mobility within an organizational hierarchy but on a succession of assignments, none of which would define his professional identity or confer formal status. Rather than a sequence of positions, his career had become a circuitous path guided by a need to remain employable in an occupational labor market.

Adapting to the options available, contractors claim credit for their flexibility, which they equate with professional judgment in applying their expertise. Extra-organizational careers thus reflect a broader cultural emphasis associated with responsiveness in a market economy that promises little more than the prospect of ongoing change. Comparing their trajectories with careers in standard employment, my informants stressed resilience over rigidity and considered their mix of skills and experience an advantage in navigating uncertainty. Responsive to their clients, they would remain flexible, demonstrating an agility that they believed would propel them forward, to the next assignment and the next stage of a career. Their accounts, therefore, represent a strategic appropriation of flexibility, a cultural response to the shifting of risk and responsibility to individuals, who must adapt to external forces that remain well beyond their control.

Work Relations Reconsidered

Contract employment is far from problem free, and its practitioners do voice complaints. Some of their difficulties, however, affect contractors and employees alike. A standard job is hardly a buffer against volatility and change, and employees as well as contractors face uncertain labor markets. But employees, unlike contractors, have access to systems of legal rights and benefits. For them, a job more often comes with formal procedures in case of unresolved disputes. In contrast, problems specific to contracting stem largely from a lack of applicable social policy or institutional support. What, then, do contract professionals forgo in an external labor market? What new institutions might fill the breach and enhance this form of nonstandard work?

Supported by public policy, the standard job promotes predictability, so that employees can depend on some measure of assistance from employers or the state. In contrast, the fluidity that characterizes contracting offers little assurance or assistance and virtually no protection. Even formal documents that spell out terms for payment and dates for deliverables are no guarantee that a project and the employment relationship it created will proceed as planned. Changes in schedules, budgets, specifications, and myriad matters at the level of the firm may alter any formal contract, leaving the contractor with little leverage for protest. Day to day, the agreements that contract professionals forge with their clients remain subject to decisions beyond their control.

The norms and practices of contracting also leave all contractors vulnerable, to some degree, to client default. Clients responsible for late payment, nonpayment, or unilateral changes to agreed-on terms face few sanctions. Just as they lack formal mechanisms for professional governance, contractors also lack ready access to legal redress. Formal rights, together with social insurance, accrue all but exclusively to employees. Contractors working through staffing agencies may, in some circumstances, access the benefits of insurance, but without the continuity of a single employer, they too must find stopgap solutions during periods of need. Distinguished from employees both in practice and in law, contract professionals are clearly on their own. For contractors, therefore, work relations require vigilance, not only to maintain client relations but also to avoid the risks of unequal exchange.

Although many of the contractors I met expressed skepticism about the prospects for new social policies, most recognized the limits of their individual leverage. Better institutional support, they suggested, might extend social protection, enforce fair employment practices, and resolve the occasional intractable dispute. Yet, in these occupations, only a few small-scale instances of collective action have addressed such concerns. Work relations, these efforts suggest, might better encompass new forms of market mediation, beyond the system of agency contracting, with its corresponding constraints. New institutional forms might further accommodate differences across labor market structures and so promote greater equality for the workforce as a whole.

Working without a Net

Employment policies in the United States depend, in different combinations, on mandated guarantees, employer practices, and collective bargaining to provide rights, benefits, and the means for worker participation.

Statutes and regulations, however, offer legal protection to only specified segments of the workforce. Although a single standard has never been universal, employment policies have accommodated nonstandard arrangements unevenly, with specific provisions covering different groups of workers.[1] Most important for contract professionals is the exclusion of independent contracting—all U.S. labor and employment laws apply only to employees. Most statutes are explicit, although they rarely spell out the criteria that determine employee status.[2]

For example, employees, but not contractors, have the right to sue for discrimination and the right to bargain collectively over wages and working conditions. Only employees receive unemployment compensation in case of layoff. Even contractors working steadily for one client over many years remain outside the bounds of the legal mandates that apply to employees. This lack of legal and social protection has led some analysts to suggest that the growth of the contingent workforce more broadly has been spurred by employers' desire to circumvent regulation.[3] Contract employment may thus provide a loophole for employers seeking to limit their liability.

These statutory exclusions apply most clearly to contractors hired directly by their clients and paid "on 1099." In contrast, a contractor hired through a staffing agency, even an agency acting only as a payroll agent, becomes nominally an employee of the agency and is, potentially, covered by the regulatory framework that supports standard employment. In principle, the staffing agency, as employer of record, is liable for adhering to employment regulations. In practice, however, the triangular arrangement—among agency, contractor, and client—generates much ambiguity. *Joint employment,* as the arrangement is called, can leave the worker in legal limbo, with the agency and client sharing liability. Court rulings in cases of joint employment vary widely.[4] To be covered by U.S. statutes, however, contractors must first establish that they are employees under the law.

Despite these legal limits, most of my informants expressed little regard for formal rights. Rather, they had learned to navigate a system based on "gentlemen's agreements." Although some had, on occasion, sought advice from an attorney or could recount a serious client conflict, no one I interviewed cited a current need for legal redress, and those who spoke of past discrimination or sexual harassment were often referring to their experiences as employees. A few voiced a desire for union representation, although none had ever been a union member represented at a work site.[5] Most had implicitly accepted the conditions of contracting and had few clearly articulated grievances for which they might seek formal advocacy.

Gaps in Social Insurance

Of greater concern to a segment of my informants was lack of a package of benefits that come with standard employment. Although neither uniform nor legally mandated,[6] benefits might include health, disability, and life insurance; contributions to a retirement plan; and paid sick and vacation time. For some employees, especially in newer high-technology companies, benefits might also include stock options, which could significantly augment a salary. None of my informants reported receiving any client-sponsored benefits when working "on 1099" as an independent contractor, even when employed full-time and on-site for an extended period. Having decided to contract for at least a while, many had purchased their own insurance and funded their own retirement accounts. Others could depend on spouses or partners for family health coverage, an arrangement that spared them considerable expense.

Janice, a writer, editor, and project manager, described the difference that marital status had made: "Insurance isn't a problem for me now, but it was when I first started contracting.... I had to COBRA.[7] That was hideously expensive. So health benefits can be a real serious problem, and to me that seems silly. Why shouldn't they be more reasonable? ... I don't know many couples where both people contract. I know a lot where one person contracts and the other has the benefits." Once married to someone with a standard job, Janice had seen her expenses decrease. Although many of the contractors I met considered insurance a cost of doing business—and believed they earned incomes that offset the expense—a need for benefits could be a factor in charting a career. For Katlin, an editor and production manager, the costs were becoming prohibitive: "I'm single, and as a freelancer,...there are some significant benefits you miss out on...sick time, extremely limited vacations.... Ya, profit sharing, matching 401(k) funds. None of that stuff is available to me as a contractor.... And I'm not making significantly that much more than my counterpart at the company.... So those are things to consider." A higher hourly rate, Katlin thought, would better compensate for a lack of insurance, but paid sick time, too, was weighing on her sense of security. "I've never been sick," she reflected, "but, well, the other thing is I don't get paid if I'm sick."

Sick time, like insurance, could be critical to sustaining an income, but the short-term support that sick days provide is unavailable to contractors. Even after years with a single client, a contractor rarely, if ever, receives compensation for time away from work because of illness. When asked what would make his working life better, Blaine, a programmer and test engineer, quickly responded, "Sick leave would be nice." A minor illness had cost him several days at work, he continued, and the loss of income had been notable. "That's a little dollar sign with a circle around it and a line through it," he elaborated, "no sick days, no holidays, no vacation for contractors." The contractors I interviewed emphasized this difference: a contractor is paid only for the time devoted to work and must fund any unplanned downtime, including time spent for health care. Lack of vacation time was a similar problem, but vacations were, at least, voluntary. Illness, in contrast, could be devastating.

Brenda, a programmer and systems analyst, was my only informant who revealed a medical condition that had cost months away from work. "About half my clients know about my health condition," she explained, "and the other half don't. It all depends on the character of the client." Aware that a chronic illness might affect her employability, Brenda always concealed her condition until she had established a working relationship she could trust. Fortunately, long periods of remission had allowed her illness to go unnoticed. "I'm very lucky to be working at all," she reflected. "I also have a gold-plated disability policy,... and if I had remained somebody else's employee, I couldn't even have been eligible to buy it." Paradoxically, Brenda believed she was better insured as a contractor. "I needed to go contract to get control of my insurance," she mused.

Left alone to navigate the market, however, a contractor can just as easily come up short. When describing the limits of available insurance, my informants cited a number of compromises and stopgap measures. Some had found scaled-down health plans at lower cost. Some had established special savings accounts as a hedge against future need. Others were cutting corners in ways that could prove costly. Jason, a programmer and single parent, had decided to buy health insurance only for his children. "I don't take life insurance or disability insurance," he explained, "and I'm continuing with health insurance for my two kids but not myself.... I just figure my health is pretty good, and maybe in another year I'll get it." Although his choice was atypical among the contractors I interviewed, Jason's predicament—rising costs and no affordable benefits—was all too common. Faced with few desirable options, contractors can find themselves assuming considerable risk.

Staffing agencies sometimes offer health insurance and other benefits, which may approximate the packages available to employees. A few of my informants described benefit packages that had improved during economic upturns, as recruiters competed for contractors in a tight labor market. Contractors who depended on staffing agencies for insurance, however, were either tied to the agency as a constant source of work or forced to make frequent changes, which often meant incurring waiting periods until coverage became available. Roland, a programmer and project manager, described the gaps in health care he had incurred: "Most of the recruiting agencies that I've dealt with and all the ones I've signed on with have a medical package.... Generally you get pretty much the same benefit package you do working for a regular employer.... [But] since I've never stayed with any recruiting agency...they generally don't have another job available right afterwards.... I end up canceling coverage." High mobility makes any employer-sponsored insurance a patchwork arrangement of short-term coverage and transitional gaps, which not all contractors can fill on their own.

A lack of insurance extends to transitional income between assignments, to cover the downtime that most contractors face at some point in their careers. During downtime, a contractor can approximate a laid-off employee experiencing "frictional" unemployment while seeking a new job. An employee, however, might be eligible to collect unemployment insurance for some defined period.[8] As a system of income support, unemployment insurance is premised on the recognition that workers occasionally lose their jobs for reasons beyond their control. This system, however, presumes a standard job with a single employer. Independent contactors "on 1099" are thus consistently excluded.

For contractors "on W-2," usually working through staffing agencies, defining a layoff and eligibility for benefits is a judgment call. Bernice, an editor and indexer, described her struggle to collect compensation:

> I got a letter from the unemployment office saying that my unemployment
> claim was being contested because the agency said that I wasn't laid off; I had

quit. And so then I had to contact the unemployment office and say no, that I actually was laid off, but as it turned out, what had happened...was that they had called me, oh, the day after my contract had ended and said that, oh, you know, they could probably find me something else. And I said no.

Bernice's story illustrates the mismatch between contract work and a system of unemployment compensation designed for those with standard jobs. With insurance available only after working on an agency payroll, she could be deemed ineligible for refusing a new assignment. As her employer, therefore, the agency could redefine the terms of her employment and, having offered her a new contract for a much lower wage, could claim that she had precipitously quit. In this case, Bernice had prevailed. "I just had to write a statement explaining my situation and what I was doing to find a job," she explained.

The varying regulations across the United States make collecting unemployment insurance haphazard. Not only can employee status be contested, but also, in some states, a staffing agency would probably have succeeded in denying Bernice's claim.[9] For agency contractors, access to unemployment insurance might come only after having acquiesced to lower wages or undesirable assignments. Yet few of my informants voiced these concerns, and most seemed unaware that they might sometimes claim coverage, at least under certain circumstances. Only two described investigating the possibility but had decided not to try, fearing that they might jeopardize their prospects for future work.

Problems with Payment

My informants described far more assertiveness when clients were late in paying their bills, occasionally by many months. Billing clients after finishing projects or segments of work, contractors typically receive their money at least a few weeks after earning it. Having met their part of the bargain, they expect timely payment. Problems with payment were not the norm among my informants, but almost half raised the issue at some point in our interview. Late payment seemed both insulting and unjust. Kevin, an editor and translator, described his frustration:

With agencies, you know, I've only really been burned once or twice. Once by a company in California that owed me like $2,000 or something, and you know, I jumped on, I got on the phone finally, after 75 or 80 days, and I demanded my money, and I told them what I would do if I didn't get it.... And I started yelling all over the phone. I was livid, and I said, you know, give me your finance person, whatever the term was. So she gave me the person, and I went ballistic, and she said OK. And, you know, next morning it was there.

With staffing agencies in particular, Kevin saw no reason for delay. The agency was in business as a broker, and paying contractors should have been routine.

Even with contracting well institutionalized, several of my informants had faced obstacles affecting payment, both when contracting through an agency and when working "on 1099." Sam, an editor and proofreader, described a client with procedures so complex that he sometimes waited months: "I often don't get paid on time.... And that organization is pretty well organized, but there are so many different possible points at which things can get bottlenecked that in the case of getting a timesheet approved—since it has to go through two or three different people—if one person sits on it, then I don't get paid. And it's the powerlessness that's really annoying." Although he had learned much about his client's internal system, Sam had been unable to speed up the process. Appealing for assistance, he had been doubly offended when one manager described "having to fight" to have his paperwork approved. "That's irresponsible," he exclaimed. "I mean I think I do my work, basically. They should be able to pay me,... [but] the message is 'be thankful you get paid.'"

Myra, an editor and project manager, attributed an especially long delay to an employee's personal crisis: "Right now I'm having a problem with a totally overwhelmed client, and it's ridiculous. I call her now and again, but at this point it's six months, and it's like I just sent her an e-mail—and I felt badly because her mother just died, and I'd really like to stay out of her face—but basically saying, 'Can you get me my payment before quarterly taxes are due, please?'" Like Sam, Myra felt the double standard acutely; she had produced as promised, but the client had failed to pay as they had agreed. Such problems were unusual, Myra assured me, and she was sure they were no reflection on the quality of her work. Rather, the problem rested with the client—an individual employee could affect a contractor's cash flow merely by ignoring a backlog of paperwork. Linda, a software and database developer, reflected on delinquent clients: "How quickly they pay us is much more a function of their competence in paying their bills, rather than how well they think we've done."

The contractors I interviewed described different strategies to prevent late payments. If the assignment was ongoing, they might threaten to stop work until outstanding bills were paid. Some made sure that they documented a payment schedule when agreeing to take the assignment. Most indicated payment terms on their invoices. Once a payment was late, a second invoice, marked overdue, was an appropriate reminder, and two of my informants reported adding interest charges, which underscored their concerns. Although clients rarely, if ever, paid the interest, these contractors hoped the sight of mounting expenses would serve as a warning of pending legal action. When problems arise, contractors have little recourse beyond an appeal to good faith or, if the problem proves intractable, hiring a collection agency or filing a lawsuit for contractual breach.[10]

A few of my informants had managed to forge agreements for immediate payment. Bill, a writer, had established a training business and, for his "training clients," insisted on a down payment and the balance due on the day of a session. "Independent contractors in this industry are finding that we have to say, up front, fifty down now and balance on delivery," he explained. "Go back to what plumbers do, you know." Bill's comparison with plumbers, however, highlights the influence of occupational norms. When working as a writer, he had little choice but to submit his work and wait for payment, but when offering a new service to a larger clientele, he could insist on different terms. Most contractors face similar constraints. Unlike attorneys who deposit retainers and bill against client accounts, few contractors manage to begin work with collected funds. As Darrell, a programmer and project manager, explained, "It's easiest to get somebody to write a check if there's a deliverable that goes along with the check."

During economic downturns, my informants explained, contractors tended to have more problems. For the purposes of cost accounting, they are suppliers of services, technically vendors rather than workers, and when clients manage their cash flow by delaying payments to vendors, contractors also wait. Sherry, an editor, translator, and project manager, had even been warned by her clients: "I actually had editors write me an e-mail and say, 'Bill us. You know, you've been working a long time. Bill us.'" Submitting invoices more often, Sherry had offset some of the delay and had also, she thought, asserted her expertise. "I'm pretty good about billing," she explained. "If I turn in a project, I bill the next day. If I haven't been paid in thirty days, I'll do a follow up."

The most serious problems occurred when a client declared bankruptcy and sought legally to restructure debt. In such cases, a contractor becomes one of many creditors and can be at significant risk of losing all outstanding payments. When the debts of a client reach this stage, they assume an order of priority under law, so that contractors "on 1099" have less standing than employees and less than contractors "on W-2," for whom staffing agencies assume at least a portion of the legal liability. Darrell described "taking a big hit" when one of his clients filed for bankruptcy. "I didn't lose my shirt exactly, but I learned to pay attention to the client's state of affairs," he remembered. The experience, although unusual, remained a stark reminder of market risk.

Problems with payment illustrate a contractor's limited leverage. When a project goes well and all parties are satisfied, a contractor can ignore the risks of contractual status. But a client that fails to meet the terms of an agreement can force a contractor to accommodate. My informants' accounts document many such difficulties: projects cancelled midstream, promised work that never materialized, changes in schedules that left them scrambling either to meet their obligations or to find new work on short notice. These difficulties were frustrating and certainly unfair. But they rarely provoked the raw anger that problems with payment could generate. Compensating for unforeseen problems, a contractor might still negotiate, but waiting for a check from a delinquent client, a contractor can feel all but powerless. A failure in work relations leaves contractors with few options for redress.

The Prospects for Collective Advocacy

The risk of nonpayment suggests a need for formal advocacy, but for contract professionals, few mechanisms exist. Individual litigation is time consuming and expensive; collective advocacy is largely unavailable. Among my informants, the possibility of formal advocacy seemed sometimes attractive, yet the idea, for many, seemed almost far-fetched. In neither occupation does a sizable organization provide significant support to contractors. Nor does either occupation support a professional organization that monitors employment practices. These contract professionals thus have no formal representation for their material interests, much as the industries that employ them similarly include very few unionized employees. As a result, my informants had little experience with work-site advocacy, and their attitudes toward collective organization reflected an individualism consistent with their experience in both contract employment and standard jobs.

Attitudes and Impediments

Ruminating about client conflict, Ezra, a software developer, considered a contractor's mobility the most likely resolution. "If the relationship between me and my employer reaches the point where we need a third-party mediator, we've already failed," he reflected. "I wouldn't want to stay in a job where I thought the only way that I could function with my managers is I need a mediator to keep the relationship going." With a favorable labor market and an expansive network, Ezra saw little reason to invest in resolving disputes. If a working relationship proved too contentious, he could cut his losses and move on. Pay levels, too, were more than adequate in his field, "even ridiculously high sometimes," he believed. Yet on further reflection, he added, "I've managed to stay in a situation where I don't feel the need [for collective representation], but when I look at the overall situation, it's well, you know, there's something not right here that needs to be fixed ... for at least some people, ... employees especially."

Ezra was one of several contractors who considered collective advocacy more critical for employees. Jackie, a software engineer recalled her experience in a series of standard jobs:

> When I was full time [an employee] now, I believed that they needed a union; I really did. They were being pressured, or I was being pressured, into fitting ten pounds of potatoes in a five-pound bag, and you can't do it. I mean you cannot work ten, twelve, fourteen hours a day, seven days a week, every day of the week, every month of the year. And yet they [her employer] thought that was OK on salary, and they thought their little bonuses, extra vacation days were worth it.

Although a standard job might come with perks, Jackie considered the demands "abusive." Like many of my informants, she believed that employers exploited salaried employees more than they did contractors, who were at least paid for the time they worked. Employees, she noted, more often "burned out" or lost their jobs before they could collect their promised rewards. Her choice to contract, in this context, was a kind of individual protest.

Ellie, a writer and editor, concurred. "I do think that the people who are in production at [client's name] might very much need advocacy, and I would support that to the absolute max," she explained. Employees, she believed, should "band together when they need to." Yet for contractors her attitude was equivocal. "It's hard for me to imagine advocacy for a class of freelance editors unless there are some standards to which editors have [been] held," she reflected. "How can you demand rights for a group when there's no way of knowing who's in the group,... whether these people, you know, you would want to advocate for them?" For Ellie, as for several of my informants, advocacy for contractors should depend on occupational performance. A willingness to join with colleagues and support collective advocacy would thus depend on the company she might keep.

Ellie's concern reflects the self-regulation that contractors assume. Cognizant of their reputations, many of the contractors I interviewed seemed similarly loath to join forces with colleagues whose abilities or reputations they did not know. Although they might share common interests, need similar services, and even enjoy one another's company, formal advocacy on behalf of an individual could constitute an endorsement of someone who had failed to measure up. Katherine, a programmer and database manager, made the point succinctly. "You'd have to know who you're supporting, whether you'd want to go to bat for them in a situation," she cautioned. Such wariness may help to explain the lack of occupation-based collective action among contract professionals. The same informal mechanisms that promote self-regulation may also undermine solidarity and support.[11]

Although few of my informants had sought some form of advocacy, an awareness of risk caused many to be circumspect. Terry, a programmer and project manager, acknowledged the pervasive inequality between contractor and client:

> One of the things you find out as a contractor very quickly if you're not totally oblivious of the world around you is that the reason anybody out there for the most part cares a whole hell of a lot about your individual situation is

the employer wants somebody to do the work. If they run out of money, the fact that your kid is still in college or you have this big medical debt doesn't matter. Contract's done. Business decision. You're out of here.

Contractors, Terry knew from experience, can be dismissed precipitously, sometimes without regard for a formal written agreement. Tony, a software developer and systems designer, reflected on the irony of having a contract, which in principle binds the client as well as the contractor. "A contractor doesn't have a *real* contract," he emphasized. "You don't have that kind of security."

A "real contract," Tony implied, would be fully enforceable. If the contract stipulated a period of employment, then the client would be responsible for providing at least partial payment. The norms of contracting, however, give the client the leverage to renege, sometimes with impunity, and the need for future work can make contractors wary about asserting the contractual terms, even when they might prevail. Many of my informants reflected on this disparity. During good times, when work was plentiful, a capable contractor could recover quickly from the shock of a cancelled contract. When the labor market was slack, however, the loss of work could become a serious blow. Considering the consequences, Tony continued, "Then there are people…who don't have any leverage,…so it would be useful in that sense to have some organization backing you up."

Donald, an editor and production manager, was facing just such a situation on the day of our interview. His principal client, a publishing firm, had been sold, and he was anticipating change: "I might lose my job in a day to somebody who was just hired by the company that bought them [his client] out," he complained. "I mean that I should have some level of security, knowing that I've put in this time and I do good work. But I don't because I'm a contractor, and the person who will replace me will be a contractor, just maybe a contractor hired by the new parent company." A laid-off employee, Donald noted, would be eligible for unemployment compensation, but as a contractor, he had no comparable support. Without terms that forced his client to pay for canceling their agreement, he alone assumed the risks of dismissal without cause. Considering the problem, Donald proposed as an alternative: "a minimal amount of security," he suggested, the same idea as severance. You [the client] should have to pay to get rid of me. We should be able to demand that."

Cancellation fees might accomplish the same purpose, but these were far from common in either occupational group. A contractor might be paid a "kill fee"[12] when a client rejected work already completed, but always in such cases the contractor was short-changed. Janice had expected a project fee, payable on completion, but the client had by then deleted her segment of the project. "They were pleased with it, but they had decided that they weren't going to use it," she elaborated. "What happened was I said, 'Look, I'm going to take you to court, and I'm really, really angry about this.' And so basically, they said, 'How about if we offer you $200 less?' So I said, 'Fine. I'll take it,' 'cause I really didn't want to spend a lot of time in court." Janice faced a trade-off: even without an attorney, a legal challenge would cost more in unbillable time than the $200 she had lost. A few years later, she was "still very angry" and noted in passing, "That would be a good reason for an advocacy group."

Disputes with clients—at least overt conflicts—were rare among my informants. Conflict avoidance, their accounts suggest, is one component of a contractor's expertise. Some thus expressed discomfort with the notion of unqualified support for their colleagues' individual grievances. Contractors, they implied, "should" be able to manage relationships and "should" keep their skills and networks current and be ready to move on. But a delinquent client that reneged on an agreement was for them a social problem that no one should have to solve alone. Recognizing the limits of individual assertion, they could support a collective effort that addressed at least this common concern.

Structural barriers, however, curtail collective advocacy. Most notable in U.S. law is the statutory exclusion that denies independent contractors a legal right to collective bargaining.[13] Contractors "on W-2" and nominally employees might, technically, organize to bargain collectively, but their dispersal across work sites and their status as joint employees—of both staffing agencies and client firms—renders this right all but inaccessible. In the United States, union representation sanctioned by labor law typically requires a single employer and a defined unit of employees who share a "community of interest."[14] Across this stable community, contract terms render work relations uniform. For contract professionals, in contrast, mobile occupational communities span multiple clients; contract terms differ from one setting to the next; and market mediation through staffing agencies defines some contractors as employees. These formal distinctions and malleable, cross-cutting networks are an exceedingly poor fit for the current system of collective representation.

Small-Scale Efforts, Limited Results

Only a few occupation-based organizations have made advocacy for contractors a central mission. Rather, most local and national associations that include these contract professionals have a broader membership, including employees, managers, and sometimes educators who share topical interests in an industry, technology, or area of expertise. Usually focused on specific occupational segments, these organizations can be valuable for networking, and some further provide educational forums or training programs of interest to contractors. Very few, however, offer any form of collective representation that might enforce agreements with clients. The few organizations seeking to represent contractors in specific occupations have instead been local projects, often with scant resources or a limited geographical reach.[15]

Two such organizations have been, at different times, the Freelance Editorial Association, based in Boston from 1983 to 1999,[16] and the Washington Alliance of Technology Workers (WashTech),[17] based in Seattle and founded in 1998. From its inception, each organization sought to advocate for contractors. Most members of the Freelance Editorial Association were editorial professionals with a range of related skills and a varied clientele. In its first few years, WashTech focused principally on technical contractors, including programmers and writers who produced technical documents. Although their members constitute different labor market segments, these organizations illustrate similar possibilities and limitations for representing contractors' interests.

Both organizations remained small, relative to the population of potential members,[18] and both sought to recruit members by offering services—forums, meetings, information—to anyone interested in the message.[19] Casting a wide net gained visibility but also created a free-rider problem because a segment of services became available to those not paying dues.[20] To develop incentives for membership, WashTech developed training programs covering occupational trends, and the Freelance Editorial Association created a "members' network" that connected individuals seeking specific kinds of information. Both organizations thus sought to attract and retain members by appealing to work-related needs.

For both organizations, however, concerted challenges to specific clients proved difficult to mount. Resource constraints posed some problems, but a constantly changing membership, with no definite count of its potential size, meant neither organization could claim a significant segment of contractors working for any client, industry, or sector. Both organizations, therefore, turned to targeted media and popular education to challenge practices that members deemed unfair. WashTech established a website to post research and news supporting policy initiatives on issues affecting technical workers. The Freelance Editorial Association published a *Code of Fair Practice* that defined fair contract terms, including cancellation fees when clients pulled projects and reservation fees when a delayed start date incurred unplanned downtime.[21] In different ways, both organizations sought to address collective interests by influencing occupational norms.

Both organizations also sought to build communities of interest by linking contractors across multiple work sites and types of clients. With a mobile—and potentially global—workforce, occupational connections could fill ongoing needs for information and assistance. Programs that provide these services represent a form of mutual aid, elsewhere associated with member involvement to generate relationships and promote intra-organizational cohesion.[22] Still, for these organizations of contractors, limited membership and legal obstacles effectively prevented formal negotiation, which might more directly represent collective interests. Without a shift in policy promoting multiple models for representation, a small, fluid membership constrains collective clout.

Market Mediation as Representation

The constraints to collective advocacy faced by these contractors' organizations contrast sharply with the system of representation associated with the staffing industry. By placing contractors on their payrolls, staffing agencies act as employers, but by negotiating agreements, they also mediate work relations, claiming to address the interests of both contractors and clients.[23] Although the staffing industry as a whole encompasses day labor and low-wage temporary work, for which exploitative practices are well documented,[24] many agencies that mediate higher-wage employment also provide services that can meet contractors' needs.[25] Packages of benefits, access to training, even backstage support for a contractor's performance can be important to some contractors, in some circumstances. These services, however, come at the cost of the agency markup, essentially a fee paid as a percentage of the contractor's hourly rate.

The agency contractors I interviewed knew that the bill rate paid to an agency was always higher than the rates they received, and although they could only speculate about the markup, many believed that staffing agencies, in general, received far more than they had earned. Lori, a programmer, considered the markup "an enormous cut...I mean it's probably twenty-five percent. Sometimes I've heard it's as high as forty percent." Although Lori did use the services of recruiters when looking for work, she also took assignments that lasted months, or even years. For an agency, therefore, she represented a significant source of revenue: "I mean maybe, let's just say they spend a week even, one person placing me, and then maybe they have to have a payroll. They pay me, so there's some small cost incurred there. But they're probably making $30,000, $40,000, $50,000 a year off me for at most probably forty hours a year worth of work." Such a profit margin, Lori thought, should buy her some support in case of conflict with a client, but a recent altercation had shown her the limits of the willingness of one agency to intervene.

Her track record with this agency, Lori knew, had proved her competent and reliable, and despite a few difficulties, she had not complained. At one site, however, she and another contractor had been directly threatened by a manager. "He'd talk about all these guns and everything," she remembered, "and then he'd like be in your face, like five inches from your face, with this maniacal laugh....I was really, actually a little afraid of him." Lori and her colleague had responded to the bullying by asking the agency to intervene, but in response, they received only sympathy: "We knew the agency, the people there, and said, 'Look, this is not a good situation.'...And they said, 'OK, we'll try to help you out. We'll try to make things better. We'll try to solve some of these issues.' And things just weren't happening. Things were not getting solved, and I was really worried about this guy." As the threats escalated, Lori decided to leave. "I'd never done that, but I just felt that, I really felt uncomfortable there," she recalled. Lori had anticipated protracted downtime, but to her surprise, the agency quickly offered another assignment. "The agency placed me on the job that I'm here on now that following Monday, for more money," she noted.

The readiness of the agency to replace a problem client—and in the process to raise her hourly rate—indicated to Lori that the recruiter had understood. This time, at least, her recent track record had provided leverage. The lack of support, however, indicated the priorities of the agency, and as long as she was willing to remain with the client, Lori now believed, no agency would be likely to assist. Even when she might have been in danger, the agency had an incentive to retain her at a client site. Depending on the markup on services for their revenues, staffing agencies share with the contractors on their payrolls a concern for good performance. Their longer-term interests, however, align with their clients. When conflicts arise, therefore, an agency is rarely prepared to represent the contractor.

When their clients, together with the U.S. tax code, demanded the intercession of an agency, the contractors I interviewed had come to accept the formalities of working "on W-2." Some, too, had established relationships with recruiters who had helped to keep them employed. More often, however, they described these relations as business transactions. Jeffrey, a software engineer, applied a more graphic metaphor. "I look at the temporary help companies; really they're no different than the pimp on the street," he explained. "They take a large percentage of the money. And when I'm done and no longer usable, they ditch me." Gary, an editor and production manager, considered the agency's markup a form of "skimming," and he elaborated, "I know that most of the people [agencies] can make big bucks for their services.... It just means we're underpaid." If a client could pay the agency bill rate, Gary implied, more of the fee should go to the contractor.

In a study of staffing industry practices, Isabel Fernandez-Mateo (2007) finds that agencies designated as preferred vendors lowered contractors' wages by passing on the discounts they offered their client firms. These findings confirm the suspicions expressed by several of my informants. Agency practices, they speculated, rarely promoted contractors' interests, despite the appearance of negotiating on their behalf. Most threatening to some were restrictions on individual mobility imposed by the ubiquitous noncompete clauses, which prevent a contractor from accepting repeat business from a client without the intercession of the same agency. Non-compete clauses apply these restrictions for different periods, some as short as six months, others as long as several years, and the language is often so vague that the contractor is left unsure of its scope, which might apply only to a single department or more broadly to an entire firm or even to the subsidiaries of a large client. Linda, a software and database developer, summarized these concerns: "Agencies are very restrictive agreements. They limit your right to contract within the company. So I mean that's your life blood, is meeting people and impressing people and have them bring you in to do work. And you can't go back. You can't do this. You can't do that. And then they don't pay you anywhere near as well."

Noncompete clauses and the restrictions they impose represent a mechanism through which staffing industry practices formalize contract employment and inhibit a contractor's scope of action.[26] Such terms, my informants asserted, undermine the fluidity of contracting, which gives them the advantage of participating in establishing client relations. In contrast, when dealing with staffing agencies, many faced formal constraints. Rebecca, a writer and editor, recalled two agencies at which "pay grades" had established her hourly rate and then prevented her from "jumping a grade" for a subsequent assignment, even one involving far more responsibility. "I was handicapped by [name of agency] because they were in charge of negotiation," she explained. "So I couldn't just say, 'Let's take a look at what I'm doing and how I'm doing it and what your objectives are.'...I feel I came to use my skills,...but they definitely wanted me to get less money or, well, keep it the same....They had these rules about increments." Frustrated by the intransigence and unable to represent herself, Rebecca had moved on when her contract expired. "My job was actually ongoing," she explained, "but they just didn't have the professionalism."

Professionalism, Rebecca implied, would have allowed her the latitude to identify the needs of the client and apply her skills to agreed-on goals. Some of the recruiters she knew had indeed encouraged her to negotiate with clients over the work required, sometimes before she agreed to a rate. In contrast, an agency with job categories and gradations of pay seemed less like a mediator and more like an employer with an internal hierarchy and a system of work rules. Classifying her "skill level" and limiting the pace at which her rate could rise further approximated the formal systems associated with internal labor markets, but without the legal rights or structural authority that came with a standard job.

Bernice had encountered similar rigidities. "The only way I've been able to negotiate anything with them is based on past salary," she explained, "that I was making a certain amount and then like going to a new position that I would like to be making more." Because of her earlier rate, however, Bernice had been told to "wait a year or so" before receiving a higher fee, which seemed far from automatic. "It all depends, you know, so they'll tell me later on." The regulations seemed similar to the conditions of standard employment, but nowhere were the specifics spelled out. "The agencies need to come clean," she complained, "because...they hide these little things that they're doing." With agency incentives to limit both her fees and her mobility, Bernice saw little likelihood that these market intermediaries would represent her fairly.

My informants' accounts lead to the same conclusions. At best, a recruiter is a benign broker, trafficking information and providing a service that both contractor and client might need. As a business, however, a staffing agency has interests that conflict fundamentally with a contractor's efforts to develop client relations and negotiate project terms. A contractor's viability depends largely on the latitude to navigate an external labor market. Bernice thus proposed new policies. "What we need are better standards, but at least standards," she believed. "That way the agencies won't be so much in control."

Standards and Regulations

Standards, Bernice implied, might provide leverage when staffing agencies or clients firms failed to adhere to an agreement. Standards for contract professionals might codify occupational norms that allow a contactor to assess a project before accepting the terms of the client. Standards might define as billable time the work-based communication and social interaction required to maintain client relations. Standards would most certainly hold clients to payment schedules and might even promote late fees when a bill went unpaid. Formal standards would provide a solid basis for establishing client relations and for appeals in case of dispute. Lacking formal mechanisms for enforcement, however, standards alone can do little to protect contractors' interests or change the conditions of their employment.

When the contractors I interviewed spoke of standards, they often meant professional competence and accountability to their clients, the standards to which they held themselves and one another. Familiar with occupational practices that had taught them the norms of contracting, most linked their personal standards to their employability and expertise. High standards, they believed, maintained their positions in the external labor market and protected their autonomy. Talk of formal standards, in this context, seemed unnecessary or even threatening. To codify occupational standards, some of my informants implied, was to challenge their status as expert practitioners. Many associated standards with the relative rigidity of standard employment, a system of work relations that had frequently failed to deliver on promises of fairness, security, or success.

The prospect of standards for contract employment can thus provoke simultaneous antipathy and appeal. Standards, my informants knew, can provide a means for establishing accountability and measuring performance, but the development and application of standards depend on who sets and enforces them. Standards offer protection, but their control also limits autonomy. The prospect of standardization, in turn, invokes the specter of uniformity, symbolized by the industrial assembly line or the rabbit warren of individual cubicles. Standards, these images suggest, can diminish individuals' influence over decisions affecting their work. For many of the contract professionals I met, nonstandard work represented an escape from standards and from the rationalized organizations that contained standard jobs. Any process of standard setting, therefore, was potentially a source of conflict.

Indeed, standard employment, as understood through much of the twentieth century, is itself an outcome of class conflict and political compromise. The standard job that emerged in the United States and elsewhere once facilitated regulation, providing a basis for extending legal rights and social benefits. With jobs structures defined, policies could apply to broad segments of the workforce, and the resulting regulations could define principles, such as fair labor standards, which guaranteed minimum wages and maximum hours, and antidiscrimination, which offered redress for disparities in hiring, pay, and promotion. Standard employment thus became a mechanism for promoting social and economic equality.

The diminishing reach of standard employment points to a need to re-consider a system based on a single standard. Nonstandard work and con-tingent status necessitate new policies to promote inclusion and equality in a workforce increasingly marked by both social diversity and structural difference. No single standard can accommodate this complexity. Nor can singular notions of contingent status as subordinate and substandard cap-ture the variety of work arrangements, which now range across a broad spectrum of occupations and industries. Nonstandard employment thus represents a segment of workers whose experiences policymakers have largely ignored.

For contract professionals in particular, new policies might sustain em-ployability by offering greater security and support. A system of insurance either universally available or tied to occupation or employment sector, rather than employer, would be an important first step. Left to the mar-ket to meet individual needs, contractors face the twin prospects of grow-ing risks and rising costs. Packages of portable benefits would sever the connection between social insurance and standard employment and thus provide ongoing protection without constantly opening gaps. Bundles of benefits might include the equivalent of unemployment compensation, perhaps a kind of wage insurance, for unwanted downtime. By administer-ing social insurance, new occupational mechanisms might further provide the basis for a system of collective representation and support in occasional disputes.[27]

Occupational representation might also offer ongoing access to infor-mation about clients and trends. A clearinghouse of connections—which in the twenty-first century would most certainly be online—might link disparate groups of contractors and support the informal exchanges in which these practitioners engage. Information might extend to postings of available contract assignments or notices about clients with upcoming needs. Such a mechanism would, in turn, curtail the control of staffing agencies and support contractors' individual agency to act on their own be-half. Meeting individual needs, such a resource would probably gain cred-ibility among large numbers of contractors. New institutions supporting occupational mobility could, in turn, reconstruct opportunities, providing larger groups of workers with a greater range of options.

The divided labor markets in which contractors move now present a stark contrast: the rigidity of standard employment versus the fluidity of contracting with all its attendant risks. Attention to the risks, rights, and benefits across these and other occupations might ultimately mean greater convergence, erasing some of the sharp distinctions that now mark these two forms of work.[28] Equality, however, need not depend on uniformity. Nor should flexibility demand trade-offs that institutionalize disadvantage. Standardization, as this book suggests, no longer serves to raise standards for large segments of the workforce. A reconsideration of employment relations, therefore, should accommodate structural differences across multiple work arrangements.

Conclusion

What, then, can the accounts of these contract professionals reveal about the new economy? How might their experiences explain new patterns of autonomy and constraint? What might they portend for employment relations in a global age? The expansion of contracting represents one dimension of the new economy, a structural shift in paid employment in which flexibility has become the byword, signifying the malleability of work relations and the ever-present possibility of change. All workers, even those who remain firmly lodged in standard jobs, now confront, in some form, the unpredictability of a volatile economy. The security once implied by a full-time regular job with a stable employer has become increasingly rare.

Flexibility further encapsulates a cultural shift that demands resilience in the face of change. Gone are the well-defined terms of standard employment, which offered the commitment of an employer in return for good performance. Instead, exposed to the risks of the market, workers shoulder the responsibility for remaining employable. In the new economy, individuals might exercise a range of options, but when change comes fast or frequently, they may have little choice but to adapt. For the contractors in this study, the imperatives of flexibility rationalized their position outside an internal labor market. Charting their own course, they might accommodate family life and other pursuits. Outside the boundaries of employing organizations, they could forge occupational connections and develop shared norms. Marginalized in client firms, they could defend their professional standards. Far from an isolated, atomized workforce, these professionals established infrastructures that supported external labor markets and occupational cultures that regulated their working lives.

Contracting in Practice

Contractors, by their own accounts, are strategic actors, presenting themselves as skilled, capable, and ready to meet the needs of their clients. To maintain their viability in the market, they maintain ties with colleagues, managers, and recruiters at staffing agencies, which in some cases act as intermediaries between contractors and client firms. The interactional processes that produce and sustain these relationships require an expertise beyond the execution of work-related tasks. A contractor needs to be capable but needs also to gain the confidence of the client and establish authority over occupational practice. Contracting, for those who do it, is a command performance through which a careful self-presentation promotes trust in a contractor's abilities and supports an assertion of expertise.

The occupational dynamics of contracting constitute a relational system with its own norms, processes, and mechanisms of control. In contradistinction to the standard job, fixed within an organizational hierarchy, contracting is fluid and flexible. The processes that sustain it further support a dual system of employment relations encompassing internal and external labor markets. For managers in employing organizations, contracting offers staffing options, with a segment of an occupational workforce situated outside the formal regulation of much public policy and organizational practice. For contractors, the same system offers an alternative opportunity structure based on negotiated agreements and lateral mobility across multiple client firms. Outside formal systems of organizational status and authority, contractors depend on occupational networks of similarly situated colleagues who become sources of social identity and informal professional oversight.

Despite its apparent informality, contracting is a well-institutionalized arrangement. Operating in tandem with standard employment and organization-based jobs, it is also a temporal construction: short term and wage based, distinct from the salaried careers of employees who perform much the same work. Hour for hour, contractors can net comparable, or even higher, incomes than their salaried counterparts in standard jobs, whose rewards for long hours and good performance come principally—when they come at all—as raises and promotions at some future time. In contrast, contracting offers a quicker market exchange and an orderly series of related processes through which practitioners find clients, negotiate the scope of their authority, and then move on to new assignments and new clients. These processes promote contractors' mobility across multiple employing organizations. They also demand a working knowledge of occupational practices and an awareness of internal organizational structures that can affect individual success.

When these contract professionals judged themselves successful, they credited both their expertise and their abilities to establish professional credibility. For them, flexible work relations required vigilance. Negotiating terms and tasks for each new assignment, they navigated the contradictions between participation in client firms and disengagement from internal conflict. Charting careers outside the more established paths offering incremental promotions, they sought to leverage their experience, one project at a time, to find professional challenge and financial reward. By attending to the microprocesses that sustained client relations, they sought to remain employable. Aware of their marginal position relative to employees, they reinforced the status distinctions of contracting. However engaging the project or congenial the environment, they were always prepared to move on.

Released from the strictures of the standard job, most of the contractors who informed this study prized the relative flexibility of their contractual status. None, however, voiced the grand claims of free agency, unencumbered by external constraints, so audible in segments of the popular press. Rather, these practitioners consciously exercised an autonomy constrained by prevailing practices, client expectations, and labor market conditions. Outside the more formal systems that define the terms of organizational membership, they adhered to occupational norms that could exert considerable control. When accounting for their time, they tracked their billable hours or, when receiving project-based fees, enforced an efficiency not required of their counterparts in standard jobs. Flexibility, their accounts reveal, is a relative phenomenon, experienced not as an absolute set of criteria but as a contrast to the rigidities of standard employment in these two occupational groups.

What, then, can these practitioners reveal about the system of contract employment? Contracting is both a social location and an experiential condition. On the margins of client firms, contractors face exposure to the market, without even the promise of security or the protection of formal regulation. Yet, left alone to manage the ambiguities of their contractual status, they develop strategies to establish their expertise and maintain their employability. The contractors in this study presented themselves as experts, asserted authority over tasks, reassured their clients, and engendered trust in their abilities. Managing the expectations of their clients, they also managed the impressions they conveyed. Whereas a confident performance could sustain client relations, expertise was a social accomplishment, the outcome of effective work-based interaction.

Even a well-honed performance, however, requires a contractor to navigate contradictions between autonomy and constraint. Narrowly focused on the content of their work, contract professionals must remain accountable for their time and progress toward meeting the goals of their clients. Aware of internal conflict that might affect their success, the contractors I met monitored the boundaries that marked the limits of their involvement in client organizations. Attentive to interactional cues that signal the terms of participation, they relied on informal exchange to assure consent for goals, tasks, and time lines. Disengaged from the politics that seemed to inform the exercise of managerial authority, they actively maintained their distance. Patterns of interaction thus supported the structural distinction between contract work and the standard job.

Although they remained marginal in client firms, these contractors were active participants in their respective occupations. All had, to some degree, established networks of boundary-spanning relationships that supported ongoing, reciprocal exchange. Networks might buffer a contractor from protracted periods of unemployment, or downtime, with referrals to new clients. Networks could provide information about new developments in a field. Although exposed to an unfettered market, which offered no promises of ongoing demand for their services, these contingent workers had found refuge in networks that constituted informal work-based communities. There they might achieve occupational status outside the formal authority of an organizational position.

With experience in volatile organizations, these practitioners had come to see contract employment as a sensible alternative, a choice most often informed by their experiences as employees. Their choices thus depended on the available options in their respective occupations. Far from the cultural ideal promising stability and opportunity in return for hard work and compliance with employer demands, the standard jobs they knew were more often located in unstable, ever-changing environments. When uncertainty prevailed, reconfigured hierarchies could obstruct opportunity; internal conflict could impede individual progress; and distant decision makers could undermine prospects for successful careers. In this context, contracting appeared no less tenuous than standard employment. The choice to contract, as these practitioners understood it, was an implicit critique of employing organizations and the conditions imposed by the standard job.

The Context of Contingent Work: What Distinguishes Contracting?

Contract employment in these two occupations is distinctly different from many other forms of nonstandard, contingent work. Its form may be similar to much temporary employment—short term, tenuous, and sometimes mediated by a staffing agency—but its labor market structures and occupational processes present important contrasts. Clerical and industrial temps, the prototype for the contingent worker, are more often subject to multiple processes of external control that render them subordinate, both in markets for their services and in client firms. Most earn less than their counterparts in standard jobs; few have incomes adequate to buy the benefits of standard employment; most have little chance to earn the respect of colleagues, including managers and employees; and most depend exclusively on staffing agencies, which can demand adherence to formal policies that limit their options and devalue their abilities. Clearly, much temporary employment has institutionalized new workforce inequalities and so informed claims that contingent status in any form is a social problem.

The experiences of these contract professionals confound this claim. Although contractors' tenuous agreements with clients are no less contingent than those of most temps, the contractors in this study described greater negotiating leverage in their dealings with both clients and recruiters. Some used their contractual status to meet personal needs for temporal flexibility, often to accommodate paid work with family responsibilities or to pursue personal interests. Others considered their lack of formal position an asset that removed them from organizational conflict that might otherwise limit their professional development. Even those who depended principally on staffing agencies as sources of work described greater autonomy to chart their own course than temporary workers have in clerical and industrial settings. What, then, accounts for this difference?

Expertise, often defined as human capital, provides a common explanation. Contract professionals bring to their assignments identifiable skills and knowledge. They have invested considerable time and effort learning their occupations, sometimes through formal education and usually through years of experience in standard jobs where they learned the norms and processes that facilitate their mobility. Their expertise is thus a combination of knowledge, skill, and capacity to learn, which produces value and provides labor market leverage. By attending to their occupations, contractors maintain their abilities with an eye toward market exchange. High market demand, in turn, enhances their prospects for long-term viability outside standard employment.

But high demand and expertise are only a partial explanation for contractors' market leverage. Demand can be highly variable, especially in industries vulnerable to boom-and-bust cycles, and in economic downturns, oversupplied human capital may fail to sustain practitioners' livelihoods. Despite extensive workforce experience and well-documented expertise, contract professionals face the ever-present prospect of downtime and the possibility that their human capital will depreciate. The expertise associated with specific technologies might become obsolete, or occupational change might demand a grasp of new practices. An investment in human capital alone cannot account for the differences between the labor markets for these contract professionals and the markets for lower-wage temporary workers.

The portability of skills also fails fully to explain these differences. Although contractors do, indeed, move readily across the boundaries of multiple client firms, other skilled workers in nonstandard arrangements move just as readily, but at a significant disadvantage. The conditions for adjunct faculty offer a clear comparative case. Despite years of educational investment, advanced degrees, and, for some instructors, much professional experience, contingent faculty have little leverage in an occupational labor market for academic services. Like clerical and industrial temps, their work is devalued relative to their counterparts in standard jobs, and although many move easily from one institutional setting to the next, mobility into standard employment is far more difficult. For most adjunct faculty, the lack of a stable affiliation is a mark of subordination in both their employing organizations and their academic fields. Here the value of human capital depends not only on expertise but also on the practitioner's relationship to a formal organization, which further informs occupational status.

Across occupations, therefore, different labor market structures create different conditions for individual agency. Distinguishing factors include the relative valuation of standard and nonstandard employment and the ease with which workers may move, without social or economic penalty, across the boundary between the internal and external segments of an occupational labor market. The contract professionals in this study reported few such penalties. With incomes equivalent to the employees they saw as peers, they considered their work to be valued comparably, although rewarded differently, and they considered themselves equals in their respective occupations. They further described multiple avenues for career mobility, including a return to standard employment, which might occur several times in a career. For them, the options for professional practice remained open, with fewer labor market obstacles than other contingent workers face. Contingent status is thus neither a mark of subordination nor a barrier to career advancement over time.

Labor market structures also promote contractors' participation in their respective occupations. With their boundary-spanning networks of colleagues, clients, and recruiters, contract professionals can demonstrate their competence among a range of social actors. In collegial interaction—whether at work or "off the clock"—they can claim authority by performing expertise. Embedded in occupational communities, they can establish occupational status despite the lack of stable affiliations and formal titles that signal authority. Unlike occupations in which a nonstandard work arrangement signifies subordination, contingent status here carries little, if any, stigma.

Differences across labor market structures, therefore, offer a more comprehensive explanation for the relative agency of these contract professionals. Unlike markets that construct disadvantage, the structures that these contractors navigate promote their mobility without the subordination typical of much contingent work. A lack of market control by staffing agencies is one important factor. Although some contractors do turn to agencies when seeking new assignments, they may also find work on their own, and even when relying entirely on recruiters, most maintain other occupational connections from which opportunities for employment might also arise. In contrast to other forms of temporary work, these labor markets remain accessible through multiple channels. Networks of similarly situated practitioners mitigate the social closure that staffing agencies have established in markets for temporary clerical and industrial services.

The occupational culture sustained by these networks also constrains and controls occupational practice. Network dynamics allow contractors to act as gatekeepers who monitor the performances of colleagues as they determine whom to refer. Whether in person or online, collegial communication becomes a forum for professional scrutiny as contractors assess their colleagues' abilities and seek to present themselves as capable. The processes associated with networking, therefore, might address individual needs but also serve the interests of clients, who depend on reliable sources of information when procuring contractors' services. Accountable and self-regulating, contractors can be trusted, at least in part, because concern for a good reputation provides an incentive for adhering to occupational norms and addressing the goals of the client.

Paradoxically, these same regulatory processes promote contractors' autonomy. Although a performance may, on occasion, require backstage support, contractors' concern for reputation and their expressed commitment to high standards purchase an independence from direct managerial scrutiny. Developing their own resources and mobilizing their networks, these contract professionals are individual agents, conveying confidence in their abilities. Like their counterparts in standard jobs, they exercise considerable latitude in the execution and coordination of tasks. They can then approach each new client, setting, or project with a presumption of autonomy that renders them less vulnerable than lower-wage contingent workers. Labor market structures facilitate decentralized occupational processes that enhance their individual agency.

Risk and Opportunity: How Do They Intersect?

A growing body of research now attests to variation in the operation of external labor markets and points to differences in risks and opportunities across segments of the contingent workforce. Most contingent workers, however, remain organizational outsiders, with only limited access to internal opportunity structures that might enhance their long-term prospects. Most also remain subject, to some degree, to the control of market intermediaries or to an ever-changing demand for their specific sets of skills. Outside the shelter of standard employment, they assume a structural risk that leaves them vulnerable to periods of downtime—whether unemployment or underemployment—caused by any number of factors beyond their control.

Contract professionals share some of this structural vulnerability. Despite their calculated choices, tenuous client relations provide them with few protections and no guarantees. For those who informed this study, however, opting for an arrangement with little or no formal support was less an act of risk taking than an indictment of the employing organizations they had known and the positions available to them there. The risks of standard employment, they explained, could be just as significant as the dangers of contingent status. Weighing risks and considering options, these occupational practitioners had made choices that were themselves contingent, reflecting an awareness of the shifting structures of risk and opportunity that might alter their calculus of decision making over time.

Like most workers, these professionals had witnessed the development of new flexible work relations, much heralded since the final decades of the twentieth century. Flexible organizations had expanded the system of contracting and had created the conditions that informed their options. Institutionalized across a range of client firms, flexible staffing provided an opportunity structure, an alternative to the series of fixed positions that constitute an organizational career in an internal labor market. There they had witnessed diminishing aspirations and truncated careers. There standard employment had also become tenuous, with the script that once marked the stages of a career now open to revision. Lacking a single cultural template for tracing a career trajectory, these practitioners had imposed their own coherence on their separate paths and sought occupational advancement through extra-organizational careers.

For many, contracting further offered a temporal arrangement with greater control over daily schedules and a more proportionate return for time spent at work. Unlike salaried employees, they could avoid the risks of investment in a single employer, manifest in countless hours spent meeting deadlines, displaying loyalty, and promoting organizational goals. As contractors, in contrast, they tallied their hours and billed for their time. Employers, they explained, too often failed to compensate employees for an up-front investment in time and commitment. The erosion of job security, the breaking of the "psychological contract," the lack of stability in most organizational settings were for them an intractable social problem, a set of conditions for which they could see no solution within the boundaries of organizational life. To understand their individual choices, therefore, is to recognize the context in which they determined which set of risks appeared most salient and which they would decide to assume.

The flexibility that these contractors embraced shielded them, to some degree, from ongoing organizational volatility. Exposed to the risks of the market—which standard employment can still, in part, subsume—they sought to mitigate risk by generating their own opportunities. The risks they perceived as salient then depended on their experiences in standard jobs and their perceptions of prospects among available clients. In an occupational context that had become inherently riskier, with employing organizations straying far from the ideal type that absorbs most risks of market transaction, they had sought to appropriate risk, shaping it to their own ends and developing occupational connections as a hedge against future need. Drawing on larger cultural themes, they championed their adaptability in the face of pervasive risk.

Across the boundary between internal and external segments, labor market structures allocate risk, spreading and differentiating its terms. Although the standard job might still shelter employees from the shocks of external change, employees risk internal restructuring, which can eliminate jobs and undermine careers. Although contractors might hedge their bets with multiple clients and prospects, they risk the prospect of downtime during which their networks might prove inadequate. The allocation of risk in the new economy is thus one focus for a reexamination of work relations and related social policies. Nonstandard work may offer opportunities in some occupations, but social policies remain based on the standard job. Unlike employees, who are protected by legal rights and social insurance, contractors have little protection and few means for advocacy in cases of intractable dispute. All of these elements need attention if the current gaps are to be closed.

The current system of fragmentary rights and benefits, applying to some but not to others, can also keep groups of workers from finding common ground. Differences in contractual status divide workers from one another, generating fault lines that can undermine the potential for a collective response to common conditions. Lacking the prospect of coherent political action—or even the language with which to describe it—workers act individually, seeking the best available option, despite its drawbacks and despite the risks they still incur. Divided labor markets may thus pose obstacles to the development of new models of representation, which might bridge contractual distinctions and lead to new policies and practices. In this broader context, contract professionals are only one group of workers affected by a patchwork system with frayed edges and many holes.

To date, the lack of consensus over problems related to nonstandard, contingent work has impeded progress toward new policies that might better represent workers' interests. Attention to occupational, as well as organizational, structures is now necessary to encompass a broader swath of workers. Narrowly focused on organization-based employment, the current system of rights and protections—as variously constituted across industrialized countries—excludes large segments of the workforce. Those employed in lower-wage, intermittent work arrangements are especially vulnerable to changing conditions, and most have little recourse for collective response. A more comprehensive approach to employment policy would bridge divisions and promote greater inclusion. Together with new models of worker representation, social policies need to address the multiple forms of employment that have proliferated in the new economy.

Contracting in the New Economy: What Implications Might Emerge?

In a period of ever-accelerating change—technological innovation, capital mobility, globalization—this form of contracting is only one of many models of employment that have assumed new significance. Among analysts of the new economy, contracting among higher-wage workers is most closely associated with the development of new technologies and related technical work. Sometimes termed the *knowledge* or *information economy,* industries and services that develop and apply technologies have indeed spurred the proliferation of new practices and modes of working. Technological innovation, in turn, has accelerated the pace of change in many industries and employment sectors.

The association between technological change and contract employment, however, is inexact. Contracting, as a system of work relations, need not depend on specific technologies. Nor is it limited to technical workers. Contract employment in some occupations and industries, especially those that employ programmers and engineers, did, of course, develop in tandem with the commercialization of computing, which generated a rapidly growing need for technical workers in the second half of the twentieth century. Yet writers and editors in nontechnical fields are also part of the contract workforce, and as I explain in chapter 1, some were employed on a contract (or freelance) basis as early as the nineteenth century, with the expansion of literacy and a market for print publications. The historical antecedents of contracting thus point to long-standing variation in the social organization of work and the relations of paid employment, independent of any specific technologies. Rather than a manifestation of technological development, contracting is an enduring social arrangement, structured by relations between contractors and clients.

As it has with standard employment, however, technological change has altered long-standing work practices. Most often cited among experienced practitioners in this study was the advent of e-mail as a tool for informal exchange. E-mail, contractors explained, offered a means of accountability while maintaining a written record of decisions made and questions still to address. Contractors working off-site had found online exchange especially useful for transmitting up-to-date materials, keeping apprised of internal decisions, and facilitating work-related discussion. Information technology, they explained, could mitigate the exclusion from organizational life that can adversely affect a contractor's performance. By facilitating communication and coordination among dispersed team members, the same technology might also, presumably, have propelled the expansion of contracting in the last decades of the twentieth century.

Deploying these technological developments may also decentralize labor processes and so facilitate new modes of working. The practice of telecommuting, for example, may appear superficially like home-based contracting. Telecommuters work away from a central work site for at least part of a workweek, and some work from a distance too far for a physical commute. Although telecommuters do hold organizational positions, with the prerogatives and expectations of membership, the conditions of their work can also exclude them from internal processes and decisions that affect their performance. Like home-based contractors, telecommuters need effective lines of communication with the colleagues and managers with whom they work.

For contractors, however, online communication further facilitates the broader exchange that constitutes occupational networks. Collegial ties, once limited to geographical proximity, can now extend their reach through virtual communities whose members may never meet face to face. With collegial networks so important for finding work and staying abreast of occupational practice, Listservs and websites now expand the scope of these connections. On the Listservs that I monitored, contractors used the web to post questions, offer advice, and discuss topics related to both the substance of their work and the experience of contracting. Interaction online, which might include contractors and employees, could extend across widely dispersed locales. Decentralized exchange can thus contribute to the centrality of occupation, rather than employing organization, as a basis for work-based connection and social identity.

The proliferation of virtual communities might, in turn, enhance the prospects for organization among self-identified practitioners. Although contract professionals, as a constituency, have rarely engaged in collective action, the possibilities for mobilization increase with the prospect of greater numbers and a broader reach. Across a range of occupations with a significant segment of contractors, support for new social policies could enhance the prospects for reform. Online communication related to expanding legal rights and social protections might engage a broad swath of similarly situated workers, beyond the two occupations considered in this book. Mobilization for policy change could then stem, eventually, from connections among widely dispersed social actors who share a common set of interests.

Global Connections, Local Communities

With its decentralized processes of connection, communication, and exchange, contract employment contributes to the reconfiguring of temporal and spatial boundaries in a global economy. Through occupational networks, dispersed members of the workforce not only forge connections outside the bounds of employing organizations but also, to different degrees, escape the temporal constraints of face-to-face communication. In the cybersettings of online interaction, patterns of communication may more closely resemble a sequence of attenuated exchanges than an interactive discussion among social actors convened for a specific purpose. In the give and take of written responses, however, even quiet voices can be heard.

Bridging time and space, telecommunication also facilitates the decentralization of project teams, whose members might be spread across time zones and national boundaries. As widely dispersed collaborators move information and materials quickly and easily around the globe, processes of communication can drive day-to-day expectations. Hours of work may be adjusted. Coordination and completion of tasks may come to supplant "face time" at a central location as a measure of individual progress. Such arrangements, in turn, challenge long-standing features of the standard job. Rather than a requisite schedule at a designated work site, for example, employment under such conditions might offer the discretion to adjust working time to meet project needs. When coordination requires flexibility, challenges to the temporal organization of work may, in turn, redefine employment practices.

Flexibility, enhanced through cyberconnections, is most often associated with ever-increasing mobility in the new economy. Mobility, in turn, may approximate the "itinerant professionalism" that Barley and Kunda (2004, 285) identify with contract employment. Whereas regional networks promote mobility between firms, for example, occupational links facilitate employees' mobility from one organizational position to the next, so that across employing organizations occupation assumes significance regardless of contractual status. Although online discussion seems to augment, rather than supplant, these local and regional connections, the scope of cyberexchanges further facilitates the construction of far-ranging careers. Global connections and cybercommunities thus contribute to new patterns of mobility, now evident among many segments of the workforce.

For two subgroups of these contract professionals, the availability of work across geographical regions—and potentially around the world—has promoted two markedly different patterns of mobility. One subgroup is geographically mobile, with practitioners relocating with each new assignment. Ready access to information has expanded this population of transient contractors, who typically work on-site for one client at a time, most often through staffing agencies that specialize in longer-term assignments. In contrast, another subgroup works principally off-site, usually from home offices, and avoids even a daily commute to work. For home-based practitioners, wide-ranging connections facilitate working from a distance while remaining rooted in a specific locale. For geographically mobile contractors, frequent relocation enhances options beyond the range of local employers. The mobility associated with contracting may in these ways expand a contractor's geographical reach, disembedding practitioners from the limits of local environments.

Contract professionals thus embed themselves in spaces that may be at once local and global. Their communities of practice might include both colleagues with whom they share specific experiences and those identified in cyberspace, with whom they share little more than an occupational identity and an occasional exchange. These mediating connections—sometimes understood as social capital—can lead to employment opportunities well beyond a commuting radius in a single community or geographical region. Beyond new mechanisms for organizing work relations, such occupational links also pose the possibility of new forms of community development. Local communities, they suggest, might invest in developing economies of scope that can generate multiple means of employment for local residents.

In contrast, local efforts at job creation more often depend on attracting and retaining financial capital. Based on a singular definition of *job,* policies to promote employment typically call for the creation of standard jobs and for workforce development to meet the needs of local employers. Measuring the effectiveness of such policies then depends on charting job growth and decline by enumerating and evaluating organizational positions. Such calculations clearly ignore much nonstandard employment, including contract work, which encompasses different legal definitions, crosses census categories, and remains all but invisible to policymakers. As a system of work relations, the features of contracting remain largely unexamined for their potential to provide employment options and to develop the capacities of local and regional economies.

The proliferation of occupational communities, potentially with a global reach, may thus generate new possibilities for local development. Beyond common associations between contract employment and high-tech firms, a great many of which do engage the services of contractors, multiple forms of employment offer options for an increasingly diverse workforce. The institutions that sustain contracting, however, have so far been either informally constituted by contractors themselves or incorporated as for-profit market intermediaries, which support workforce mobility at considerable cost. Alternative institutions might address contractors' needs, both individually and collectively, by offering not only the benefits commonly packaged with standard employment but also an infrastructure that could foster cross-occupational connections and address common concerns. New institutions—accountable to workers' needs and interests—might, in turn, establish mechanisms that support communities of practitioners, variously deployed in a number of occupations and work arrangements.

Equality in Difference

The cultural shift that valorizes flexibility continues to beg an important question: Can options for workers create opportunities without disadvantages for those who need or choose them? More broadly, does the new economy necessarily place some segments of the workforce at ever-increasing risk? The new economy is less a break with an older order than a multiplicity of arrangements that are reshaping work relations and employment practices. These have been proliferating in a period of dynamic change marked by pervasively stagnant wages, an assault on unions, and eroding social welfare. Along with the heightened insecurity associated with these conditions, the growing gap between those who benefit and those who lose ground has generated much analysis and debate. Although the growing inequality has many causes, the proliferation of nonstandard work in lower-wage occupations is clearly a contributing factor, and since the last decades of the twentieth century, much social policy and organizational practice have facilitated the growth of a lower-wage contingent workforce.

This trend has, in turn, underscored common correlation, in both discourse and policy, between employment status and social characteristics. Short-term or seasonal work, irregular schedules, casual labor—all are associated in some way with specific, often disadvantaged populations. The logic of matching work arrangements with demographic categories identifies women as only secondary earners and youth as needing only stopgap employment. It presumes that older workers are collecting pensions or are somehow easing out of the workforce. Demographically driven assumptions function to perpetuate the recruitment of specific racial and immigrant groups for low-wage work, with few protections of any kind. Despite much academic analysis of segmented labor markets and access to employment, such practices continue to go unchallenged.

These associations have far-reaching consequences for the structure of the workforce and for the experiences of workers at all socioeconomic locations. Divided labor markets can provide a pretext for segregation on the basis of race or gender and so exacerbate social inequalities. To equate temporary or part-time work with opportunities for women, for example, is to institutionalize gender inequality in most occupations and organizational settings. True, women more often than men assume domestic responsibilities and experience work-family conflict. Shorter workweeks and flexible schedules do permit more women to meet these obligations. Yet like the "mommy track" jobs that some contractors had eschewed, these arrangements more often pay less for hours at work and offer fewer opportunities for advancement than comparable full-time employment. Disadvantages thus come packaged with the flexibility needed for those seeking to accommodate paid work with family and other obligations.

The structures of contracting, in contrast, challenge the correlation between flexibility and disadvantage and even blur the distinctions between full-time and part-time work. For contractors, full-time work can mean any number of configurations, from on-site arrangements that approximate the daily rhythms of an organization-based job to billable hours, sometimes spread across several projects and clients, which aggregate an equivalent income. Whether measured in billable time or in total hours that include time spent maintaining skills, knowledge, and networks, working time for contract professionals rarely conforms, consistently, to any discernible standard. Rather, the autonomy of contracting provides one means for achieving the "customized time" that Meiksins and Whalley (2002, 11) identify as a strategy for balancing work with family obligations and other aspects of life. Contractors' schedules thus confound temporal distinctions that mark some jobs as full-time and others as only fractions of a whole.

Yet in common parlance, sometimes echoed by contractors themselves, a full-time job is still a proxy for standard employment. A full-time job signifies a single employer, an organizational position, and for some workers a healthy measure of stability. To work full-time is to be fully engaged and firmly attached to the labor market. For much of the workforce, too, full-time employment determines eligibility for social insurance and access to legal rights. Against this backdrop of policy and practice, contract professionals are but one group of workers who can appear deviant, violating the full-time norm that connotes workforce legitimacy. Together with those holding part-time organization-based jobs, they risk common cultural assumptions that they are less than fully capable or less committed to their occupations than their full-time counterparts with standard jobs.

In the globally connected workplace, however, such temporal distinctions are fast becoming obsolete. Demands for time extend well beyond any full-time standard, and the call of e-mail, cell phones, and text messages are constant reminders that work might be beckoning at any hour of the day. This encroachment of paid employment on the rest of life is for some a social problem, variously associated with individual stress, organizational tyranny, or family dysfunction. Whatever its effects, the demands of work for a great many salaried employees have long since eroded the spatial and temporal boundaries that once separated work from home and public from private life. The standard job, in many settings and for many workers, has been stretched almost beyond recognition.

Today's employees, therefore, share with contract professionals the effects of a broader cultural shift in which paid employment exacts constant—and often unacknowledged—demands. The resulting inflexibility can be a barrier to entry, especially for those with family responsibilities. Separately challenging the temporal norms of much standard employment, contractors may achieve a greater measure of flexibility than their counterparts in standard jobs, but these arrangements remain individually negotiated, informed by individual perceptions of market conditions and prospects for future work. A more comprehensive challenge to temporal demands in the new economy would instead seek solutions that apply to workers across the spectrum of paid employment, regardless of contractual status.

The problem of workforce inequality, therefore, is best addressed by meeting the needs for flexibility, shared in different ways by both workers and employers, without subordinating nonstandard work arrangements to a single standard of employment. Rather than a pretext for lower wages and pervasive insecurity, such arrangements might reconfigure working time without differentially distributing risk or limiting opportunity for specific groups of workers. With equivalent incomes and possibilities for professional growth, the contractors who contributed to this study could well be pioneers in identifying terms on which workforce equality might allow for differences across an occupation without resorting to standards that demand conformity. The practices they develop might promote new terms by which flexibility can be negotiated rather than imposed.

Nonstandard work, as this book suggests, can provide an alternative opportunity structure, different but not necessarily subordinate to the standard job. Although among the more advantaged members of the contingent workforce, contract professionals raise the prospect of equivalence across segments of a divided workforce, and their experiences point to new principles for promoting equality and inclusion in employment relations. Rather than a single standard that defines a job, policies and practices should seek to establish an equality that provides multiple options rather than a single norm. Work relations should leave room for reconfiguration, to accommodate workers' as well as employers' needs. Reconsidering employment relations, to accommodate contractual diversity, could thus hold the promise of greater equality for employees and contingent workers alike.

APPENDIX
CONTRACTORS INTERVIEWED

TABLE 1. Writers and Editors

Pseudonym	Type of work	Time as contractor	Age (years)	Gender	Race	Income (in thousands of dollars)	Education	Household composition
Bernice	Editing, indexing	4 years	46	F	W	55	MA	Single
Bill	Writing, training	6 years	48	M	W	60	MS	Partner
Carla	Writing, editing	9 years[a]	61	F	W	73	MA	Single
Carol	Writing, editing	5 years	42	F	W	50	BS	Single
Charles	Writing, editing, training	4 years[a]	47	M	W	80	PhD	Spouse, one child
Darla	Editing, proofreading	2 years	31	F	W	35	BA	Roommate
Donald	Editing, production management	1 year	35	M	W	45	PhD	Spouse
Ellie	Editing, writing	4 years	50	F	W	55	MA	Partner
Emily	Editing, proofreading	1 year	46	F	W	43	BA	Single
Gary	Editing, production management	9 years[a]	47	M	W	45	MA	Spouse, two children
Grant	Indexing, editing	8 years[a]	44	M	W	45	MA	Partner
Heather	Editing, training	20 years	51	F	W	30	EdD	Spouse
Holly	Editing, project management	15 years	50	F	W	60	MA	One child
Janice	Writing, editing, project management	6 years[a]	41	F	W	N/A	BA	Spouse, one child
Jon	Writing, editing	10 months	23	M	W	48	BA	Roommate
Katlin	Editing, production management	1 year	42	F	W	44	BA	Single
Kevin	Translating, editing	6 years[a]	54	M	W	40	Courses	Partner
Lisa	Writing, editing, project management	7 years[a]	57	F	W	50	MA	Spouse, two grown children[b]
Martin	Editing, proofreading	6 months	28	M	W	N/A	BA	Single

Name	Type of work	Experience	Age	Sex	Race	Income	Education	Household
Melanie	Writing, editing	17 years	50	F	W	35	MBA	Two children
Michael	Editing, proofreading	25 years	63	M	W	45	BA	Spouse, two children (one grown)[b]
Myra	Editing, project management	10 years	36	F	W	N/A	BA	Spouse, two children
Noreen	Writing, editing	4 years[a]	46	F	W	N/A	BA	Spouse
Pat	Writing	5 years	52	F	W	40	BA	Spouse, two children
Phil	Writing, project management	8 years[a]	42	M	W	90	MA	Partner
Rebecca	Writing, editing	14 years[a]	60	F	W	65	MA	Single
Sam	Editing, proofreading	2 years	57	M	W	30	BA	Spouse
Seth	Editing, production management	3 years[a]	46	M	W	70	AA	Single
Sherry	Editing, translating, project management	2 years[a]	30	F	W	50	MA	Partner
Sylvia	Writing, editing	11 years	39	F	W	52	MA	Spouse, two children
Ted	Writing, editing	3 months	28	M	W	30	MFA	Partner
Thomas	Writing, training	6 years[a]	45	M	W	70	Courses	Spouse, two children
Valerie	Writing, production management	5 years[a]	51	F	W	48	BA	Partner
Yolanda	Writing, editing, project management	6 years	42	F	A	45	BA	Spouse

Notes: N/A, not available. Type of work represents informants' characterizations of their typical responsibilities and range of skills. "Project management" or "production management" thus denotes the oversight of projects, supervision of other staff, or both. In designating race, A = Asian; L = Latino; W = White. Incomes are self-reports only and do not distinguish between gross and net amounts.

[a] Most recent period of contracting.

[b] Grown children formerly in household.

TABLE 2. Programmers and Engineers

Pseudonym	Type of work	Time as contractor	Age (years)	Gender	Race	Income (in thousands of dollars)	Education	Household composition
Anna	Programming	7 years[a]	52	F	W	95	BS	Parent
Ben	Software engineering, project management	6 years	42	M	W	125	MS	Spouse, two children
Bennett	Software engineering	19 years	46	M	W	N/A	MS	Single
Blaine	Programming, test engineering	6 years[a]	53	M	W	100	BS	Spouse
Brenda	Programming, systems analysis	14 years	43	F	W	150	BS	Single
Brent	Software engineering, project management	2 years[a]	32	M	W	60	MS	Spouse
Bruce	Software engineering, systems analysis	5 years	53	M	W	125	MS	Partner, two children
Bryan	Programming, systems engineering	10 years[a]	62	M	W	80	BA	Single
Carl	Programming	3 years	45	M	W	60	MS	Spouse, two children
Daniel	Software engineering	2 years	48	M	W	100	BA	Spouse
Darrell	Programming, project management	10 years[a]	61	M	W	100	BS	Spouse, five grown children[b]
Ezra	Software development	8 years	43	M	W	70	MA	Partner
Jackie	Software engineering	5 years	50	F	W	90	BA, additional courses	Single
Jason	Programming	2 years	45	M	W	40	BA	Two children
Jeffrey	Software engineering	30 years	57	M	W	125	BS	Spouse, two grown children[b]
Joseph	Software engineering, systems analysis	22 years[a]	67	M	W	80	MS	Spouse, two grown children[b]
Karen	Software development, training	1 year[a]	44	F	W	70	BA	Spouse

Name	Type of work	Experience	Sex	Race	Income	Degree	Family status
Katherine	Programming, database management	5 years	F	W	48	MA	Spouse, one child
Lauren	Programming, systems analysis	6 years	F	W	62	BS	Spouse, two children
Linda	Software and database development	3 years	F	W	120	MS	Spouse, two children
Lori	Programming	7 years	F	W	70	BS	One child
Marta	Software development	1 year	F	L	100	MS	Spouse, one child
Max	Programming, tech support	1 year	M	W	50	PhD	Spouse
Melinda	Programming	15 years	F	A	90	MBA	One child
Meredith	Programming, database, development, training	5 years	F	W	70	MS	Partner, two children
Patrick	Programming, systems analysis	3 years	M	W	120	BA	Spouse, three children
Peggy	Programming	9 years[a]	F	W	100	BA	Partner
Pete	Software development	13 years	M	W	100	BA	Spouse, two children
Richard	Programming	8 months	M	W	40	BA	Single
Rita	Programming, training	4 years[a]	F	W	90	MA	Spouse, two children
Roland	Programming, project management	2.5 years	M	L	90	BA	Partner
Terry	Programming, project management	4 years[a]	M	W	90	MS	Two children
Tony	Software development, systems design	2 years[a]	M	W	150	BS	Single, grown children[b]
Vincent	Programming	10 months	M	A	N/A	BS	Single

Note: N/A, not available. Type of work represents informants' characterization of their typical responsibilities and range of skills. "Project management" or "production management" thus denotes the oversight of projects, supervision of other staff, or both. In designating race, A = Asian; L = Latino; W = White. Incomes are self-reports only and do not distinguish between gross and net amounts.

[a] Most recent period of contracting.

[b] Grown children formerly in household.

NOTES

Introduction

1. The erosion of job security has received much attention among scholars, journalists, and managerial consultants (Ehrenreich 2005; Hammer and Champy 1993; Harrison 1994; Head 2003; Osterman 1999b; Ross 2009; Uchitelle 2006). Periods of rising unemployment have historically been associated with lower-wage work, but organizational downsizing and layoffs now appear at all levels of the workforce hierarchy.

2. Among the best-known books promoting the prospects for financial success and personal growth is *Free Agent Nation* (Pink 2001). The author also sponsors a website that promotes independence from organizational life. Among books that have offered a mix of analysis and advice are Bridges (1994); Gould, Weiner, and Levin (1997); McGovern and Russell (2001); Reinhold (2001); Whittlesey (1982); Winter (1993). Advice books directed to the occupations under study here, some of which date back further, concern marketing services, negotiating terms, and maintaining skills. Among these are Consulting Engineers Council of Texas (1972); Kent (1992); O'Neill and Ruder (1974); Powell (1999); Rogers (1995); Watlington and Radeloff (1997). Yet another stream of advice literature offers guidance for managers engaging the services of contractors. See, for example, Allen and Yablok (2005); Gubman (2003).

3. The variable definitions of self-employment make the designation slippery at best. Confusion over legal definitions stems in part from different criteria imposed by federal and state-level agencies as well as different interpretations of the law (Linder 1999). The Current Population Survey (CPS), conducted by the U.S. Census Bureau, identifies two groups of the self-employed: those who receive wages and salaries and small business owners who derive income from revenues (Cohany 1996).

4. In their study of technical contracting, conducted during the dot-com boom of the 1990s, Barley and Kunda (2004) draw the same conclusion: contract employment represents an enduring structural phenomenon. The number of contractors may rise or fall with changing economic conditions, along with overall employment, but contractors now represent a stable segment of the workforce.

5. The U.S. system of legal rights applies principally to standard employment, without which a range of exclusions and impediments apply (Carnevale, Eisenmann, and Jennings 1998; Carré, duRivage, and Tilly 1994; Stone 2006). For those whose employment is in some way nonstandard, access to legal redress is often unavailable, either because a statute explicitly excludes a category of workers or because the law establishes a threshold or conditions that leave workers unprotected by its provisions.

6. Although standard employment could provide lifelong security, mid-twentieth-century analyses also decried the authoritarian bureaucracies of organizational employment, which offered little space for individual autonomy (Mills 1956; Whyte 1956).

7. In the ideal-type internal labor market, entry points are strictly limited, and hiring depends on prior employment within the firm (Baron and Kreps 1999). Osterman (1988) distinguishes further between an industrial model that bases job security on seniority, sometimes enforced through collective bargaining, and a salaried model that depends on an employer's implicit commitment to job security in return for cooperation with managerial prerogatives.

8. An extensive literature has identified rationales governing internal labor markets. Doeringer and Piore's (1971, 58) classic analysis focuses on "lines of progression," with screening for entry-level workers and on-the-job training for those hired. Other analysts have emphasized incentives for good performance (Segal 1986; Williamson 1985) or investment in human capital (Becker 1975). Stone (2004) traces the development of a quasi-contractual agreement whereby workers share their knowledge and skills in return for an implicit promise of steady employment. A work-site-based system of collective bargaining, institutionalized in the United States in the 1930s, applied this logic. Job security thus depended on a commitment, sometimes codified in a union contract, rather than association with a craft or trade.

9. Since the mid-1980s, many researchers have examined the extent, processes, and effects of downsizing and restructuring (Cappelli et al. 1997; Gallie et al. 1998; Osterman 1999a). The dislocation that results may affect the various segments of the workforce differently (Gardner 1995; Hipple 1997), but the result has been an overall decline in job tenure among all demographic groups, evident by the 1990s (Bureau of Labor Statistics 1998; Swinnerton and Wial 1995). Unclear, however, is the extent to which long-term employment within a single organization has been supplanted by new models of career mobility (Hirsch and Naquin 2001; Jacoby 1999).

10. Heckscher and Donnellon (1994) identify work relations in less hierarchical environments as "post-bureaucratic." Surveying both aggregate data and work-site case studies, other analysts see a similar trend toward the decentralization of authority (Cornfield, Campbell, and McCammon 2001; Leicht 1998; Marsden, Cook, and Kalleberg 1996; Smith 1997). Decentered control within the firm is consistent with the broader proliferation of networks for production and distribution (Harrison 1994; Harvey 1989). Control is thus diffuse, although systems of management may remain authoritarian.

11. Implementing more general job descriptions is consistent with efforts to develop cross-functional teams and dismantle rigid boundaries between departments and divisions (Miner and Robinson 1994). Appropriating the language of a digital age, some firms have applied the notion of "broadbanding" to place employees' responsibilities within broad bands of general expectations (Stone 2004). Workers may then move horizontally and, in some cases, vertically without the frequent reclassification of jobs.

12. Analysts of "boundarylessness" identify various patterns of mobility that differ from organizational careers (Arthur and Rousseau 1996; Nicholson 1996). Although some analysts see

the dismantling of internal labor markets as the principal cause of change (DiTomaso 2001; Osterman 1999a), others emphasize extra-organizational factors, among them the prevalence of dual-earner households, needs for family care, and increased geographical mobility (Moen and Roehling 2005).

13. Job changing might also indicate worker control through professionalization, which can promote mobility by establishing skill sets for specific occupational groups (Heckscher 1995; Kanter 1989). DiTomaso (2001), however, cautions that, without adequate mechanisms for professional governance, workers can expect little protection from the adverse effects of unfettered markets and organizational change.

14. Among knowledge workers in some industries and occupations, patterns of lateral mobility have long been common, with mobility across organizational boundaries considered appropriate for gaining valuable experience and building a career (Colclough and Tolbert 1992; Mosco and McKercher 2007; Powell 1985; Royal and Althauser 2003; Saxenian 1994; Tang, Jacobs, and Lai 2000).

15. The notion of employability shifts responsibility for the ongoing acquisition of knowledge and skills from the employer to the employee. The logic of employability suggests that workers who invest in their own human capital will find work, even if forced to leave their jobs (Kanter 1989; Johnston and Lawrence 1988; Katzenbach and Beckett 1995; Womack, Jones, and Roos 1990). Studies of downsizing and reemployment, however, suggest that outcomes differ across populations of workers with different social characteristics and in different social classes (Rubin and Smith 2001).

16. The term *contingent work* was coined in the mid-1980s by Audrey Freeman, an economist, who used it to identify a set of work arrangements that depend on an employer's ongoing need for an employee's services (Freeman 1996). In this broad sense, the term might apply to any employment not covered by formal contractual terms. In both academic and policy circles, however, contingent work is equated with some segment of nonstandard work arrangements, regardless of workers' relative security. The term is most common in the United States, but the prevalence of short-term and contract-based work has expanded to a global scale. In other industrialized economies, the terms *atypical work* and *precarious work* are more common (Bronstein 1991; Vosko 2000; Houseman and Osawa 2003; Ross 2009).

17. Some of these forms of employment are identified with the informal economy, or informal sector (Leonard 1998; Portes, Castells, and Benton 1989). Informal work, however, is principally defined by a lack of regulation; unreported taxable income; and evasion of licensing, permits, and insurance. Long equated with ethnic enclaves and immigrant populations, informal work may also include personal services in middle-class communities (Snyder 2004).

18. Although structurally similar, these two arrangements differ somewhat in practice. A staffing agency, or temporary help agency, matches individual workers with client firms and, in most cases, shares the legal responsibilities of an employer with its client (Gonos 1998; Vosko 2000). Contracting companies provide businesses with services and often a workforce as well; contracting out, then, eliminates ancillary functions, such as building maintenance, food service, mailing, and data processing, from direct, centralized management (Holmes 1986; Kalleberg 2000).

19. Many part-time workers are employees working voluntarily reduced hours in stable jobs, some of them in professional occupations (Meiksins and Whalley 2002). The U.S. Bureau of Labor Statistics (BLS) distinguishes between voluntary and involuntary part-time employment and suggests that only involuntary part-time work is legitimately contingent because such work fails to match the workers' preferences. Tilly (1996) offers a perspective that distinguishes, instead, between kinds of jobs. His typology defines *secondary part-time work* as peripheral and relatively unstable and *retention part-time work* as stable and equivalent in most ways to standard employment. This perspective is consistent with broader analyses of labor market segmentation (Gordon, Edwards, and Reich 1992).

20. The U.S. Senate Subcommittee on Labor of the Committee on Labor and Human Resources convened two Senate hearings, one in 1993 and the other in 1994. Senator Howard Metzenbaum (D-Ohio), the subcommittee chair, opened the first day of hearings by warning, "if this trend continues, we may wake up one morning to find that the American dream has slipped away" (U.S. Senate 1993, 2). At the second hearing, Secretary of Labor Robert Reich announced the decision to collect data on the contingent workforce: "The new data will help us answer questions regarding the number of workers and different contingent work relations" (U.S. Senate 1994, 7).

21. The CPS is a monthly survey of U.S. households. The additional questions appear in the "Supplement on Contingent Work" (Polivka 1996a).

22. Kalleberg, Reskin, and Hudson (2000) challenge the BLS definition of *contingent work* and argue that limiting it to those employed in nonstandard arrangements for less than one year fails to capture the size and scope of the contingent workforce. Equating contingent work with nonstandard employment, these researchers include part-time work, contracting, and self-employment in their estimate. Analyses applying similar definitions include an early study by Belous (1989) and reviews by the U.S. Government Accounting Office (GAO) (2000, 2006).

23. For analyses of data collected from 1995 to 2005, see GAO (2000, 2006); Hipple (2001); Wenger (2003).

24. See Canter (1988); DiNatale (2001); Polivka (1996b); Polivka and Nardone (1989). These analysts argue that contingent work is a demand-driven phenomenon—that is, it reflects the preferences of a segment of the workforce.

25. See Appelbaum et al. (1997); Kalleberg, Reskin, and Hudson (2000); Wenger (2003). Earlier analyses similarly argued that nonstandard employment limits opportunities for those already socially and economically disadvantaged (Golden and Appelbaum 1992; Harrison 1994).

26. Although part-time workers, under certain conditions, may be covered by some regulations, workers with nonstandard jobs in the United States are excluded from much of the labor and employment law, including statutes addressing discrimination, occupational safety and health, and family and medical leave (Carnevale, Jennings, and Eisenmann 1998; Carre, duRivage, and Tilly 1994; Stone 2006).

27. The equation between nonstandard work and substandard jobs marks a number of analyses of polarized employment in which structural divisions are becoming wider and deeper (Harrison 1994; Kalleberg, Reskin, and Hudson 2000; Mishel, Bernstein, and Shierholz 2009; Rassell and Appelbaum 1997).

28. Smith (2001a) compares a series of case studies, each of which represents some aspect of work relations in the new economy. Although only one of these cases represents contingent work in any of the senses usually applied, the comparison draws theoretical links that apply broadly to many forms of employment.

29. Studies of clerical and industrial temps and contractors draw on labor process theory to explain mechanisms of control and subordination, and they conclude that these contingent workers fare worse than their counterparts in standard jobs. See Gottfried (1991, 1992); Henson (1996); McAllister (1998); Parker (1994); Rebitzer (1998); Rogers (2000).

30. For analyses of gender and racial inequality in the social relations of temporary clerical work, see Gottfried (1991); Rogers (1995); Rogers and Henson (1997).

31. Kahne (1985) challenges gendered assumptions about part-time schedules and the relative value of part-time work implicit in some analyses of the contingent workforce (Polivka 1996b). Meiksins and Whalley (2002) similarly find a preponderance of women among technical professionals with reduced working hours.

32. Historical and contemporary accounts of home-based work document the marginality of home workers worldwide, despite variation across social class and individual circumstances (Daniels 1989; Felstead and Jewson 2000; Jurik 1998). All home workers share a historically constructed legacy of gender that equates women's work with domestic obligations.

33. Case studies of home-based contingent workers document practices that allow individuals to integrate, or at least intersperse, paid work with family responsibilities (Dangler 1994; Gringeri 1994; Osnowitz 2005). In these studies, the workers' latitude to control their daily schedules contrasts with the relative rigidity of standard employment.

34. Rogers (2000) compares attorneys working on temporary assignments, through staffing agencies, with clerical temps and documents the differences between these two groups, which may otherwise appear to be structurally similar.

35. Henson (2003) identifies both a nursing shortage and agency contractors' mandating overtime as sources of leverage used to limit work hours.

36. Barker (1998) applies the notion of moral exclusion to explain the interactional processes that rationalize the subordination of adjunct faculty, whose ranks have grown significantly over the past three decades (Gappa and Leslie 1993; Finkelstein, Seal, and Schuster 1998). Rajagopal (2002) further documents patterns of limited opportunity in Canadian universities.

37. Definitions of *professionals* and *professionalism* carry theoretical connotations that have generated much analysis (Leicht and Fennell 1997). Freidson (2001) associates professionalism with occupational control, with practitioners responsible to a professional body that determines standards of practice and manages labor market entry through certification and formal credentials. Applied here, however, is a "common language" definition (Abbott 1991, 17), based on a shared understanding among members of an occupational group. Such a definition applies to organizational professionals, subject to managerial control (Whalley 1986a).

38. In a study of engineers in standard, organization-based jobs, Whalley (1986b) links employers' trust to an ideology of professionalism in which engineers internalize employers' goals without overt direction and control.

39. Labor markets that promote mobility from project to project are evident in the arts and creative industries. See, for example, Bechky (2006); Bielby and Bielby (1999); Ekinsmyth (2002); Faulkner and Anderson (1987); Menger (1999).

40. Stone (2004) argues that job structures associated with craft-based production prevailed into the late nineteenth century, until this system was broken by large employers seeking to impose a model of industrial capitalism. The advent of the digital age and the new economy, she suggests, are an equivalent turning point.

41. Both groups of researchers focused on the transitions from standard employment to contract work. The study of translators (Fraser and Gold 2001; Gold and Fraser 2002) cites a broader clientele than copy editors and proofreaders apparently find available (Granger, Stanworth, and Stanworth 1995; Stanworth and Stanworth 1997b). Taken together, these analyses suggest that limited labor market options are an obstacle to a contractor's prospering over time.

42. Meiksins and Whalley's (2002) larger study addresses part-time work among organization-based professionals, all in technical occupations.

43. For facets of this study, see Barley and Kunda (2004); Evans, Kunda, and Barley (2004); Kunda, Barley, and Evans (2002).

44. In some organizational settings, subordinate employees are charged with managing relationships between professionals and their clients. In law firms, for example, paralegals may be required to relieve attorneys of responsibility for keeping clients informed and satisfied with the progress of their cases (Pierce 1995).

45. All of my informants worked in the United States in the English language, but a few had been educated elsewhere or had worked outside the United States in another language or in a bilingual context. Translators, of course, had facility in at least two languages.

46. As Barley and Kunda (2004) explain, technical contractors acknowledge a hierarchy, with engineers and programmers in the upper strata and administrators toward the bottom. Status distinctions are also evident among programmers and engineers: developing operating systems or architecture places a practitioner at the top of a hierarchy; applications programming and testing

place a practitioner a few notches below. These gradations are apparent in both employees' salaries and contractors' rates.

47. The work of technicians, according to some analysts, differs from that of technical professionals (Whalley and Barley 1997). Technicians support professionals. They may, for example, operate, repair, and maintain machinery. Barley and Orr (1997) conceive of technicians as mediating between technology and society, shielding professionals from the implementation of technical innovation.

48. For an overview of portfolio work, see Cohen and Mallon (1999).

1. Two Occupations with Divided Labor Markets

1. Many analysts have documented the development of the flexible organization, sometimes termed post-Fordism. See, for example, Gouliequer (2000); Houseman (2001); Kalleberg (2001); Vallas (1999).

2. Martin (1994) charts the development of flexible forms across the cultural landscape, linking the imagery of science and medicine with practices in human resource management, exercise training, and advertising for consumer goods, all of which convey messages about the virtues of flexibility. A science of complexity, she asserts, places individuals in ever-changing environments and demands adaptability in an unpredictable world.

3. A number of analysts have associated nonstandard, contingent work with mechanisms that lower wages and employment standards across the workforce. See, for example, Kalleberg (2003); Harrison (1994); Rassell and Appelbaum (1997).

4. My informants' accounts suggest that external factors promoting flexible staffing include the scrutiny of investment managers, whose analyses affect share prices. Despite my informants' familiarity with "management by head count," the rationale is largely absent from the literature on staffing strategies in flexible firms.

5. Staffing agencies that mediate contract employment differ from headhunters, who recruit personnel to fill openings for standard jobs (Finlay and Coverdill 2002).

6. Gonos (1998, 2001) chronicles the history of the staffing industry in the 1970s and 1980s, when deregulation promoted both its expansion and a redefinition of temporary employment. As the industry grew, some staffing agencies came to mediate in specific labor markets (Benner, Leete, and Pastor 2007; Ofstead 1999; Peck and Theodore 2002; Vosko 2000).

7. A stream of studies identifies staffing agencies as sources of subordination for clerical and industrial temps. See Gottfried (1991); Henson (1996); McAllister (1998); Parker (1994); Rogers (2000).

8. Henson (2003) attributes the relative responsiveness of staffing agencies that recruit traveling nurses to these workers' market leverage. Unhappy with one agency, a nurse can easily find work with another.

9. Rogers (2000) cites staffing agency practices that differ markedly between clerical workers and attorneys.

10. Barley and Kunda (2004) provide a detailed ethnographic account of agencies placing technical contractors.

11. See Cohany (1996) for an explanation of definitions used by the U.S. Census Bureau and the BLS.

12. In distinguishing between wage and salary workers and those who are self-employed, the BLS applies a definition that hinges on whether the worker solicits work or responds to unsolicited offers (Cohany 1996). The data depend on respondents' self-reports. Many of the contract professionals in this study would probably place themselves in both of these categories.

13. These options for the self-employed to participate in tax-deferred retirement savings in the United States have gradually expanded, most recently with the Economic Growth and Tax Reconciliation Act of 2001.

14. In a much publicized legal case, *Vizcaino v. Microsoft,* the IRS criteria led to a settlement through which contractors who had been reclassified as employees received compensation for benefits, including stock options, that would have been available to them as employees. Several of my informants mentioned this case, often ruefully noting that it had further eroded the possibilities for working "on 1099."

15. See, for example, Lenz (1999) for the perspective of the staffing industry on business liability. The story of Section 1706, both its insertion into the Tax Reform Act of 1986 and the subsequent controversy, is chronicled in Biemesderfer (1999).

16. Gonos (1998) chronicles the contested definition of the employment relationship in the United States, noting that periods of socioeconomic change have historically been associated with new forms of labor market mediation. In the decades after World War II, that contest focused on the deregulation of employment agencies, which sought legitimacy as employers of record as well as labor market intermediaries.

17. The agency markup replaced the employment agency fees that had been standard practice for market intermediaries in an earlier period (Gonos 2001). Consequently, staffing agencies could advertise their services as "free" to workers. The result of this shift, however, has been a markup of the worker's hourly wage, which agencies rarely disclose to either workers or client firms (Gottfried 1991; Henson 1996; Parker 1994; Rogers 2000).

18. Fernandez-Mateo (2007, 2009) finds that staffing agencies transferred the cost of the discounts that they offered as preferred vendors to the workers in the form of lower wages and that women's wages rose more slowly than men's, despite similar experience. Staffing agencies thus exercise considerable control in setting prices in the market for temporary employment.

19. Benefits available through a staffing agency, my informants explained, were rarely, if ever, portable, so that contractors who depended on them were tied to a single agency. Needing multiple clients to maintain their viability, most of my informants resisted such arrangements, which constrained their mobility.

20. A growing postwar school-age population made textbook publishing the segment of greatest growth (Coser, Kadushin, and Powell 1982; Tebbel 1981), but scholarly publishing also expanded with the growth of higher education (Powell 1985). Government contracts and defense spending during the same decades underwrote the development of computer software and hardware and so spurred the development of a new industry, which soon expanded with commercial applications as well (Kraft 1977; Langlois and Mowery 1996; Tarallo 1987).

21. Coser, Kadushin, and Powell (1982) chart the commercialization of the publishing industry, a process that Tebbel (1981) chronicles as "the great change."

22. Greenbaum (1979) and Kraft (1977) exemplify analyses in the Bravermanian tradition.

23. See Orlikowski (1988) for a review of literature suggesting variation across segments of an expanding technology sector.

24. Beirne, Ramsay, and Pantelli (1998) identify "control and contradiction" in computer work. Business organizations dictate product specifications, they explain, but technical professionals continue to exercise discretion over tasks and processes.

25. The expansion of editorial freelancing in the 1960s and 1970s occurred in tandem with increasing pressures to cut costs and with legal challenges to women's status in the publishing industry (Caplette 1981; Osnowitz 2000, 2007; Stanworth and Stanworth 1997a). As early as the 1880s, however, trade publishers had been engaging the services of first readers to review their "slush piles" of unsolicited manuscripts (Sheehan 1952). For this service, Henry Holt, a publisher, reportedly paid an hourly fee for occasional work: $1.00 for men and $0.50 for women.

26. See, for example, Kunda (1992) and Tarallo (1987), who note the presence of contractors.

27. Heckscher and Donnellon (1994) present multiple manifestations of "post-bureaucratic" organizations, with increasing emphasis on self-directed teams as a unit of productivity, evident by the late twentieth century. See, for example, Orsburn et al. (1990); Wellins, Byham, and Wilson (1991).

28. Off-site contracting represents one form of distributed, or virtual, teams in which members are dispersed across multiple sites (Hinds and Kiesler 2002; Pauleen 2004). Decentralized collaboration in many forms has become increasingly common as businesses extend their global reach (Shapiro et al. 2002). Yet, despite the growing prevalence of decentralized collaboration, research suggests greater conflict in distributed teams (Hinds and Bailey 2003).

29. The notion of codification, elaborated by Bridges and Villemez (1991), differs from standardization associated with the expansion of new technology (Greenbaum 1979; Kraft 1977; Kraft and Dubnoff 1986). Standardization creates conditions for appropriation of skill, consistent with Braverman's (1974) analysis of deskilling and intensified control. Occupations that allow high discretion, however, may be more resistant to standardization (Orlikowski 1988).

30. The notion of a community of practice equates group identity with social learning and the negotiation of meaning through participation in certain activities (Lave and Wenger 1991; Wenger 1998). The concept has been applied and differentiated in a variety of contexts, including virtual communities established or maintained online (Amin and Roberts 2008).

31. For further analysis of home-based contracting, see Osnowitz (2005).

32. Until it ceased publication in 2002, the magazine *Contract Professional* carried advertising for short-term rental housing that offered amenities for professionals with short-term assignments in a number of locales.

33. Ness (2007) chronicles the growth of the workforce on H-1B visas and offers evidence of U.S. worker displacement, despite regulations that prohibit employers from replacing U.S. citizens with temporary immigrants or employing them as strike breakers. For analyses of the subordination of technical contractors from India working in the United States with H-1B visas, see Aneesh (2006); Banerjee (2006).

34. The Washington Alliance of Technology Workers (WashTech) maintains an online archive of news reports related to H-1B visas and employment trends (see www.WashTech.org). Aneesh (2006) suggests that "virtual migration," or outsourcing, is likely to accelerate among programmers and engineers. Dahlmann and Huws (2006–2007) identify similar trends for editorial workers in the United Kingdom.

35. On the culture of new media companies and the associated dot-com expansion of the 1990s, see Neff (2007); Ross (2003).

36. Florida (2002) and Reich (1992) equate knowledge work with the manipulation and analysis of symbols, prominently including computer code.

37. Occupation and work-site case studies attest to the white cast of these two occupations (Kunda 1992; Meiksins and Whalley 2002; Osnowitz 2000), as do my observational data and informants' accounts.

38. Analyses of the effects of networks in other contexts include Coverdill (1998); McGuire (2000). Benner, Leete, and Pastor (2007) further analyze the effects of market intermediaries and associated networks in shaping employment access for disadvantaged groups.

39. Warburg (1960) describes book publishing before its commercialization, when editorial work was less a profession than an elite vocation.

40. Feminization in book publishing established gendered hierarchies, in which men occupied higher positions and women had jobs that were defined as supportive and subordinate (Caplette 1981; Colgan and Tomlinson 1996; Reskin 1990).

41. Reskin and Roos (1990) apply queuing theory to explain this process. Industry expansion, they argue, creates new opportunities, and having exhausted the supply of qualified men—or, in many cases, white men—employers turn to women to fill jobs.

42. On the experience of women in publishing during the 1970s and 1980s, see Colgan and Tomlinson (1996); Johnson (1976); Osnowitz (2000, 2007).

43. Reskin (1990) cites a personal communication from John Tebbel, a book industry chronicler, indicating that in 1987 women in editorial freelancing appeared to outnumber men three to one.

Counting entries in *Literary Market Place,* Caplette (1981) suggests that women outnumber men two to one. Membership records from the Boston-based Freelance Editorial Association suggest an even higher percentage of women: 92 percent in 1984 and 85 percent in 1998 (Osnowitz 2000).

44. On the roots of computing in engineering, see Hughes (1987); McIlwee and Robinson (1992).

45. Donato (1990) associates the feminization of some segments of computer programming with queuing theory. Glenn and Tolbert (1987) place feminization in the broader context of race and gender segregation.

46. On the masculinity associated with computing and associated impediments for women, see Grundy and Grundy (1996); Wright (1996). On the entry of women into some segments of computer work, see Donato (1990).

47. A few of my informants distinguished between programming and software engineering, usually by reserving the title *engineer* for those who had engineering degrees, designed operating systems, or developed software based on complex computing languages. Although these definitions were far from uniform, they indicated a hierarchy of skills in which engineer designated high status.

48. Bailyn (1987), Cockburn (1988), and Woodfield (2001) document organizational cultures that reward long hours and interpersonal competition and so inhibit women's participation and success. Kuhn and Rayman (2007) cite work-family concerns as key issues in the IT sector.

49. Despite working in closely integrated teams in which success depends on collaboration, employees in many settings succeed by exhibiting individual prowess (Dryburgh 1999; Tarallo 1987; Wright 1996).

50. Van Maanen and Barley (1984) define an occupational community using four criteria: people engaged in the same work, who draw identity from their work, who share a culture that extends beyond the work itself, and whose social relations meld work and leisure to some degree.

51. Of thirty-four programmers and engineers, twenty-three (or about two-thirds) lived and worked in New England or New York; seven (or about 20 percent) were based on the West Coast, from Silicon Valley to Seattle; two lived in the Southeast; and another two lived in the Southwest. Of the thirty-four writers and editors, twenty-four (or about 70 percent) lived and worked in New England or New York; six were based on the West Coast, in or near Los Angeles, San Francisco, or Seattle; two lived in the upper Midwest; one lived in the Southeast; and one lived in the Southwest.

52. For example, Silicon Valley is well known for software development. Technical professionals working in the Southwest, however, might more readily find work in the petrochemical industry; those living on the central East Coast might work in health care. Practitioners in both occupational groups reported industry-specific applications, which varied somewhat from one region to another.

53. I did not report their colleagues' assessments to these informants. Rather, in all cases, I promised confidentiality (also required of all institutional review boards) and so carefully avoided trafficking information between informants. To do so would also probably have foreclosed their cooperation.

54. Two of these companies were regional offices of large software development firms. One was a start-up company specializing in software for Internet sales. The fourth was a biotechnology firm that produced computer-aided medical devices.

2. Assessing Options, Making Choices

1. Coser (1974) develops the notion of a greedy institution as an ideal type that shapes the lives of subordinates subject to institutional control. Greedy institutions demand unflagging commitment, limit individual autonomy, and appropriate the resources of their subjects to serve institutional goals.

2. Hammer and Champy (1993) provide a vocabulary and rationale that several informants cited in their accounts of restructuring. Cornfield, Campbell, and McCammon conceive of workplace restructuring as "the devolution of decision making, the casualization of the employment relationship, and a shift from collective bargaining to individual bargaining" (2001, xiii–xiv). As they imply, an expansion of contract employment is itself a likely result of workplace restructuring. Many of my informants had reached the same conclusion.

3. Robinson and Rousseau (1994) and Rousseau (1995) define the *psychological contract* as a set of beliefs regarding employment obligations, and they associate violations of the psychological contract with employers' reneging on employees' expectations. For an overview of the development and elaboration of the concept, see Anderson and Schalk (1998).

4. Evan's experience echoes dilemmas that Smith (2001b) describes in her study of first-line managers at a manufacturing plant employing temporary workers. There, too, the integration of contingent workers posed problems for supervisors who sought to create cohesive teams. Workplace policies that interfered with these efforts can thus undermine productivity and contribute to the complexities of supervision.

5. On the development of the core-ring model for organizational staffing, see Harrison (1994); Harvey (1989); Osterman (1988).

6. In a study of technical contractors, only some of whom represent the occupations in this study, Bidwell and Briscoe (2008) find the incidence of long-term contracting to be higher among professionals with greater experience. Contracting was also more likely to occur immediately after a layoff or after a job in the technology industry and was less likely among married men with children. On transitions to contract employment, see Granger, Stanworth, and Stanworth (1995); Kunda, Barley, and Evans (2002).

7. Although the Fair Labor Standards Act, passed in 1938, established the eight-hour day and forty-hour week as the standard for full-time employment in the United States, most professionals and managers are exempt from these limits. For most salaried employees, overtime hours do not garner additional hourly pay.

8. In a case study of one high-tech firm, Schellenberg (1996) finds that organizational instability contributed to greater turnover among employees with options outside the firm. As an exit option for employees, therefore, contracting may promote turnover, even for employees whose jobs are not directly affected.

9. A series of studies focusing on working time in the United States have attributed a time shortage to various causes: an overall increase in working hours (Schor 1991); work-family conflicts (Hansen 2005; Hochschild 1997; Jacobs and Gerson 2001); and organizational culture, especially among those in professional occupations (Bailyn 1993; Epstein et al. 1999; Fried 1998; Perlow 1997; Seron and Ferris 1995). Contract professionals in this study reported evidence supporting all three causes, which might, in many cases, be mutually reinforcing.

10. Interspersing paid work with unpaid tasks, home-based contractors share some characteristics of teleworkers or telecommuters, who spend part of the standard workweek working from home (Haddon and Lewis 1994; Kraut 1989; Mirchandani 1998, 1999; Sullivan and Lewis 2001). Telecommuters, however, hold standard jobs. In contrast, contracting relieves workers of the expectation that they should adhere to the temporal norms of employing organizations.

11. With home-based freelancing long established, some publishers employ staff only to recruit freelancers and coordinate project teams (Stanworth and Stanworth 1997a). Some segments of the publishing industry—for example, publishers of school textbooks—more often expect freelancers to work at client sites.

12. Most of my informants reported hourly rates of pay. Projects that they willingly accepted for project fees typically allowed them to exercise control over the scope and depth of work to be done. Indexing a document, for example, is usually paid on a per-page basis, which allows a contractor to adjust the task to the fee.

13. In a study of engineering work in Silicon Valley, Shih (2004) identifies the demands of "project time" as a system of domination that controls workers through temporal manipulation that disrupts their daily life. My informants would probably concur.

14. Goffman (1961) associates role distancing with a "disdainful detachment" that social actors assume when a role is too constraining or somehow undesirable. Role distancing separates the individual from the performance of a role.

3. Performing Expertise

1. See Fletcher (1999) for an analysis of invisible helping behaviors, O'Riain (2000) for an account of interaction across dispersed work groups, and Perlow (1997) for an analysis of time management in a software firm. All three studies illustrate collaborative processes. Sonnentag (1998) further found engineers' collaboration associated with high performance, although Perlow and Weeks (2002) found that Indian engineers, more than their U.S. counterparts, viewed assistance as opportunity to develop skills and reputations to enhance interfirm mobility.

2. On the dimensions of risk, see Beck (1992); Luhmann (1990).

3. On the relationship between risk and uncertainty, see Gambetta (1988); Kollock (1994); Lane and Bachmann (1996); Williamson (1985).

4. On the relationship between risk and trust, see Lewis and Weigert (1985); Sabel (1993).

5. Despite looser mechanisms of control in the postbureaucratic organization, employees continue to hold jobs defined by position in a hierarchy (Grey and Garsten 2001; Heckscher and Donnellon 1994; Powell 1996).

6. Technically, this distinction is inaccurate. Any agreement, even informal terms undocumented in writing, constitutes a contract, and the failure to meet its terms could lead to a legal challenge. In practice, contractors maintain written documents in many forms, including correspondence, proposals, e-mail exchanges, and status reports. As evidence of a working relationship, these document the agreement and in this sense constitute a contract.

7. Rogers (2000) analyzes discursive mechanisms of control exercised by staffing agency personnel.

4. Managing Marginality

1. Surveillance technology has made worker monitoring increasingly possible, yet none of my informants reported experience with client surveillance. Rather, they believed themselves trusted to meet the expectations of their clients without the monitoring that has become pervasive for workers in other occupations.

2. Yakura (2001) analyzes the processes for billable hours in a consulting firm and similarly shows that the manipulation of time is one means for maintaining equivalence between time and the value of professional services.

3. Of the sixty-eight contractors I interviewed, only one described padding a bill, and this contractor then quickly qualified the response by explaining that the padding amounted only to "rounding up" a fraction of an hour. The day after the interview, I received an e-mail message from this informant asking that I eliminate this segment of the response from the audiotape and that I avoid any attribution to this contractor, even with a pseudonym, in referring to the practice of bill padding.

4. This view is consistent with Buroway's (1979) elaboration of "consent" as an analytical tool in understanding worker compliance under capitalist relations of production. The notion of consent has since undergone extensive critique and elaboration; see, for example, Gottfried et al. (2001); Sturdy, Knights, and Wilmott (1992).

5. A large literature analyzes organizational culture. See, for example, Alvesson (2002); Fine (1984); Kunda (1992); Ouchi and Wilkins (1985); Vaughan (2002); Wilson (1999).

6. Contractors' concern for honesty rarely involves illegality or potential harm to others, perhaps because clients are unlikely to expose contractors to organizational misconduct. Although whistleblowing, which takes concerns and grievances public (Graham 1986; Rothschild and Miethe 1994), is unlikely, some informants speculated that outright personal abuse or severely compromised professional standards might be so egregious that they would terminate a contract. A few informants also cited moral offense, usually drawing the line at associating themselves with racist, sexist, or homophobic content or behavior.

7. In contrast, studies of telecommuting employees indicate that spatial distance from a work site need not affect involvement in an organization. As employees, however, telecommuters are organizational members, and many exert extra effort to remain connected to their employers and part of a work-site culture (Felstead and Jewson 2000; Mirchandani 1998; Sullivan and Lewis 2001).

8. In its original formulation, emotional labor was externally focused, enacted by workers who interacted with customers and clients (Hochschild 1983). Later elaborations of the concept have applied it to work performed within the bounds of an organization, across the strata of a hierarchy, as supervisors and subordinates manage relationships (Kunda 1992; Lively 2002; Pierce 1995). Although not all emotion work is performed by women, the concept is linked to many female-typed occupations, in which women are charged with responsibility for others' feelings (Bailyn 2000; Jackson 1999; Steinberg and Fiegart 1999).

5. Collegial Networking, Occupational Control

1. Van Maanen and Barley (1984) characterize occupational communities as collegial forms of organizing work, distinct from rational administrative organization. As sites for sharing values, norms, and perspective, occupational communities create and sustain work-specific cultures.

2. Joseph's self-reported success with a broad and diverse network is consistent with Granovetter's (1995) notion of weak ties as a mechanism for job seeking. Unlike strong ties, which replicate connections, weak ties more often diversify and expand an individual's network (Powell and Smith-Doerr 1994).

3. The aggregate effect of such decisions generates what some theorists have termed *social capital,* variously defined as social resources, access to resources, and the process by which social actors acquire and exchange resources (Bourdieu 1986; Burt 1992; Coleman 1988; Portes 1998). Trust, obligation, and exchange produce social capital, but the process by which it circulates depends on structures of social relations. Hierarchical arrangements, for example, can impede exchange (Polodny and Baron 1997), but networks of horizontal connections provide a ready mechanism for reciprocal interaction.

4. Analyses of respect focus variously on social interaction (Lawrence-Lightfoot 1999), structural inequality (Miller and Savoie 2002), and autobiography (Sennett 2003), but all have similarly identified respect as a manifestation of relative equality between individuals and groups.

5. As this manager explained, most of the resumes were likely to be "cold"—that is, the contractor was probably busy elsewhere but had in the past submitted a resume to the agency. Several of the managers I interviewed complained that many agencies provided little more than access to large files of resumes representing a great range of experience and skill.

6. Rationales for employers' hiring through informal networks include reliable information (Coverdill 1998), an available infrastructure for accessing it (Miller and Rosenbaum 1997), and the perception that recruits hired through informal means will be accountable to those who made the connection (Mencken and Winfield 1998).

7. Stone (2004) cites human capital theory as rationale for an "implicit contract" between employer and employee. As a firm invests in human capital, an employee receives a lower-than-market wage, but the employee can then expect steady employment, despite any decline in productivity later in life (Becker 1975; Williamson 1985). The prospect of a career in an internal labor market is

thus both a mode of control and a promise of job security (Heckscher 1995; Segal 1986). This implicit contract underpins the psychological contract, more recently described by theorists of organizational behavior as a set of expectations rooted in organizational membership (Rousseau 1995).

8. Individual names do, occasionally, appear in finished products, although the scope of individual contributions is rarely specified. Some book publishers, for example, list the names of staff, sometimes including contractors, on copyright pages. Authors may also thank individuals in print. Programmers' names are occasionally listed on software, most often on open-source code or shareware.

9. The dismantling of internal labor markets is associated with the decentering of workplace control, together with less rigidity and greater informality (Smith 1997). Many analysts associate this trend with greater flexibility for both employers and employees. See, for example, Heckscher and Donnellon (1994); Kanter (1989).

10. Cultural means of control, in which informal norms and sanctions serve a machanism of regulations, are evident across contexts. See, for example, Ezzy (2001); Grugulis, Dundon, and Wilkinson (2000); Kunda (1992).

11. *Professionalism,* like the designation *professional,* carries theoretical connotations and has generated much analysis of professional practice and organizational control (Leicht and Fennell 1997). Occupational practice may, in some cases, be governed by formal standards that apply to independent practitioners (Seron 1996). Applied here, however, is a common-language definition (Abbott 1991), which takes as its point of departure the shared understanding of groups of occupational practitioners. Professionalism is, in this sense, embedded in a cultural context that creates and perpetuates meaning (Tolbert and Barley 1991).

12. For analyses of professionalization processes, see Abbott (1988); Freidson (2001); Larson (1977). All indicate that professional status is subject to challenge and change.

6. Extra-Organizational Careers

1. The notion of a "boundaryless career" distinguishes multiple trajectories from organization-based careers that depend on a single firm (Arthur, Inkson, and Pringle 1999; Arthur and Rousseau 1996; Cohen and Mallon 1999; Handy 1989; Mirvis and Hall 1994). With an emphasis on individual agency, analyses of "boundarylessness" often echo the calls for free agency evident in popular culture. Conceptually, however, "boundaryless careers" encompass standard employment in which employees cross the boundaries of multiple employing organizations.

2. On the salience of occupation, even for those in standard employment, see Kanter (1989); Tolbert (1996); Weick (1996).

3. I spoke with two managers who reported prohibiting contractors from working simultaneously for more than one client, and one related an incident in which a contractor had been dismissed for "carrying on" with another project months after having promised to complete it. Several of the contractors I interviewed described inquiries, by both clients and recruiters, about their work-related commitments. Many had found such inquiries intrusive, or even threatening. As long as they met their commitments, they believed, their use of uncommitted time was no one's business but their own.

4. Using multiple staffing agencies approximates the practice of coregistration used by temporary clerical workers (Gottfried 1991; Henson 1996).

5. In this study, other factors limiting flexibility included project pressures, opportunity costs, and unbilled time spent to please particular clients (Evans, Kunda, and Barley 2004). Unlike my informants, most of these technical contractors reported "a sizable number of unbillable hours" (19). They also represented a broader range of occupations for which the common element was technology, and only a portion of them exercised the autonomy associated with software engineering and technical writing. Still, these researchers find a striking disjuncture between their informants' claims of temporal flexibility and their findings of significant constraints.

6. In their larger study of reduced working time, Meiksins and Whalley (2002) analyze accounts of part-time technical professionals, principally engineers and writers, who exercised considerable autonomy, frequently worked for multiple clients, and rarely turned to staffing agencies. All these factors promote flexibility and individual agency.

7. O'Mahony and Bechky (2006) identify four tactics for acquiring stretchwork common to their two occupational groups: differentiating competence, acquiring referrals, framing and bluffing, and discounting.

8. In a U.K. survey of professionals in nonstandard work arrangements, Hoque and Kirkpatrick (2003) find the lack of access to training, especially for women, to be evidence of marginality.

9. Contractors "on 1099," who are self-employed for tax purposes, and those who are employees of their own corporations can usually deduct the costs of training from their incomes or revenues and so lower their tax payments.

10. Aneesh (2006) characterizes the growth of these global connections for programming as "virtual migration," which conflates labor with trade and poses new challenges for advocates and policymakers. Dahlmann and Huws (2006–2007) point to the downgrading of employment standards as editorial jobs move from the United Kingdom to India. O'Riain (2004) explains the emergence of a globally integrated high-tech workforce as the outcome of economic development strategies that promote global networks.

11. Studies of part-time professional work have documented considerable obstacles for practitioners who seek to return to full-time standard jobs. On academic faculty, for example, see Barker (1998). On attorneys, see Epstein et al. (1999); Rogers (2000). In contrast, Meiksins and Whalley (2002) find part-time technical professionals who sometimes felt pressured to return to full-time status.

12. See, for example, Eaton and Bailyn (1999); Royal and Althauser (2003).

13. On the challenges that women face when trying to combine work and family, see Bailyn (1993); Blair-Loy (2003); Williams (2000).

14. Home-based work carries a historically constructed legacy of gender, evident in both legal codes and social norms; see, for example, Christensen (1988); Prugl (1999); Sullivan and Lewis (2001). For an analysis of gender and home-based contracting, see Osnowitz (2005).

15. On technology workers' career options, see Stinchcombe and Heimer (1988).

16. Stone (2004) elaborates the legal difficulties that can plague workers who move from job to job, taking their human capital with them, and she argues that case law has failed to account for changes in the employment relationship, which have shifted the terms of investment in human capital to workers, regardless of contractual status. Noncompete clauses, she explains, are not limited to contractors.

17. On this career quandary for engineers, see Hughes (1958); Meiksins and Smith (1996); Perlow and Bailyn (1997); Tang, Jacobs, and Lai (2000); Zussman (1985).

18. In an expanding the book-publishing industry, the feminization of editorial work provided a rationale for truncated career ladders (Osnowitz 2000).

19. Harrison (1994) documents the development of production networks, which Harvey (1989) identifies as economies of scope, supplanting the economies of scale associated with mass production and the vertically integrated firm.

7. Work Relations Reconsidered

1. For example, many part-time employees are covered by the wage provisions of the Fair Labor Standards Act, enacted in 1938 and later amended with such provisions as the Equal Pay Act, passed in 1963. Most of the same part-time employees, however, are excluded from coverage under the Family and Medical Leave Act, signed into law in 1993 (Carnevale, Jennings, and Eisenmann 1998).

2. Carlson (2001) charts a long history of contest over the definition of an employee in the United States, in which Congress and the Supreme Court have often been at odds, and argues that employee status is an inappropriate criterion for determining coverage under labor and employment law.

3. On the expansion of nonstandard employment, especially lower-wage contract work, and related rationales, see Carré and Wilson (2004); Maltby and Yamada (1997); Rasell and Appelbaum (1997).

4. On the ambiguities and contradictions of joint employment, sometimes called coemployment, see Feldman and Klaas (1996); Hiatt and Jackson (1997); Stone (2006); Tansky and Veglahn (1995).

5. Four of the writers I interviewed self-identified as members of the National Writers Union, which includes both employees and contractors who make their living by writing. Since its founding in the early 1980s, the National Writers Union has addressed a number of issues concerning freelance journalists and book authors, most notably regulations governing the copyright and distribution of published work. The writers who were part of this study, in contrast, engaged in "work for hire" and sold their services to clients who retained ownership of the work. To address this constituency, the union also has a "biz-tech" section that offers information and guidance regarding contract terms.

6. The U.S. Employee Retirement Income Security Act (ERISA), passed in 1974, does set minimum standards for health and pension plans in private industry, and antidiscrimination statutes also apply. Employers cannot legally discriminate on the basis of a social category that has been given statutory protection by, for example, providing fewer benefits for women or for workers over age forty. When a segment of a workforce is employed in a nonstandard arrangement, however, contractual status can mask discriminatory practices that would otherwise be illegal. The growth of contingent employment can thus undermine the applicability of discrimination law (Stone 2004).

7. The Consolidated Omnibus Budget Reconciliation Act (COBRA) dates from 1986. This U.S. law allows former employees, under certain conditions, to continue to have health insurance coverage through a former employer at group rates for a specified period. Many of my informants spoke of "doing COBRA" or "COBRAing" after leaving a standard job. Most had found the law effective in providing some transitional assistance while they became contractors. Because they were responsible for the full amount, however, the insurance was more expensive than the portion they had paid as employees.

8. In the United States, the unemployment insurance system is regulated at the state level, with federal oversight, and varies from state to state. Established as a system of wage replacement, unemployment insurance is funded by employers, which typically contribute in proportion to their size and the frequency of their employees' claims.

9. For example, in 2003 Massachusetts passed a law that denies unemployment insurance to any temporary worker employed through a staffing agency unless that worker can prove an inability to find work through the same agency. The law thus allows a staffing agency to deny a claim for unemployment compensation merely by offering a worker a new assignment at reduced wages, a longer commute, or any other terms that might be unacceptable.

10. One informant reported having successfully used his state Small Claims Court to collect from a delinquent client, and in most states, individuals can use a small claims procedure to seek legal redress without an attorney. Specific criteria, such as limits to the amount sought, usually apply. Contractors living in states far from their clients are also likely to find the procedures inconvenient at best.

11. Mechanisms of collegial control in these two occupations thus subvert the possibility of the kind of "occupational unionism" that Cobble (1991, 1996) has proposed and elaborated for service

workers in a postindustrial economy. Cobble draws from her study of a waitresses' union, which negotiated prehire agreements and mediated work relations through local hiring halls. The labor market structures and occupational processes for these workers, however, differ from the conditions of contracting for the practitioners discussed here (Osnowitz 2007).

12. "Kill fees" are sometimes paid to journalists who submit completed articles, only to have the newspaper, magazine, or website decide not to publish them.

13. The National Labor Relations Act (NLRA) has, since 1935, provided regulatory oversight for workers forming unions. The statute, however, excludes independent contractors, who must depend on other sources of leverage if they wish to bargain collectively (Carré, duRivage, and Tilly 1994).

14. The exception to this work-site model of union representation is the hiring hall, which the NLRA sanctioned only for specific industries in which hiring halls had already been established by the mid-1930s, when the law was enacted.

15. One organization with a different strategy is the Freelancers Union, based in New York City, which offers various services to a range of independent workers. By mobilizing those working outside standard employment, the organization seeks to affect policy in a number of areas, including unpaid wages, social insurance, unemployment support, worker classification, and taxation.

16. After the mid-1990s, the Freelance Editorial Association lost membership and eventually disappeared (Osnowitz 2007).

17. WashTech soon became Local 37083 of the Communications Workers of America and is supported as a pilot project for organizing new economy workers (van Jaarsveld 2004). Its efforts have more recently encompassed workers in a number of technical occupations, both contractors and employees, for whom it also engages in collective bargaining.

18. At its height in the early 1990s, the Freelance Editorial Association included over 1,600 dues-paying members (Osnowitz 2007). In 2001, WashTech had just over 300 members, not all of whom were contractors (personal communication, Marcus Courtney, staff member, July 28, 2001).

19. On organizational strategies, see Osnowitz (2007); Rodino-Colocino (2007); van Jaarsveld (2004).

20. As articulated by Mancur Olson (1965), the free-rider dilemma is a problem of mobilization occurring when those who opt out of participation will also reap the benefits of collective action. A rational individual, therefore, will choose to "ride free," allowing others to act for the collective good. To address this problem, Olson proposes selective incentives, rewards made available only to those who contribute to the collective effort.

21. A pared-back version of its *Code of Fair Practice* was eventually posted on the website for the Editorial Freelancers Association (EFA), based in New York (www.the-efa.org). Although similar in name, the EFA has focused less on advocacy than on enhancing professional status.

22. On traditions and prospects of mutual aid, see Bacharach, Bamberg, and Sonnenstuhl (2001); Jarley (2005).

23. On the staffing agency model, see Gonos (1998, 2001); Peck and Theodore (2002); Vosko (2000).

24. On exploitative agency practices in lower-wage labor markets, see McAllister (1998); Parker (1994); Valenzuela (2003).

25. For analyses of agency practices in labor markets for technical contractors, see Barley and Kunda (2004); for attorneys, see Rogers (2000).

26. The staffing industry operates with minimal regulation, a lack of oversight that contrasts sharply with the regulations that apply to union hiring halls, which serve essentially the same function—providing access to short-term employment in a specific labor market (Freeman and Gonos 2005; Gonos 1998).

27. A model for this form of collective representation is in the film and television industry, which for decades has administered employment benefits and, for some creative artists, payment for "residuals" when work appears in new venues. Organized on the basis of occupation, outside the more common model of work-site representation, these unions have sustained membership by providing essential services (Carpenter 2007; Paul and Kleingartner 1994).

28. Stone (2006) presents an agenda for legal reform that would encompass much of the workforce with nonstandard, contingent arrangements.

REFERENCES

Abbott, Andrew. 1988. *The System of Professions: An Essay on the Division of Expert Labor*. Chicago: University of Chicago Press.

———. 1991. "The Future of Professions: Occupation and Expertise in the Age of Organization." *Research in the Sociology of Organization* 8:17–43.

Allen, Jamerson C., and Nina Yablok. 2005. *Working with Independent Contractors, Leased Workers, and Outsourcing: How and When to Do It*. Berkeley: Regents of the University of California.

Alvesson, Mats. 2002. *Understanding Organizational Culture*. Thousand Oaks: Sage.

Amin, Ash, and Joanne Roberts. 2008. "Knowing in Action: Beyond Communities of Practice." *Research Policy* 37(2): 353–69.

Anderson, Neil, and Rene Schalk. 1998. "The Psychological Contract in Retrospect and Prospect." *Journal of Organizational Behavior* 19(special issue): 637–47.

Aneesh, Aneesh. 2006. *Virtual Migration: The Programming of Globalization*. Durham: Duke University Press.

Appelbaum, Eileen, Naomi Cassirer, Betty L. Dooley, Ken Hudson, Arne L. Kalleberg, Edith Rassell, Barbara F. Reskin, Roberta M. Spalter-Roth, and David Webster. 1997. *Managing Work and Family: Nonstandard Work Arrangements among Managers and Professionals*. Washington, D.C.: Economic Policy Institute.

Arthur, Michael B., Kerr Inkson, and Judith K. Pringle. 1999. *The New Careers: Individual Action and Economic Change.* London: Sage.

Arthur, Michael B., and Denise M. Rousseau. 1996. "Introduction: The Boundaryless Career as a New Employment Principle." In *The Boundaryless Career: A New Employment Principle for a New Organizational Era,* edited by Michael B. Arthur and Denise M. Rousseau, 3–22. New York: Oxford University Press.

Bacharach, Samuel, Peter D. Bamberger, and William J. Sonnenstuhl. 2001. *Mutual Aid and Union Renewal: Cycles of Logics of Action.* Ithaca: Cornell University Press.

Bailyn, Lotte. 1987. "Experiencing Technical Work: A Comparison of Male and Female Engineers." *Human Relations* 40(5): 299–312.

———. 1993. *Breaking the Mold: Women, Men, and Time in the New Corporate World.* New York: The Free Press.

———. 2000. "Time in Organizations: Constraints on, and Possibilities for, Gender Equity in the Workplace." Working Paper no. 4142, Sloan School of Management, Massachusetts Institute of Technology, Cambridge, Mass.

Banerjee, Payal. 2006. "Indian Information Technology Workers in the United States: The H-1B Visa, Flexible Production, and the Racialization of Labor." *Critical Sociology* 32(2–3): 425–45.

Barker, Kathleen. 1998. "Toiling for Piece-Rates and Accumulating Deficits: Contingent Work in Higher Education." In *Contingent Work: Employment Relations in Transition,* edited by Kathleen Barker and Kathleen Christensen, 195–220. Ithaca: Cornell University Press.

Barley, Stephen R., and Gideon Kunda. 2004. *Gurus, Hired Guns, and Warm Bodies: Itinerant Experts in a Knowledge Economy.* Princeton: Princeton University Press.

Barley, Stephen R., and Julian E. Orr. 1997. "The Neglected Workforce: An Introduction." In *Between Craft and Science: Technical Work in U.S. Settings,* edited by Stephen R. Barley and Julian E. Orr, 1–19. Ithaca: Cornell University Press.

Baron, James N., and David M. Kreps. 1999. *Strategic Human Resources: Frameworks for General Managers.* New York: John Wiley & Sons.

Bechky, Beth A. 2006. "Gaffers, Gofers, and Grips: Role-Based Coordination in Temporary Organizations." *Organization Science* 17(1): 3–21.

Beck, Ulrich. 1992. *Risk Society: Towards a New Modernity.* Trans. by Mark Ritter. Newbury Park, Calif.: Sage.

Becker, Gary S. 1975. *Human Capital: A Theoretical and Empirical Analysis, With Special Reference to Education.* 2nd ed. New York: National Bureau of Economic Research/Columbia University Press.

Beirne, Martin, Harvie Ramsay, and Androvniki Panteli. 1998. "Developments in Computing Work: Control and Contradiction in the Software Labour Process." In *Workplaces of the Future,* edited by Paul Thompson and Chris Warhurst, 142–62. Houndsmills, UK: Macmillan.

Belous, Richard S. 1989. *The Contingent Economy: The Growth of the Temporary, Part-Time and Subcontracted Workforce.* Washington, D.C.: National Planning Association.

Benner, Chris, Laura Leete, and Manuel Pastor. 2007. *Staircases or Treadmills?: Labor Market Intermediaries and Economic Opportunity in a Changing Economy.* New York: Russell Sage Foundation.

Bidwell, Matthew, and Forrest Briscoe. 2008. "Contracting and Careers: Determinants of Decisions to Work as Independent Contractors among Information Technology Workers." Unpublished paper presented at the annual meeting of the American Sociological Association, Boston.

Bielby, William T., and Denise D. Bielby. 1999. "Organizational Mediation of Project-Based Labor Markets: Talent Agencies and the Careers of Screenwriters." *American Sociological Review* 64(1): 64–85.

Biemesderfer, S. C. 1999. "1706: The Little Law That Shadows Your Career." *Contract Professional,* March 1999. Available at: www.cpuniverse.com/newsite/arhcives/1999/mar/1706/html (accessed July 19, 2001).

Blair-Loy, Mary. 2003. *Competing Devotions: Career and Family among Women Executives.* Cambridge, Mass.: Harvard University Press.

Bourdieu, Pierre. 1986. "The Forms of Capital." In *Handbook of Theory and Research for the Sociology of Education,* edited by John G. Richardson, 241–58. New York: Greenwood Press.

Braverman, Harry. 1974. *Labor and Monopoly Capital: The Degradation of Work in the Twentieth Century.* New York: Monthly Review Press.

Bridges, William. 1994. *Job Shift: How to Prosper in a Workplace without Jobs.* Reading, Mass.: Addison-Wesley.

Bridges, William, and Wayne J. Villemez. 1991. "Employment Relations and the Labor Market: Integrating Institutional and Market Perspectives." *American Sociological Review* 56(6): 748–64.

Bronstein, Arturo S. 1991. "Temporary Work in Western Europe: Threat or Complement to Permanent Employment?" *International Labour Review* 130(3): 293–310.

Burawoy, Michael. 1979. *Manufacturing Consent: Changes in the Labor Process under Monopoly Capitalism.* Chicago: University of Chicago Press.

Bureau of Labor Statistics, U.S. Department of Labor (BLS). 1996. "The October Review." *Monthly Labor Review* 110(10): 2.

Bureau of Labor Statistics, U.S. Department of Labor (BLS). 1998. Employee Tenure in 1998. http://stats.bls.gov/news.release/tenure.toc.htm (accessed August 2000).

Burt, Ronald S. 1992. *Structural Holes: The Social Structure of Competition.* Cambridge, Mass.: Harvard University Press.

Canter, Sharon. 1988. "The Temporary Help Industry: Filling the Needs of Workers and Business." In *Flexible Workstyles: A Look at Contingent Labor,* 46–49. Washington, D.C.: Women's Bureau, U.S. Department of Labor.

Caplette, Michele Kathleen. 1981. "Women in Publishing: A Study of Careers and Organizations." PhD diss., State University of New York, Stony Brook.

Cappelli, Peter, Laurie Bassi, Harry Katz, David Knoke, Paul Osterman, and Michael Useem. 1997. *Change at Work: How American Workers Are Coping with Corporate Restructuring and What Workers Must Do to Take Charge of Their Own Careers.* New York: Oxford University Press.

Carlson, Richard R. 2001. "Why the Law Still Can't Tell an Employee When It Sees One and How It Ought to Stop Trying." *Berkeley Journal of Employment and Labor Law* 22(2): 295–368.

Carnevale, Anthony P., Lynn A. Jennings, and James M. Eisenmann. 1998. "Contingent Workers and Employment Law." In *Contingent Work: American Employment Relations in Transition,* edited by Kathleen Barker and Kathleen Christensen, 281–305. Ithaca: Cornell University Press.

Carpenter, Tris. 2007."What Works: Organizing Freelance Professionals in the New Economy." In *Surviving the New Economy,* edited by John Amman, Tris Carpenter, and Gina Neff, 173–83. Boulder: Paradigm.

Carré, Francoise, Virginia duRivage, and Chris Tilly. 1994. "Representing the Part-Time and Contingent Workforce: Challenges for Unions and Public Policy." In *Restoring the Promise of American Labor Law,* edited by Sheldon Friedman, Richard W. Hurd, Rudolph A. Oswald, and Ronald L. Seeber, 314–23. Ithaca: Cornell University Press.

Carré, Francoise, and Randall Wilson. 2004. "The Social and Economic Costs of Employee Misclassification in Construction." Construction Policy Research Center, Labor and Worklife Program, Harvard Law School and Harvard School of Public Health.

Christensen, Kathleen. 1988. *Women and Home-Based Work: The Unspoken Contract.* New York: Henry Holt.

Cobble, Dorothy Sue. 1991. *Dishing It Out: Waitresses and Their Unions in the Twentieth Century.* Urbana: University of Illinois Press.

——. 1996. "The Prospects for Unionism in a Service Society." In *Working in the Service Society,* edited by Cameron Lynne Macdonald and Carmen Sirianni, 333–58. Philadelphia: Temple University Press.

Cockburn, Cynthia. 1988. *Machinery of Dominance: Women, Men, and Technical Know-How.* Boston: Northeastern University Press.

Cohany, Sharon P. 1996. "Workers in Alternative Employment Arrangements." *Monthly Labor Review* 119(10): 31–45.

Cohen, Laurie, and Mary Mallon. 1999. "The Transition from Organisational Employment to Portfolio Work: Perceptions of 'Boundarylessness.'" *Work, Employment & Society* 13(2): 329–52.

Colclough, Glenna, and Charles M. Tolbert II. 1992. *Work in the Fast Lane: Flexibility, Divisions of Labor, and Inequality in High-Tech Industries.* Albany: SUNY Press.

Coleman, James S. 1988. "Social Capital in the Creation of Human Capital." *American Journal of Sociology* 94(Supp.): S95–S121.

Colgan, Fiona, and Frances Tomlinson. 1996. "Women in Book Publishing—A 'Feminised' Sector?" In *Women in Organisations: Challenging Gender Politics,* edited by Sue Ledwith and Fiona Colgan, 44–77. Houndsmills, UK: Macmillan Business.

Consulting Engineers Council of Texas. 1972. *General Engineering Services: A Manual of Practice for Engaging the Services of a Consulting Engineer.* Austin: Texas Society of Professional Engineers.

Cornfield, Daniel B., Karen E. Campbell, and Holly J. McCammon. 2001. "Working in Restructured Workplaces: An Introduction." In *Working in Restructured Workplaces: Challenges and New Directions for the Sociology of Work,* edited by Daniel B. Cornfield, Karen E. Campbell, and Holly J. McCammon, xi–xxii. Thousand Oaks: Sage.

Coser, Lewis. 1974. *Greedy Institutions: Patterns of Undivided Commitment.* New York: Free Press.

Coser, Lewis, Charles Kadushin, and Walter W. Powell. 1982. *Books: The Culture and Commerce of Publishing*. Chicago: University of Chicago Press.

Coverdill, James E. 1998. "Personal Contacts and Post-Hire Job Outcomes: Theoretical and Empirical Notes on the Significance of Matching Methods." In *Research in Social Stratification and Mobility*, Vol. 16, edited by Kevin T. Leicht, 247–69. Stamford, Conn.: JAI Press.

Dahlmann, Simone, and Ursula Huws. 2006–2007. "Sunset in the West: Outsourcing Editorial Work from the UK to India—a Case Study of the Impact on Workers." *Work Organisation, Labour & Globalisation* 1(1): 59–75.

Dangler, Jamie Faricellia. 1994. *Hidden in the Home: The Role of Waged Homework in the Modern World Economy*. Albany, N.Y.: SUNY Press.

Daniels, Cynthia R. 1989. "Between Home and Factory: Homeworkers and the State." In *Homework: Historical and Contemporary Perspectives on Paid Labor at Home*, edited by Eileen Boris and Cynthia R. Daniels, 13–32. Urbana: University of Illinois Press.

DiNatale, Marisa. 2001. "Characteristics of and Preference for Alternative Work Arrangements, 1999." *Monthly Labor Review* 124(3): 28–49.

DiTomaso, Nancy. 2001. "The Loose Coupling of Jobs: The Subcontracting of Everyone." In *Sourcebook of Labor Markets: Evolving Structures and Processes*, edited by Ivar Berg and Arne L. Kalleberg, 247–70. New York: Kluwer Academic/Plenum.

Doeringer, Peter, and Michael Piore. 1971. *Internal Labor Markets and Manpower Analysis*. Lexington, Mass.: Lexington Books.

Donato, Katharine M. 1990. "Programming for Change?: The Growing Demand for Women Systems Analysts." In *Job Queues, Gender Queues: Explaining Women's Inroads into Male Occupations*, edited by Barbara Reskin and Patricia Roos, 167–82. Philadelphia: Temple University Press.

Dryburgh, Heather. 1999. "Work Hard, Play Hard: Women and Professionalization in Engineering—Adapting to the Culture." *Gender & Society* 13(5): 664–82.

Eaton, Susan C., and Lotte Bailyn. 1999. "Work and Life Strategies for Professionals in Biotechnology Firms." *Annals of the American Academy of Political and Social Science* 562(March): 159–73.

Ehrenreich, Barbara. 2005. *Bait and Switch: The (Futile) Pursuit of the American Dream*. New York: Metropolitan Books.

Ekinsmyth, Carol. 2002. "Project Organization, Embeddedness and Risk in Magazine Publishing." *Regional Studies* 36(3): 229–43.

Epstein, Cynthia Fuchs, Carroll Seron, Bonnie Oglensky, and Robert Saute. 1999. *The Part-Time Paradox: Time Norms, Professional Lives, Family, and Gender*. New York: Routledge.

Evans, James A., Gideon Kunda, and Stephen R. Barley. 2004. "Beach Time, Bridge Time, and Billable Hours: The Temporal Structure of Technical Contracting." *Administrative Science Quarterly* 49(1): 1–38.

Ezzy, Douglas. 2001. "A Simulacrum of Workplace Community: Individualism and Engineered Culture." *Sociology* 35(3): 631–50.

Faulkner, Robert R., and Andy B. Anderson. 1987. "Short-Term Projects and Emergent Careers: Evidence from Hollywood." *American Journal of Sociology* 92(4): 879–909.

Feldman, Daniel C., and Brian S. Klaas. 1996. "Temporary Workers: Employee Rights and Employer Responsibilities." *Employer Responsibilities and Rights Journal* 9(1): 1–21.

Felstead, Alan, and Nick Jewson. 2000. *In Work, at Home: Toward an Understanding of Homeworking.* New York: Routledge.

Fernandez-Mateo, Isabel. 2007. "Who Pays the Price of Brokerage?: Transferring Constraint through Price Setting in the Staffing Sector." *American Sociological Review* 72(2): 291–317.

———. 2009. "Cumulative Gender Disadvantage in Contract Employment." *American Journal of Sociology* 174(4): 871–923.

Fine, Gary Alan. 1984. "Negotiated Orders and Organizational Cultures." *Annual Review of Sociology* 10:239–62.

Finkelstein, Martin J., Robert K. Seal, and Jack H. Schuster. 1998. *The New Academic Generation: A Profession in Transformation.* Baltimore: Johns Hopkins University Press.

Finlay, William, and James E. Coverdill. 2002. *Headhunters: Matchmaking in the Labor Market.* Ithaca: Cornell University Press.

Fletcher, Joyce K. 1999. *Disappearing Acts: Gender, Power, and Relational Practice at Work.* Cambridge, Mass.: MIT Press.

Florida, Richard. 2002. *The Rise of the Creative Class and How It's Transforming Work, Leisure, Community, and Everyday Life.* New York: Basic Books.

Fraser, Janet, and Michael Gold. 2001. "'Portfolio Workers': Autonomy and Control amongst Freelance Translators." *Work, Employment & Society* 15(4): 679–97.

Freeman, Audrey. 1996. "Contingent Work and the Role of Labor Market Intermediaries." In *Of Heart and Mind: Social Policy Essays in Honor of Sar A. Levitan,* edited by Sar A. Levitan, Garth L. Mangum, and Stephen L. Mangum, 177–99. Kalamazoo: Upjohn Institute for Employment Research.

Freeman, Harris, and George Gonos. 2005. "Regulating the Employment Sharks: Reconceptualizing the Legal Status of the Commercial Temp Agency." *Working USA: The Journal of Labor and Society* 8(March): 293–314.

Freidson, Eliot. 2001. *Professionalism: The Third Logic.* Chicago: University of Chicago Press.

Fried, Mindy. 1998. *Taking Time: Parental Leave and Corporate Culture.* Philadelphia: Temple University Press.

Gallie, Duncan, Michael White, Yuan Cheng, and Mark Tomlinson. 1998. *Restructuring the Employment Relationship.* Oxford: Clarendon Press.

Gambetta, Diego. 1988. *Trust: Making and Breaking Cooperative Relations.* New York: Blackwell.

Gappa, Judith M., and David W. Leslie. 1993. *The Invisible Faculty: Improving the Status of Part-Timers in Higher Education.* San Francisco: Jossey-Bass.

Gardner, Jennifer M. 1995. "Worker Displacement: A Decade of Change." *Monthly Labor Review* 118(4): 45–57.

Glenn, Evelyn Nakano, and Charles M. Tolbert. 1987. "Technology and Emerging Patterns of Stratification for Women of Color: Race and Gender Segregation in Computer Occupations." In *Women, Work, and Technology,* edited by Barbara D. Wright, 318–31. Ann Arbor: University of Michigan Press.

Goffman, Erving. 1959. *Presentation of Self in Everyday Life.* Garden City, New York: Doubleday/Anchor Books.

———. 1961. *Encounters.* Indianapolis: Bobbs-Merrill.

———. 1969. *Strategic Interaction*. Philadelphia: University of Pennsylvania Press.

Gold, Michael, and Janet Fraser. 2002. "Managing Self-Management: Successful Transitions to Portfolio Careers." *Work, Employment & Society* 16(4): 579–97.

Golden, Lonnie, and Eileen Appelbaum. 1992. "What Was Driving the 1982–88 Boom in Temporary Employment?: Preference of Workers or Decisions and Power of Employers." *American Journal of Economics and Sociology* 51(4): 473–82.

Gonos, George. 1998. "The Interaction between Market Incentives and Government Action." *Contingent Work: American Employment Relations in Transition*, edited by Kathleen Barker and Kathleen Christensen, 170–91. Ithaca: Cornell University Press.

———. 2001. "'Never a Fee!': The Miracle of the Postmodern Temporary Help and Staffing Agency." *Working USA* 4(3): 9–36.

Gordon, David M., Richard Edwards, and Michael Reich. 1992. *Segmented Work, Divided Workers: The Historical Transformation of Labor in the United States*. New York: Cambridge University Press.

Gottfried, Heidi. 1991. "Mechanisms of Control in the Temporary Help Service Industry." *Sociological Forum* 6(4): 699–713.

———. 1992. "In the Margins: Flexibility as a Mode of Regulation in the Temporary Help Service Industry." *Work, Employment & Society* 6(3): 443–60.

Gottfried, Heidi, Robin Leidner, Steven Peter Vallas, Jennifer L. Pierce, Roger F. Freeland, Gay Seidman, Leslie Salzinger, and Michael Burawoy. 2001. "From Manufacturing Consent to Global Ethnography: A Retrospective Examination." *Contemporary Sociology* 30(5): 435–58.

Gould, Susan B., Kerry J. Weiner, and Barbara R. Levin. 1997. *Free Agents: People and Organizations Creating a New Working Community*. San Francisco: Jossey-Bass.

Gouliquer, Lynne. 2000. "Pandora's Box: The Paradox of Flexibility in Today's Work place." *Current Sociology* 48(1): 29–38.

Graham, Jill W. 1986. "Principled Organizational Dissent: A Theoretical Essay." In *Research in Organizational Behavior,* Vol. 8, edited by Barry M. Staw and L. L. Cummings, 1–52. Greenwich, Conn.: JAI Press.

Granger, Bill, John Stanworth, and Celia Stanworth. 1995. "Self-Employment Career Dynamics: The Case of 'Unemployment Push' in UK Book Publishing." *Work, Employment & Society* 9(3): 499–516.

Granovetter, Mark. 1995. *Getting a Job: A Study of Contacts and Careers*. 2nd ed. Chicago: University of Chicago Press.

Greenbaum, Joan. 1979. *In the Name of Efficiency*. Philadelphia: Temple University Press.

Grey, Chris, and Christina Garsten. 2001. "Trust, Control and Post-Bureaucracy." *Organization Studies* 22(2): 229–50.

Gringeri, Christina E. 1994. *Getting By: Women Homeworkers and Rural Economic Development*. Lawrence, Kan.: University Press of Kansas.

Grugulis, Irena, Tony Dundon, and Adrian Wilkinson. 2000. "Cultural Control and the 'Culture Manager': Employment Practices in a Consultancy." *Work, Employment and Society* 14(1): 97–116.

Grundy, Anna F., and John Grundy. 1996. *Women and Computers*. Exeter, UK: Intellect Books.

Gubman, Ed. 2003. *The Engaging Leader: Winning with Today's Free Agent Workforce.* New York: Kaplan Business.

Haddon, Leslie, and Alan Lewis. 1994. "The Experience of Teleworking: An Annotated Review." *International Journal of Human Resource Management* 5(1): 193–223.

Hammer, Michael, and James Champy. 1993. *Reengineering the Corporation: A Manifesto for Business Revolution.* New York: Harper Business.

Handy, Charles B. 1989. *The Age of Unreason.* Boston: Harvard Business School Press.

Hansen, Karen. 2005. *Not-So-Nuclear Families: Class, Gender, and Networks of Care.* New Brunswick, N.J.: Rutgers University Press.

Harrison, Bennett. 1994. *Lean and Mean: The Changing Landscape of Corporate Power in the Age of Flexibility.* New York: Basic Books.

Harvey, David. 1989. *The Condition of Postmodernity: An Enquiry into the Origins of Cultural Change.* Oxford: Basil Blackwell.

Head, Simon. 2003. *The New Ruthless Economy: Work and Power in the Digital Age.* New York: Oxford University Press.

Heckscher, Charles. 1995. *White-Collar Blues: Management Loyalties in an Age of Corporate Restructuring.* New York: Basic Books.

Heckscher, Charles, and Anne Donnellon, eds. 1994. *The Post-Bureaucratic Organization.* Thousand Oaks: Sage.

Henson, Kevin D. 1996. *Just a Temp.* Philadelphia: Temple University Press.

———. 2003. "Calling the Shots: Contingent Nursing Work and Time Sovereignty." Unpublished paper presented to the Conference on Work and Family, sponsored by Brandeis University, Orlando, Fla.

Hiatt, Jonathan P., and Lee W. Jackson. 1997. "Union Survival Strategies for the Twenty-First Century." *Journal of Labor Research* 18(fall): 487–501.

Hinds, Pamela J., and Diane E. Bailey. 2003. "Out of Sight, Out of Sync: Understanding Conflict in Distributed Teams." *Organization Science* 14(6): 615–32.

Hinds, Pamela, and Sara Kiesler. 2002. *Distributed Work.* Cambridge, Mass.: MIT Press.

Hipple, Steven. 1997. "Worker Displacement in an Expanding Economy." *Monthly Labor Review* 120(12): 22–35.

———. 2001. "Contingent Work in the Late 1990s." *Monthly Labor Review* 124(3): 3–27.

Hirsch, Paul M., and Charles E. Naquin. 2001. "The Changing Sociology of Work and the Reshaping of Careers." In *Working in Restructured Workplaces: Challenges and New Directions for the Sociology of Work,* edited by Daniel B. Cornfield, Karen E. Campbell, and Holly J. McGammon, 427–35. Thousand Oaks: Sage.

Hochschild, Arlie Russell. 1983. *The Managed Heart: Commercialization of Human Feeling.* Berkeley: University of California Press.

———. 1997. *The Time Bind: When Work Becomes Home and Home Becomes Work.* New York: Metropolitan Books.

Holmes, John. 1986. "The Organization and Locational Structure of Production Subcontracting." In *Production, Work, Territory; The Geographical Anatomy of Industrial Capitalism,* edited by Michael Storper and Allan J. Scott, 80–106. Boston: Allen and Unwin.

Hoque, Kim, and Ian Kirkpatrick. 2003. "Non-Standard Employment in the Management and Professional Workforce: Training, Consultation and Gender Implications." *Work, Employment & Society* 17(4): 667–89.

Houseman, Susan. 2001. "Why Employers Use Flexible Staffing Arrangements: Evidence from an Establishment Survey." *Industrial and Labor Relations Review* 55(1): 149–70.

Houseman, Susan, and Machiko Osawa. 2003. *Nonstandard Work in Developed Economies: Causes and Consequences.* Kalamazoo: W. E. Upjohn Institute for Employment Research.

Hughes, Everett C. 1958. *Men and Their Work.* Glencoe: The Free Press.

Hughes, Thomas P. 1987. "The Evolution of Large Technological Systems." In *The Social Construction of Technological Systems,* edited by Thomas P. Hughes and Trevor J. Pinch, 51–82. Cambridge, Mass.: MIT Press.

Jackson, Paul, Ed. 1999. *Virtual Working: Social and Organisational Dynamics.* London: Routledge.

Jacobs, Jerry A., and Kathleen Gerson. 2001. "Overworked Individuals or Overworked Families?: Explaining Trends in Work, Leisure, and Family Time." *Work and Occupations* 28(1): 40–63.

Jacoby, Sanford M. 1999. "Are Career Jobs Headed for Extinction?" *California Management Review* 42(1): 123–45.

Jarley, Paul. 2005. "Unions as Social Capital: Renewal through a Return to the Logic of Mutual Aid." *Labor Studies Journal* 29(4): 1–26.

Johnson, Gayle. 1976. "Women in Publishing." In *Perspectives on Publishing,* edited by Philip G. Altbach and Sheila McVey, 259–72. Lexington, Mass.: D. C. Heath.

Johnston, Russell, and Paul. R. Lawrence. 1988. "Beyond Vertical Integration: The Rise of the Value-Adding Partnership." *Harvard Business Review* 66(4): 94–101.

Jurik, Nancy C. 1998. "Getting Away and Getting By: The Experiences of Self-Employed Homeworkers." *Work and Occupations* 25(1): 7–35.

Kahne, Hilda. 1985. *Reconceiving Part-Time Work: New Perspectives for Older Workers and Women.* Totawa, N.J.: Rowman & Allanheld.

Kalleberg, Arne L. 2000. "Nonstandard Employment Relations: Part-time, Temporary and Contract Work." *Annual Review of Sociology* 26: 341–65.

———. 2001. "The Advent of the Flexible Workplace: Implications for Theory and Research." In *Working in Restructured Workplaces: Challenges and New Directions for the Sociology of Work,* edited by Daniel B. Cornfield, Karen E. Campbell, and Holly J. McCammon, 437–53. Thousand Oaks: Sage.

———. 2003. "Flexible Firms and Labor Market Segmentation: Effects of Workplace Restructuring on Jobs and Workers." *Work and Occupations* 30(3): 154–75.

Kalleberg, Arne L., Barbara F. Reskin, and Ken Hudson. 2000. "Bad Jobs in America: Standard and Nonstandard Employment Relations and Job Quality in the United States." *American Sociological Review* 65(2): 256–78.

Kanter, Rosabeth Moss. 1989. *When Giants Learn to Dance: Mastering the Challenge of Strategy, Management, and Careers in the 1990s.* New York: Simon and Schuster.

Katzenbach, John R., and Frederick Beckett. 1995. *Real Change Leaders: How You Can Create Growth and High Performance at Your Company.* New York: Times Business.

Kent, Peter. 1992. *Technical Writer's Freelancing Guide.* New York: Sterling Publishing.

Kollock, Peter. 1994. "The Emergence of Exchange Structures: An Experimental Study of Uncertainty, Commitment, and Trust." *American Journal of Sociology* 100(1): 313–45.

Kraft, Philip. 1977. *Programmers and Managers: The Routinization of Computer Programming in the United States.* New York: Springer-Verlag.

Kraft, Philip, and Steven Dubnoff. 1986. "Job Content, Fragmentation and Control in Computer Software Work." *Industrial Relations* 25(2): 184–96.

Kraut, Robert E. 1989. "Telecommuting: The Trade-Offs of Home Work." *Journal of Communication* 39(3): 19–47.

Kuhn, Sarah, and Paula Rayman. 2007. "Software and Internet Industry Workers." In *The Future of Work in Massachusetts,* edited by Tom Juravich, 93–109. Amherst: University of Massachusetts Press.

Kunda, Gideon. 1992. *Engineering Culture: Control and Commitment in a High-Tech Corporation.* Philadelphia: Temple University Press.

Kunda, Gideon, Stephen R. Barley, and James E. Evans. 2002. "Why Do Contractors Contract?: The Experience of Highly Skilled Technical Professionals in a Contingent Labor Market." *Industrial and Labor Relations Review* 55(2): 234–61.

Lane, Christel, and Reinhard Bachmann. 1996. "The Social Constitution of Trust: Supplier Relations in Britain and Germany." *Organization Studies* 17(3): 365–96.

Langlois, Richard N., and David C. Mowery. 1996. "The Federal Government Role in the Development of the U.S. Software Industry." In *The International Computer Software Industry: A Comparative Study of Industrial Evolution and Structure,* edited by David C. Mowery, 53–85. Oxford: Oxford University Press.

Larson, Magali S. 1977. *The Rise of Professionalism: A Sociological Analysis.* Berkeley: University of California Press.

Lave, Jean, and Etienne Wenger. 1991. *Situated Learning: Legitimate Peripheral Participation.* Cambridge, UK: Cambridge University Press.

Lawrence-Lightfoot, Sarah. 1999. *Respect.* Reading, Mass.: Perseus Books.

Leicht, Kevin T. 1998. "Work (If You Can Get It) and Occupations (If There Are Any)?: What Social Scientists Can Learn from Predictions of the End of Work and Radical Workplace Change." *Work and Occupations* 25(1): 36–48.

Leicht, Kevin T., and Mary L. Fennell. 1997. "The Changing Organizational Context of Professional Work." *Annual Review of Sociology* 23:215–31.

Lenz, Edward A. 1999. "Are Time Limits the Answer to Liability?" *Workforce* 78(11): 61–64.

Leonard, Madeleine. 1998. *Invisible Work, Invisible Workers: The Informal Economy in Europe and the United States.* New York: St. Martin's Press.

Lewis, J. David, and Andrew Weigert. 1985. "Trust as a Social Reality." *Social Forces* 63(4): 967–85.

Linder, Marc. 1999. "Employed or Self-Employed? The Role and Content of the Legal Distinction, Dependent and Independent Contractors in Recent U.S. Labor Law: An Ambiguous Dichotomy Rooted in Simulated Statutory Purposelessness." *Comparative Labor Law and Policy Journal* 21(1): 187–230.

Lively, Kathryn. 2002. "Client Contact and Emotional Labor: Upsetting the Balance and Evening the Field." *Work and Occupations* 29(2): 198–225.

Luhmann, Niklas. 1990. "Familiarity, Confidence, Trust: Problems and Alternatives." In *Trust: Making and Breaking Cooperative Relations,* edited by Diego Gambetta, 94–108. Oxford: Basil Blackwell.

Maltby, Lewis L., and David C. Yamada. 1997. "Beyond 'Economic Realities': The Case for Amending Federal Employment Discrimination Laws to Include Independent Contractors." *Boston College Law Review* 38(2): 239–74.

Marsden, Peter V., Cynthia R. Cook, and Arne L. Kalleberg. 1996. "Bureaucratic Structures for Coordination and Control." In *Organizations in America: Analyzing Their Structures and Human Resources Practices,* edited by Arne L. Kalleberg, David Knoke, Peter V. Marsden, and Joe L. Spaeth, 69–86. Thousand Oaks: Sage.

Martin, Emily. 1994. *Flexible Bodies: Tracking Immunity in American Culture—From the Days of Polio to the Age of AIDS.* Boston: Beacon Press.

McAllister, Jean. 1998. "Sisyphus at Work in the Warehouse: Temporary Employment in Greenville, South Carolina." In *Contingent Work: American Employment Relations in Transition,* edited by Kathleen Christensen and Kathleen Barker, 221–42. Ithaca: Cornell University Press.

McGovern, Marion, and Dennis Russell. 2001. *A New Brand of Expertise: How Independent Consultants, Free Agents, and Interim Managers Are Transforming the World of Work.* Boston: Butterworth-Heinemann.

McGuire, Gail M. 2000. "Gender, Race, Ethnicity, and Networks: The Factors Affecting the Structure of Employees' Network Members." *Work and Occupations* 27(4): 501–23.

McIlwee, Judith S., and J. Gregg Robinson. 1992. *Women in Engineering: Gender, Power, and Workplace Culture.* Albany: SUNY Press.

Meiksins, Peter, and Chris Smith (with Boel Berner, Stephen Crawford, Kees Gispen, Kevin McCornick, and Peter Whalley). 1996. *Engineering Labour: Technical Workers in Comparative Perspective.* London: Verso.

Meiksins, Peter, and Peter Whalley. 2002. *Putting Work in Its Place: A Quiet Revolution.* Ithaca: Cornell University Press.

Mencken, F. Carson, and Idee Winfield. 1998. "In Search of the 'Right Stuff': The Advantages and Disadvantages of Informal and Formal Recruiting Practices in External Labor Markets." *American Journal of Economics and Sociology* 57(2): 135–53.

Menger, Pierre-Michel. 1999. "Artistic Labor Markets and Careers." *Annual Review of Sociology* 25:541–74.

Miller, Seymour M., and Anthony J. Savoie. 2002. *Respect and Rights: Class, Race, and Gender Today.* Lanham, Md.: Rowman & Littlefield.

Miller, Shzia Rafiullah, and James E. Rosenbaum. 1997. "Hiring in a Hobbesian World: Social Infrastructure and Employers' Use of Information." *Work and Occupations* 24(4): 498–523.

Mills, C. Wright. 1956. *White Collar: The American Middle Classes.* New York: Oxford University Press.

Miner, Anne S., and David F. Robinson. 1994. "Organizational and Population Level Learning as Engines for Career Transitions." *Journal of Organizational Behavior* 15(4): 345–64.

Mirchandani, Kiran. 1998. "Protecting the Boundary: Teleworker Insights on the Expansive Concept of 'Work.'" *Gender & Society* 12(2): 168–87.

———. 1999. "Legitimizing Work: Telework and the Gendered Reification of the Work-Nonwork Dichotomy." *Canadian Review of Sociology and Anthropology* 36(1): 87–107.

Mirvis, Philip H., and Douglas T. Hall. 1994. "Psychological Success and the Boundaryless Career." *Journal of Organizational Behavior* 15(4): 365–80.

Mishel, Lawrence, Jared Bernstein, and Heidi Shierholz. 2009. *The State of Working America 2008–2009.* Washington, D.C.: Economic Policy Institute.

Moen, Phyllis, and Patricia Roehling. 2005. *The Career Mystique: Cracks in the American Dream.* Lanham, Md.: Rowman & Littlefield.

Mosco, Vincent, and Catherine McKercher. 2007. "Introduction: Theorizing Knowledge Labor and the Information Society." In *Knowledge Workers in the Information Society,* edited by Catherine McKercher and Vincent Mosco, vii–xxiii. Lanham, Md.: Lexington Books.

Neff, Gina. 2007. "The Lure of Risk: Surviving and Welcoming Uncertainty in the New Economy." In *Surviving the New Economy,* edited by John Amman, Tris Carpenter, and Gina Neff, 33–46. Boulder: Paradigm.

Ness, Immanuel. 2007. "Globalization and Labor Resistance." In *Surviving the New Economy,* edited by John Amman, Tris Carpenter, and Gina Neff, 99–117. Boulder: Paradigm.

Nicholson, Nigel. 1996. "Career Systems in Crisis: Change and Opportunity in the Information Age." *Academy of Management Executive* 10(3): 40–51.

Ofstead, Cynthia M. 1999. "Temporary Help Firms as Entrepreneurial Actors." *Sociological Forum* 14(2): 273–94.

Olson, Mancur. 1965. *The Logic of Collective Action: Public Goods and the Theory of Groups.* Cambridge, Mass.: Harvard University Press.

O'Mahony, Siobhan, and Beth A. Bechky. 2006. "Stretchwork: Managing the Career Progression Paradox in External Labor Markets." *Academy of Management Journal* 49(5): 918–41.

O'Neill, Carol L., and Avima Ruder. 1974. *The Complete Guide to Editorial Freelancing.* New York: Dodd, Mead.

O'Riain, Sean. 2000. "Net-Working for a Living: Irish Software Developers in the Global Workplace." In *Global Ethnography: Forces, Connections, and Imaginations in a Postmodern World,* edited by Michael Burawoy, Joseph A. Blum, Sheba George, Zsuzsa Gille, Teresa Gowan, Lynn Haney, Maren Klawiter, Steven H. Lopez, Sean O'Riain, and Millie Thayer, 175–202. Berkeley: University of California Press.

———. 2004. *The Politics of High-Tech Growth: Developmental Network States in the Global Economy.* Cambridge, UK: Cambridge University Press.

Orlikowski, Wanda J. 1988. "The Data Processing Occupation: Professionalization or Proletarianization?" In *High Tech Work: A Research Annual,* edited by Richard L. Simpson and Ida Harper Simpson, 95–124. (Research in the Sociology of Work 4.) Greenwich, Conn.: JAI Press.

Orsburn, Jack D., Linda Moran, Ed Musselwhite, and John H. Zenger. 1990. *Self-Directed Work Teams: The New American Challenge.* Homewood, Ill.: Irwin.

Osnowitz, Debra. 2000. "Out of House, Out of Mind: The Negotiated Work of Editorial Freelancing." In *Unusual Occupations,* edited by Helena Z. Lopata and Kevin D. Henson, 127–50. (Current Research in Occupations and Professions 11.) Stamford, Conn.: JAI Press.

———. 2005. "Managing Time in Domestic Space: Home-Based Contractors and Household Work." *Gender & Society* 19(1): 83–103.

——. 2007. "Individual Needs versus Collective Interests: Network Dynamics in the Freelance Editorial Association." *Qualitative Sociology* 30:459–79.

Osterman, Paul. 1988. *Employment Futures: Reorganization, Dislocation, and Public Policy.* New York: Oxford University Press.

——, ed. 1999a. *Broken Ladders: Managerial Careers in the New Economy.* New York: Oxford University Press.

——. 1999b. *Securing Prosperity: The American Labor Market: How It Has Changed and What to Do about It.* Princeton: Princeton University Press.

Ouchi, William G., and Alan L. Wilkins. 1985. "Organizational Culture." *Annual Review of Sociology* 11:457–83.

Parker, Robert E. 1994. *Flesh Peddlers and Warm Bodies: The Temporary Help Industry and Its Workers.* New Brunswick, N.J.: Rutgers University Press.

Paul, Alan, and Archie Kleingartner. 1994. "Flexible Production and the Transformation of Industrial Relations in the Motion Picture and Television Industry." *Industrial and Labor Relations Review* 43(1): 663–78.

Pauleen, David J. 2004. *Virtual Teams: Projects, Protocols and Processes.* Hershey, Penn.: Idea Group.

Peck, Jamie A., and Nikolas Theodore. 2002. "Temped Out?: Industry Rhetoric, Labor Regulation and Economic Restructuring in the Temporary Staffing Business." *Economic and Industrial Democracy* 23(2): 143–75.

Perlow, Leslie. 1997. *Finding Time: How Corporations, Individuals, and Families Can Benefit from New Work Practices.* Ithaca: Cornell University Press.

Perlow, Leslie, and Lotte Bailyn. 1997. "Engineering Education and Engineering Practice: Improving the Fit." In *Between Craft and Science: Technical Work in U.S. Settings,* edited by Stephen R. Barley and Julian E. Orr, 210–29. Ithaca: Cornell University Press.

Perlow, Leslie, and John Weeks. 2002. "Who's Helping Whom: A Comparison of Helping Behavior among American and Indian Software Engineers." *Journal of Organizational Behavior* 23(3): 345–61.

Pierce, Jennifer L. 1995. *Gender Trials: Emotional Labor in Contemporary Law Firms.* Berkeley: University of California Press.

Pink, Daniel H. 2001. *Free Agent Nation.* New York: Warner Books.

Polivka, Anne E. 1996a. "Contingent and Alternative Work Arrangements Defined." *Monthly Labor Review* 119(10): 3–9.

——. 1996b. "A Profile of Contingent Workers." *Monthly Labor Review* 119(10): 10–21.

Polivka, Anne E., and Thomas Nardone. 1989. "On the Definition of 'Contingent Work.'" *Monthly Labor Review* 112(12): 9–16.

Polodny, Joel M., and James N. Baron. 1997. "Resources and Relationships: Social Networks and Mobility in the Workplace." *American Sociological Review* 62(5): 673–93.

Portes, Alejandro. 1998. "Social Capital: Its Origins and Applications in Modern Sociology." *Annual Review of Sociology* 24:1–24.

Portes, Alejandro, Manuel Castells, and Lauren A. Benton. 1989. *The Informal Economy: Studies in Advanced and Less Developed Countries.* Baltimore: Johns Hopkins University Press.

Powell, Michael. 1999. *Considering Computer Contracting: How to Become a Freelance Computer Professional.* Boston: Butterworth Heinemann.

Powell, Walter W. 1985. *Getting Into Print: The Decision-Making Process in Scholarly Publishing.* Chicago: University of Chicago Press.

———. 1990. "Neither Market nor Hierarchy: Network Forms of Organization." In *Research in Organizational Behavior,* Vol. 12, edited by Barry M. Staw and L. L. Cummings, 295–336. New York: JAI Press.

———. 1996. "Trust-Based Forms of Governance." In *Trust in Organizations: Frontiers of Theory and Research,* edited by Roderick M. Kramer and Tom R. Tyler, 51–67. Thousand Oaks: Sage.

Powell, Walter W., and Laurel Smith-Doerr. 1994. "Networks and Economic Life." In *The Handbook of Economic Sociology,* edited by Neil J. Smelser and Richard Swedbergs, 368–402. Princeton/New York: Princeton University Press/Russell Sage Foundation.

Prugl, Elisabeth. 1999. *The Global Construction of Gender: Home-Based Work in the Political Economy of the 20th Century.* New York: Columbia University Press.

Rajagopal, Indhu. 2002. *Hidden Academics: Contract Faculty in Canadian Universities.* Toronto: University of Toronto Press.

Rassell, Edie, and Eileen Appelbaum. 1997. "Nonstandard Work Arrangements: A Challenge for Workers and Labor Unions." *Social Policy* 28(2): 31–36.

Rebitzer, James B. 1998. "Toiling for Piece Rates and Accumulating Deficits: Contingent Work in Higher Education." In *Contingent Work: American Employment Relations in Transition,* edited Kathleen Barker and Kathleen Christensen, 195–220. Ithaca: Cornell University Press.

Reich, Robert B. 1992. *The Work of Nations: Preparing Ourselves for 21st-Century Capitalism.* New York: Vintage Books.

Reinhold, Barbara Bailey. 2001. *Free to Succeed: Designing the Life You Want in the New Free Agent Economy.* New York: Plume.

Reskin, Barbara F. 1990. "Culture, Commerce, and Gender: The Feminization of Book Publishing." In *Job Queues, Gender Queues: Explaining Women's Inroads into Male Occupations,* edited by Barbara F. Reskin and Patricia A. Roos, 93–110. Philadelphia: Temple University Press.

Reskin, Barbara F., and Patricia A. Roos, eds. 1990. *Job Queues, Gender Queues: Explaining Women's Inroads into Male Occupations.* Philadelphia: Temple University Press.

Robinson, Sandra L., and Denise M. Rousseau. 1994. "Violating the Psychological Contract: Not the Exception but the Norm." *Journal of Organizational Behavior* 15(3): 245–59.

Rodino-Colocino, Michelle. 2007. "High-Tech Workers of the World, Unionize!: A Case Study of WashTech's 'New Model of Unionism.'" In *Knowledge Workers in the Information Society,* edited by Catherine McKercher and Vincent Mosco, 209–227. Lanham, Md.: Lexington Books.

Rogers, Jackie Krasas. 1995. "Just a Temp: Experience and Structure of Alienation in Temporary Clerical Employment." *Work and Occupations* 22(2): 137–66.

———. 2000. *Temps: The Many Faces of the Changing Workplace.* Ithaca: ILR/Cornell University Press.

Rogers, Jackie Krasas, and Kevin D. Henson. 1997. "'Hey, Why Don't You Wear a Shorter Skirt?': Structural Vulnerability and the Organization of Sexual Harassment in Temporary Clerical Employment." *Gender & Society* 11(2): 215–37.

Rogers, Trumbull. 1995. *Editorial Freelancing: A Practical Guide.* Bayside, N.Y.: Aletheia.

Ross, Andrew. 2003. *No Collar: The Human Workplace and Its Hidden Costs.* New York: Basic Books.

———. 2009. *Nice Work If You Can Get It: Life and Labor in Precarious Times.* New York: New York University Press.

Rothschild, Joyce, and Terance D. Miethe. 1994. "Whistleblowing as Resistance in Modern Work Organizations: The Politics of Revealing Organizational Deception and Abuse." In *Resistance and Power in Organizations,* edited by John M. Jermier, David Knights, and Walter R. Nord, 252–73. London: Routledge.

Rousseau, Denise M. 1995. *Psychological Contracts in Organizations: Understanding Written and Unwritten Agreements.* Thousand Oaks: Sage.

Royal, Carol, and Robert P. Althauser. 2003. "The Labor Markets of Knowledge Workers: Investment Bankers' Careers in the Wake of Corporate Restructuring." *Work and Occupations* 30(2): 214–33.

Rubin, Beth A., and Brian T. Smith. 2001. "Reemployment in the Restructured Economy: Surviving Change, Displacement, and the Gales of Creative Destruction." In *Working in Restructured Workplaces: Challenges and New Directions for the Sociology of Work,* edited by Daniel B. Cornfield, Karen E. Campbell, and Holly J. McCammon, 323–42. Thousand Oaks: Sage.

Sabel, Charles F. 1993. "Studied Trust: Building New Forms of Cooperation in a Volatile Economy." *Human Relations* 46(9): 1133–70.

Saxenian, Annalee. 1994. *Regional Advantage: Culture and Competition in Silicon Valley and Route 128.* Cambridge, Mass.: Harvard University Press.

Schellenberg, Kathryn. 1996. "Taking It or Leaving It: Instability in a High-Tech Firm." *Work and Occupations* 23(2): 190–213.

Schor, Juliet. 1991. *The Overworked American: The Unexpected Decline of Leisure.* New York: Basic Books.

Segal, Martin. 1986. "Post-Institutionalism in Labor and Economics: The Forties and Fifties Revisited." *Industrial and Labor Relations Review* 39(3): 388–403.

Sennett, Richard. 2003. *Respect in a World of Inequality.* New York: W. W. Norton.

Seron, Carroll. 1996. *The Business of Practicing Law: The Work Lives of Solo and Small-Firm Attorneys.* Philadelphia: Temple University Press.

Seron, Carroll, and Kerry Ferris. 1995. "Negotiating Professionalism: The Gendered Social Capital of Flexible Time." *Work and Occupations* 22(1): 23–47.

Shapiro, Debra L., Stacie A. Furst, Gretchen M. Speitzer, and Mary Ann von Glinow. 2002. "Transnational Teams in the Electronic Age: Are Team Identity and High Performance at Risk?" *Journal of Organizational Behavior* 23(4): 455–67.

Sheehan, Donald. 1952. *This Was Publishing: A Chronicle of the Book Trade in the Gilded Age.* Bloomington: Indiana University Press.

Shih, Johanna. 2004. "Project Time in Silicon Valley." *Qualitative Sociology* 27(2): 223–45.

Smith, Vicki. 1997. "New Forms of Work Organization." *Annual Review of Sociology* 23:315–39.

———. 2001a. *Crossing the Great Divide: Worker Risk and Opportunity in the New Economy.* Ithaca: Cornell University Press.

———. 2001b. "Teamwork vs. Tempwork: Managers and the Dualisms of Workplace Restructuring." In *Working in Restructured Workplaces: Challenges and New Directions for the Sociology of Work,* edited by Daniel B. Cornfield, Karen E. Campbell, and Holly J. McCammon, 7–28. Thousand Oaks: Sage.

Snyder, Karrie Ann. 2004. "Route to the Informal Economy in New York's East Village: Crisis, Economics, and Identity." *Sociological Perspectives* 47(2): 215–40.

Sonnentag, Sabine. 1998. "Expertise in Professional Software Design: A Process Study." *Journal of Applied Psychology* 83(5): 703–15.

Stanworth, Celia, and John Stanworth. 1997a. "Managing an Externalised Workforce: Freelance Labour-Use in the UK Book-Publishing Industry." *Industrial Relations Journal* 28(1): 43–55.

———. 1997b. "Reluctant Entrepreneurs and Their Clients—The Case of Self-Employed Freelance Workers in the British Book Publishing Industry." *International Small Business Journal* 16(1): 58–73.

Steinberg, Ronnie J., and Deborah M. Figart. 1999. "Emotional Labor since the Managed Heart." *Annals of the American Academy of Political and Social Science* 561:8–26.

Stinchcombe, Arthur L., and Carol A. Heimer. 1988. In *High Tech Work: A Research Annual,* edited by Richard L. Simpson and Ida Harper Simpson, 179–204. (Research in the Sociology of Work 4.) Greenwich, Conn.: JAI Press.

Stone, Katherine V. W. 2004. *From Widgets to Digits: Employment Regulation for the Changing Workplace.* Cambridge, UK: Cambridge University Press.

———. 2006. "Legal Protections for Atypical Employees: Employment Law for Workers without Workplaces and Employees without Employers." *Berkeley Journal of Employment and Labor Law* 27(2): 251–80.

Sturdy, Andrew, David Knights, and Hugh Willmott. 1992. *Skill and Consent: Contemporary Studies in the Labour Process.* New York: Routledge.

Sullivan, Cath, and Suzan Lewis. 2001. "Home-Based Telework, Gender, and the Synchronization of Work and Family: Perspectives of Teleworkers and Their Co-residents." *Gender, Work and Organization* 8(2): 123–45.

Swinnerton, Kenneth. A., and Howard Wial. 1995. "Is Job Stability Declining in the U.S. Economy?" *Industrial Labor Relations Review* 48(2): 293–304.

Tang, Joyce, Jerry A. Jacobs, and Zhongwen Lai. 2000. "The Career Mobility of U.S. Engineers: Stability and Change during the 1970s and 1980s." *Unusual Occupations,* edited by Helena Z. Lopata and Kevin D. Henson, 169–93. (Current Research on Occupations and Professions 11.) Stamford, Conn.: JAI Press.

Tansky, Judith W., and Peter A Veglahn. 1995. "Legal Issues in Co-employment." *Labor Law Journal* 46(5): 293–300.

Tarallo, Bernadette Mary. 1987. "The Production of Information: An Examination of the Employment Relations of Software Engineers and Computer Programmers." PhD diss., University of California, Davis.

Tebbel, John. 1981. *A History of Book Publishing in the United States,* vol. 4: *The Great Change, 1940–1980.* New York: R. R. Bowker.

Tilly, Chris. 1996. *Half a Job: Bad and Good Part-Time Jobs in a Changing Labor Market.* Philadelphia: Temple University Press.

Tolbert, Pamela S. 1996. "Occupations, Organizations, and Boundaryless Careers." In *The Boundaryless Career: A New Employment Principle for a New Organizational Era,* edited by Michael B. Arthur and Denise M. Rousseau, 331–49. New York: Oxford University Press.

Tolbert, Pamela S., and Stephen R. Barley. 1991. "Introduction: At the Intersection of Organizations and Occupations." In *Research in the Sociology of Organizations,* Vol. 8, edited by Pamela S. Tolbert and Stephen R. Barley, 1–13. Greenwich, Conn.: JAI Press.

Uchitelle, Louis. 2006. *The Disposable American: Layoffs and Their Consequences.* New York: Alfred A. Knopf.

U.S. Government Accounting Office (GAO). 2000. "Contingent Workers: Incomes and Benefits Lag behind Those of the Rest of the Workforce." GAO-HEHS-00-76, Washington, D.C.

———. 2006. "Employment Arrangements: Improved Outreach Could Help Ensure Proper Worker Classification." GAO-06-656, Washington, D.C.

U.S. Senate. 1993. "The Increasing Use of 'Contingent' Labor." Subcommittee on Labor, Committee on Labor and Human Resources. 103rd Congress, 1st session, June 15, 1993.

———. 1994. "Conference on the Growing Contingent Work Force: Flexibility at the Price of Fairness?" Subcommittee on Labor, Committee on Labor and Human Resources. 103rd Congress, 2nd session, February 8, 1994.

Valenzuela, Abel, Jr. 2003. "Day Labor Work." *Annual Review of Sociology* 29:307–33.

Vallas, Steven P. 1999. "Rethinking Post-Fordism: The Meaning of Workplace Flexibility." *Sociological Theory* 17(1): 68–101.

Van Jaarsveld, Danielle D. 2004. "Collective Representation among High-Tech Workers at Microsoft and Beyond: Lessons from WashTech/CWA." *Industrial Relations* 43(2): 364–85.

Van Maanen, John, and Stephen R. Barley. 1984. "Occupational Communities: Culture and Control in Organizations." In *Research in Organizational Behavior,* Vol. 6, edited by Barry M. Staw and L. L. Cummings, 287–365. Greenwich, Conn.: JAI Press.

Vaughan, Diane. 2002. "Signals and Interpretive Work: The Role of Culture in a Theory of Practical Action." In *Culture in Mind: Toward a Sociology of Culture and Cognition,* edited by Karen A. Cerulo, 28–52. New York: Routledge.

Vosko, Leah F. 2000. *Temporary Work: The Gendered Rise of Precarious Employment.* Toronto: University of Toronto Press.

Warburg, Fredric. 1960. *An Occupation for a Gentleman.* Boston: Houghton Mifflin.

Watlington, Amanda G., and Roger L. Radeloff. 1997. *Contract Engineering: Start and Build a New Career.* New York: McGraw-Hill.

Weick, Karl E. 1996. "Enactment and the Boundaryless Career: Organizing as We Work." In *The Boundaryless Career: A New Employment Principle for a New Organizational Era,* edited by Michael B. Arthur and Denise M. Rousseau, 40–57. New York: Oxford University Press.

Wellins, Richard S., William C Byham, and Jeanne M. Wilson. 1991. *Empowered Teams: Creating Self-Directed Work Groups That Improve Quality, Productivity, and Participation.* San Francisco: Jossey-Bass.

Wenger, Etienne, ed. 1998. *Communities of Practice: Learning, Meaning, and Identity.* Cambridge, UK: Cambridge University Press.

Wenger, Jeffrey. 2003. "Share of Workers in 'Nonstandard' Jobs Declines: Latest Survey Shows a Narrowing—Yet Still Wide—Gap in Pay and Benefits." Economic Policy Institute, Washington, D.C.

Whalley, Peter. 1986a. "Markets, Managers, and Technical Autonomy." *Theory and Society* 15(1/2): 223–47.

——. 1986b. *The Social Production of Technical Work.* London: Macmillan.

Whalley, Peter, and Stephen R. Barley. 1997. "Technical Work in the Division of Labor: Stalking the Wiley Anomaly." In *Between Craft and Science: Technical Work in U.S. Settings,* edited by Stephen R. Barley and Julian Orr, 23–52. Ithaca: ILR/Cornell University Press.

Whittlesey, Marietta. 1982. *Freelance Forever: Successful Self-Employment.* New York: Avon Books.

Whyte, William H. 1956. *The Organization Man.* New York: Simon & Schuster.

Williams, Joan. 2000. *Unbending Gender: Why Family and Work Conflict and What to Do about It.* New York: Oxford University Press.

Williamson, Oliver E. 1985. *Economic Institutions of Capitalism.* New York: Free Press.

Wilson, Francis. 1999. "Cultural Control within the Virtual Organization." *Sociological Review* 47(4): 672–94.

Winter, Barbara. 1993. *Making a Living without a Job: Winning Ways for Creating Work That You Love.* New York: Bantam Books.

Womack, James P., Daniel T. Jones, and Daniel Roos. 1990. *The Machine That Changed the World: The Story of Lean Production.* New York: Harper Collins.

Woodfield, Ruth. 2001. *Women, Work, and Computing.* New York: Cambridge University Press.

Wright, Rosemary. 1996. "The Occupational Masculinity of Computing." In *Masculinity in Organizations,* edited by Cliff Cheng, 77–96. Thousand Oaks: Sage.

Yakura, Elaine K. 2001. "Billables: The Valorization of Time in Consulting." *American Behavioral Scientist* 44(7): 1076–95.

Zussman, Robert. 1985. *Mechanics of the Middle Class: Work and Politics among American Engineers.* Berkeley: University of California Press.

INDEX